Hollywood, hype and audiences

MANCHESTER
UNIVERSITY PRESS

Inside Popular Film

General editors Mark Jancovich and Eric Schaefer

Inside Popular Film is a forum for writers who are working to develop new ways of analysing popular film. Each book offers a critical introduction to existing debates while also exploring new approaches. In general, the books give historically informed accounts of popular film, which present this area as altogether more complex than is commonly suggested by established film theories.

Developments over the past decade have led to a broader understanding of film, which moves beyond the traditional oppositions between high and low culture, popular and avant-garde. The analysis of film has also moved beyond a concentration on the textual forms of films, to include an analysis of both the social situations within which films are consumed by audiences, and the relationship between film and other popular forms. The series therefore addresses issues such as the complex intertextual systems that link film, literature, art and music, as well as the production and consumption of film through a variety of hybrid media, including video, cable and satellite.

The authors take interdisciplinary approaches, which bring together a variety of theoretical and critical debates that have developed in film, media and cultural studies. They neither embrace nor condemn popular film, but explore specific forms and genres within the contexts of their production and consumption.

Already published:

Harry M. Benshoff *Monsters in the closet: homosexuality and the horror film*
Julia Hallam and Margaret Marshment *Realism and popular cinema*
Joanne Hollows and Mark Jancovich (eds) *Approaches to popular film*
Jacinda Read *The new avengers: feminism, femininity and the rape-revenge cycle*

Hollywood, hype and audiences

Selling and watching popular film in the 1990s

Thomas Austin

Manchester University Press
Manchester and New York
distributed exclusively in the USA by Palgrave

Published by Manchester University Press
Oxford Road, Manchester M13 9NR, UK
and Room 400, 175 Fifth Avenue, New York, NY10010, USA
www.manchesteruniversitypress.co.uk

Distributed exclusively in the USA by
Palgrave, 175 Fifth Avenue, New York,
NY 10010, USA

Distributed exclusively in Canada by
UBC Press, University of British Columbia, 2029 West Mall,
Vancouver, BC, Canada V6T 1Z2

British Library Cataloguing-in-Publication Data
A catalogue record for this book is available from the British Library

Library of Congress Cataloging-in-Publication Data applied for

ISBN 0 7190 5774 4 *hardback*
     0 7190 5775 2 *paperback*

First published 2002

10 09 08 07 06 05 04 03 02   10 9 8 7 6 5 4 3 2 1

Typeset in Sabon with Frutiger
by Northern Phototypesetting Co Ltd, Bolton

Printed in Great Britain
by Bell & Bain Ltd, Glasgow

Contents

List of illustrations

Acknowledgements

Special thanks to: Peter Kramer for his intellectual generosity, enthusiasm and advice over many years; Andrew Higson for support and supervision of the thesis from which this book derives; Mark Jancovich for patience and encouragement; Martin Barker for friendly advice; Charlotte Adcock for her insight, love and belief.

I am indebted to the British Academy for funding my three years of doctoral research. Thanks also to: Margaret Adcock, Guy Austin, Roger Austin, Sue Austin, Charles Barr, John Beyer, Helen Branwood, Pam Cook, James Donald, Lee Grieveson, John Gullidge, David Hall (for getting me started), Mike Hammond, Annette Hill, Matt Hills, Geoff King, Richard Maltby, James Montgomery, Dave Mount, Laura Mulvey, Steve Neale, Chris Nickolls, Trisha Purchas, Jamie Sexton, Roger Silverstone, Ian Strafford, Alita Thorpe, Phil Waterson, the British Film Institute library, the research department at the Cinema Advertising Association, Kelly Preedy at *Empire* magazine, Matthew Frost at Manchester University Press, and the students on the Cinema and Television in Contemporary Britain course, University of East Anglia, and on the Hollywood: Industry and Imaginary course, University of Sussex. Thanks especially to all those who returned letters and questionnaires, or agreed to be interviewed.

Earlier versions of parts of this book have appeared in the following publications:

'Gendered (dis)pleasures: *Basic Instinct* and female viewers', *Journal of Popular British Cinema*, 2 (1999); '"Desperate to see it": straight men watching *Basic Instinct*', in Melvyn Stokes and Richard Maltby (eds), *Identifying Hollywood's Audiences: Cultural Identity and the Movies* (London, British Film Institute 1999); '"*Gone With the Wind* plus fangs": genre, taste and distinction in the assembly, marketing and reception of *Bram Stoker's Dracula*', *Framework*, 41 (1999).

This book is dedicated to my Mum and Dad, and to Charlotte

Chapter 1

Introduction: a multi-dimensional approach to popular film

In a review of the state of Anglo-American film studies written in the late 1980s, Barbara Klinger noted an emerging 'recognition of the diverse contextual practices that riddle the text/viewer relation'.[1] This nascent understanding was fuelled by multiple and ongoing developments in cinema history, star studies, and work on television audiences carried out under the rubric of British cultural studies. In retrospect, it is clear that Klinger rather underestimated the efficacy of the disciplinary fire wall protecting large tracts of film studies (in teaching as well as research) from trends in cognate areas such as cultural studies and media studies. Thus, while the years since 1988 have witnessed the continuing institutionalisation of cinema history, including explorations of early audiences, contemporary film viewers remain relatively under-examined.[2] Moreover, certain traditions of textual analysis appear more or less immune to the shifts mapped by Klinger. Given these uneven trajectories, her argument constitutes a call for new investigations of film texts and the specific social and historical contexts of their production and reception which retains its relevance today.

This book is an attempt to take up that challenge. It does so by proposing a multi-dimensional approach to popular film, and proceeds by tracing the circulation of three Hollywood films – *Basic Instinct* (1992), *Bram Stoker's Dracula* (1992) and *Natural Born Killers* (1994) – from assembly and marketing to critical reception and consumption in cinemas, on home video and on television. In the process, it draws on the political economy of Hollywood in the 1990s, reception studies techniques, and empirical audience research to present an interrogation of popular film culture as a set of articulated economic, social and cultural formations and practices.[3] This pluralist mode of investigation contrasts with more

rigidly compartmentalised methods in orthodox film studies, which
have often approached cinema as a set of discrete and implicitly
autonomous mechanisms of production, textual organisation and
(more recently) consumption. Crucially, my approach also differs
from some of the latter studies, which, in focusing on the 'final
moment' in a film's life-cycle (its viewing), tend to imply that the
text precedes its audiences in a straightforward manner. By contrast,
I take account of how patterns of reception are anticipated by the
industry and feed back (via market research) into financing, production, and marketing decisions; and how practices of consumption
are informed, but never simply determined, by such strategies.[4]

My motivation in writing this book is not only to make an intervention into methodological debates. Two key and interrelated reasons why I have adopted a multi-dimensional approach are, firstly,
that it facilitates an investigation into the significance of popular
film, into how and why it matters in contemporary society, and, secondly, that it enables me to pursue issues of social and cultural power
as they arise in the circuit encompassing a film's production, its circulation, and the lived experiences of its viewers. I am attempting
here a triangulation between film texts, contexts and audiences. I
want to retain an idea of film texts as in some ways determinate,
such that their internal properties inflect, but do not fully determine,
the uses to which they are put. In the inter-discursive encounters
between audiences and film texts within specific contexts, film viewers are productive agents in the creation of meaning, pleasure and
use. But these activities are neither autonomous from textual mechanisms, institutional practices, and material and discursive settings,
nor innocent from the operations of power. (The all too common
equation of audience activity with notions of political progressive-
ness will be challenged here.) The (still somewhat limited) attention
accorded to film reception since the 1980s is both a reaction against
the long-standing disregard of cinema audiences among the majority of film scholars and a contestation of the primacy of hitherto
dominant practices of textual analysis and paradigms of textual
determinism. My project forms part of that move. However, I take
steps to avoid the consumptionist excesses found in some audience
studies. It is vital that this kind of work neither wishes away the
intricacies of textual power nor simply locates and celebrates the
achievement of commercial imperatives, including the 'successful'
act of consumption. Consumerist ideologies and rhetorics that

champion notions of audience agency and customer sovereignty need to be properly scrutinised and queried through academic study, not reproduced and legitimated.[5] Any critical inquiry into film audiences needs to examine the power relations – including unevenly distributed cultural, social and material resources – which both shape and are (re)constructed through acts of viewing. I address prevailing discourses,[6] social relations in play at specific scenarios of reception, and the film industry, its textual products and the proliferating intertextual regimes that surround them, as settings and resources for audience activity. But they are also sites of power which impact upon the actions of film viewers.

During its marketing and reception, a film is framed by a constellation of institutions, texts and practices. The commercial logic of contemporary Hollywood dictates the solicitation of multiple audiences for any single film, both across different territories and delivery systems in the global market and across different demographic segments, which are arranged into 'knowable' taste formations. I explore how the goal of financial success influences both the structure and the selling of films like the three I have selected. Films succeed commercially primarily because they are pleasurable and meaningful for viewers. Accordingly, industrial strategies aim to engineer a range of possible pleasures and meanings and advertise their presence to different audience fractions. Exploitable elements, such as stars, special effects or other generic attractions, are extracted and commodified for extra-diegetic circulation. Such operations rely upon exposure in newspapers, magazines and television shows that trade in star images, background stories, gossip and controversy. How, then, do audiences negotiate the viewing strategies cued by films such as *Basic Instinct*, *Bram Stoker's Dracula* and *Natural Born Killers*, and those proposed in associated promotional discourses and media commentaries? Watched at cinemas, on video, or on television, films are situated in countless viewing contexts, picked over and made use of in diverse acts of consumption. Some of these negotiations are encouraged by textual properties, marketing procedures and media coverage. Others are more idiosyncratic or oppositional. All take place within, and contribute to, broader social and cultural settings. In the pages that follow, I attempt to reconstruct some of the specific contexts – institutional and everyday – in which each film has been situated. My integrative methodology also allows me to make some (limited) steps towards situating these films within the complex array of mass-mediated popular culture, for example by tracing how production and marketing decisions 'piggyback' on observable trends in other cultural markets.[7] More specifically, my choice of films affords the opportunity to address questions around sexuality, gender, age and taste. How might viewing practices interact with these factors, if at all? Are industrial hierarchies of taste formations (often largely coterminous with gender, age and class distinctions) endorsed or contested by audiences? How might individual and collective identities be asserted and (re)produced through film viewing? What is the relationship between normative discourses of sexuality and gender, representations in a film such as Basic Instinct, and different viewer responses? How do popular ideologies and the commercial imperatives of the film industry interrelate?

Each of my chosen films is in some ways exceptional, and might be called an 'event' film. This term is used by the industry to designate the small number of films in any one year which achieve huge commercial success by attracting occasional cinemagoers as well as more frequent viewers. Basic Instinct and Bram Stoker's Dracula clearly fit this model: each proved highly popular with audiences, both in the United States and overseas. In the British market, Basic Instinct grossed £15.5 million in 1992, out-performing Batman Returns and Lethal Weapon 3 to become the first '18'-certificate film to top the annual box office since the similarly controversial Fatal Attraction four years earlier.[8] It was seen at the cinema by 3.9 million people.[9] Bram Stoker's Dracula grossed £11.5 million in 1993, ranking as the sixth most successful film in the United Kingdom that year.[10] A total of 3.3 million people watched it at the cinema. Natural Born Killers was a commercial hit of a lower order. In 1995 it was watched by 1.8 million people, grossing £4.7 million and reaching 19th in the box office chart.[11] However, the film became something of a cause célèbre in Britain because of anxieties about its 'violent' content and a consequent delay in its certification by the British Board of Film Classification. The two bigger hits also enjoyed widespread media coverage – Basic Instinct primarily through disputes over sex, violence and the politics of representation, Bram Stoker's Dracula largely through a marketing onslaught. While the 'event' status of the three case-study films renders them to some extent qualitatively different from less commercially successful and/or contentious films, many of the imbricating processes which I have uncovered are central to an understanding of the circulation and reception of recent and contemporary popular film in general.

My investigation centres on the dominant presence on the terrain of film culture in Britain: Hollywood. For almost a century, Hollywood films have been a highly significant integrated or 'naturalised' element of British popular culture, along with a host of other American texts and goods. This presence has led to accusations of cultural imperialism against the United States, and 'Americanisation' has become almost synonymous with the post-war expansion of commercial popular culture in Britain. While a simplistic response to these issues should be avoided, there is no escaping the dominant position occupied by American cultural producers and distributors in the British film market during the 1990s. For example, American films' share of the theatrical sector throughout the decade has been quantified at between 83 and 92 per cent.[12] My choice of films should not be taken to imply that the industrial, journalistic and social procedures under scrutiny here apply only to Hollywood pictures. Many of these mechanisms would also be found, to varying extents, in the circulation of British films. It is important not to fall into a reductive binary logic which opposes a monolithic notion of Hollywood film as always popular and commercially infallible with one of British product as always unpopular (because of elitist or miserabilist content, and/or economic and political disadvantages). However, two indisputable and interconnected factors in Hollywood's continuing dominance of the British market are, firstly, the longstanding cross-cultural appeal of many of its genres and stars; and, secondly, its economic muscle, in terms of distribution and exhibition control and marketing clout, as well as the resources it commands to fund expensive on-screen properties such as stars and special effects.[13] My three chosen films, for instance, all benefited from star presences, major advertising campaigns and large-scale theatrical openings, giving them far wider popular exposure than less well-supported rivals.[14]

The 1980s and 1990s witnessed the Hollywood studios' expansion into new markets (notably domestic and overseas video and pay-television), and their relocation within horizontally integrated transnational multimedia conglomerates. These shifts were accompanied by a continuation of some policies developed during the preceding three decades, such as the release of aggressively advertised would-be blockbusters. Since the early 1970s, tie-ins and merchan-

dising have become increasingly significant, particularly around
family-oriented 'toy movie' franchises such as the *Batman* and *Star
Wars* series. The three films in this study are adult-oriented, each
carrying an '18' certificate in Britain and supporting comparatively
small to moderate amounts of merchandising[15] (the widest array was
for *Bram Stoker's Dracula*). Nevertheless, both *Basic Instinct* and
Bram Stoker's Dracula achieved the status of event films through
securing substantial amounts of media coverage prior to successful
large-scale openings. Some of this media profile was purchased
through advertising campaigns, some came 'free' in associated print
and broadcast exposure. For all three films, attractions highlighted
in advertising were often picked up in wider popular journalism. A
number of intertextual discourses were thus mobilised around each
film, offering prospective audiences access to a range of filmic and
non-filmic background information, and to various viewing strategies. It is important to note here that there are both continuities and
differences in the ways a film is framed by the procedures of the film
industry, by the media, and among audiences. For example, marketing campaigns and film critics clearly make attempts to supervise the
meanings attributed to a film. There may be some match between
these protocols, or between them and interpretations made by viewers, but it is not complete or inevitable. Moreover, just as a film's
audience should not be conceived as an undifferentiated totality, so
industrial and critical sectors should be recognised as relatively heterogeneous rather than monolithic. A number of different promises
about a film may be made by a distributor targeting various markets.
Equally, neither critics and commentators nor viewers can be considered homogeneous in their responses. In each case study, I examine the interrelations and differences between these three
overlapping and heterogeneous areas of activity: film marketing,
media coverage and audiences.

My three case studies trace a common circuit of interrelated procedures, from production to promotion to reception. Within this
general trajectory, each inquiry takes a slightly different tack. Chapter 3 centres on *Basic Instinct*, looking at marketing strategies, accusations of homophobia directed at the film, and the discourse of
entertainment mobilised to counter these charges. Much of the
chapter addresses the gendered patterning of audience response,
and it includes a consideration of the ramifications of employing
gender as an analytical category in audience research. I also investi-

gate the ways in which *Basic Instinct* can be seen to mediate and participate in discourses of postfeminism. Alongside this line of inquiry, I track female viewers' positive and negative reactions to the film's portrayal of women, and their fantasy rewritings of its open ending. My analysis also approaches the relatively under-explored area of male heterosexual pleasures, and considers 'under-age' straight male viewers, for whom the act of watching the film became an assertion of an 'adult' identity. The chapter examines the impacts of the internal mechanisms of the film text, promotional and journalistic discourses, and macro- and micro-social contexts in shaping the viewing frames into which *Basic Instinct* was inserted. (This chapter is markedly longer than either of the other two case studies, for two reasons. Firstly, its position in the book requires that I elaborate upon certain methodological issues that also apply to the later chapters. Secondly, the range of the material I uncovered in my research requires sufficient space for sustained analysis. I have written the case study as a single chapter, as to do otherwise would interrupt the flow of my argument in such a multi-dimensional investigation.)

In chapter 4 I focus on the complex cultural and generic status of *Bram Stoker's Dracula*, via examinations of the intertextual relations between the film and other cultural forms, both those referring to Dracula or vampires directly, and those associated with its director, stars and broader artistic borrowings. I unravel how social and cultural hierarchies were erected by the film's representatives and distributors, by commentators and by viewers. Within and across each of these groupings, contesting distinctions were made, both between the genres on which the film was seen to draw, and between the assumed audiences for those genres. In tracing these taste conflicts I offer a new theorisation of audience investments in Hollywood's genre system.

Chapter 5 maps interfaces between the industry, discursive contexts and audiences by examining the marketing of *Natural Born Killers* and the ultimately beneficial effect upon this campaign of the delay in the award of a certificate by the British Board of Film Classification, a decision influenced by media allegations of 'copycat' killings inspired by the film. The delay in classification effectively authenticated *Natural Born Killers*' 'outlaw' appeal for a young and largely male audience, enhancing its box-office performance in Britain. The chapter examines Warner Bros.' strategy of crisis management, which capitalised upon the screen violence scare to both reduce advertising costs and maximise revenue from the film. I analyse various constructions of *Natural Born Killers*' audience proposed through marketing tactics and journalistic commentary, querying how prospective viewers made use of media coverage in forming expectations about the film. Continuing the previous chapter's interrogation of viewers' self-perceptions based on taste and cultural preference, this case study explores distinctions made by viewers between themselves and 'other' audience fractions. How did they negotiate and articulate self-images through watching *Natural Born Killers* and writing to me about the film? To what extent did these identities coincide with or diverge from journalistic and marketing constructions of assumed spectators? In chapter 6 I pull together my conclusions from the preceding case studies and discuss what a multi-dimensional model of popular film culture can offer for understandings of the significance of popular film and the operations of cultural and social power.

In the next chapter, I delineate in more detail the academic context from which this book has emerged, tracing signal developments within cinema history, cultural studies, reception studies, and the political economy of Hollywood in the 1990s. Readers who are less interested in an elaboration of my methodological motivations may wish to turn to chapter 3, where my first case study begins.

Notes

1 Barbara Klinger, 'In retrospect: film studies today', *Yale Journal of Criticism*, 2:1 (1988) 149.

2 See also Jostein Gripsrud, 'Film Audiences', in John Hill and Pamela Church Gibson (eds), *The Oxford Guide to Film Studies* (Oxford, Oxford University Press, 1998), pp. 202–11. Gripsrud's excellent overview is one of a burgeoning number of summaries of work on media audiences. This trend does present the risk, however, that the *idea* of audience studies may become increasingly familiar, while new empirical work on audiences beyond a relatively narrow 'canon' remains surprisingly slow to develop. On the emergence of a canon in audience research, see Sonia Livingstone, 'Audience research at the crossroads: the "implied audience" in media and cultural theory', *European Journal of Cultural Studies*, 1:2 (1998), 193–217.

3 My conception of popular film culture extends to films watched on video and television as well as at the cinema. My audience research draws on viewing experiences involving all these formats, and while I

focus largely on marketing and popular film journalism at the time of each picture's cinema release, I also take account of such processes around video launches and television broadcasts in order to track something of each title's post-theatrical career.

4 This kind of mutual relationship is most clearly apparent in the discursive 'contracts' between industry and audience central to the functioning of the star system and to notions of genre. See chapter 4.

5 See more on this point at chapter 3.

6 Following the work of Michel Foucault, I take 'discourse' to mean a (more or less sanctioned) productive and systematic way of organising thought as a social practice. See Michel Foucault, *The History of Sexuality, Volume 1: An Introduction*, trans. Robert Hurley (London, Penguin, 1979); *Power/Knowledge: Selected Interviews and Other Writings, 1972–77*, ed. Colin Gordon (Brighton, Harvester, 1980).

7 It is in part the influential stress within much of film studies on the 'uniqueness' of cinema, and an associated tendency to isolate it from other media as well as from wider patterns of everyday life, that has insulated the discipline from developments in cultural and media studies.

8 'UK top 10 films', *Screen International*, 18 December 1992, 2. *Basic Instinct* ranked as the sixth biggest film at the North American box office in 1992, grossing $117 million in the United States and Canada. 'US top 30 releases, Jan 1 – Dec 31, 1992', *Screen International*, 29 January 1993, 15.

9 All attendance figures provided by the Cinema Advertising Association, May 1997. These figures include repeat visits.

10 'UK Top 10, Dec 4, 1992 – Nov 28, 1993', *Screen International*, 14 January 1994, 50. *Bram Stoker's Dracula* grossed $82 million in the United States and Canada, ranking 13th in the rolling box office chart. 'US top grossers to date: Jan 3 1992 – Jan 3 1993', *Screen International*, 8 January 1993, 37. It was more successful in overseas markets, where it grossed $110m. Figure from imdb.com.

11 'UK Top 20 Dec 1, 1994 – Nov 26, 1995', *Screen International*, 15 December 1995, 15. *Natural Born Killers* grossed $50 million in the United States and Canada in 1994, ranking 30th in the box office chart. 'US top 100 films: Dec 29 1993 – Dec 30 1994', *Screen International*, 27 January 1995, 47.

12 A figure of 92.5 per cent is given in 'Indigenous and US films' share of national markets', *BFI Film and Television Handbook 1994* (London, British Film Institute, 1993),p. 44. Figures of 85.8 per cent for United States films, plus 4.6 per cent for 'UK–Hollywood films' such as *Alien 3* are given in 'Breakdown of 1992 UK box office by country of origin', *Ibid.*, p. 42. Respective figures for 1998 are similar, at 83.8 and 5.7 per

cent. 'Breakdown of UK box office by country of origin 1998', *BFI Film and Television Handbook 2000* (London, British Film Institute, 1999), p. 35.

13 This is not to imply that Hollywood enjoys consistent success with all of its releases. It is important to recognise that the business practices of the Hollywood industry attempt to reduce and manage risk and insecurity, but can never eradicate them.

14 *Basic Instinct* opened on 307 screens in the United Kingdom, *Bram Stoker's Dracula* on 355, and *Natural Born Killers* on 203. 'UK top 10, May 8–10', *Screen International*, 15 May 1992, 20; 'UK top 15, Jan 29–31', *Screen International*, 5 February 1993, 28; 'UK top 15, Feb 24–26', *Screen International*, 3 March 1995, 29.

15 The '18' certificate designates a film as suitable only for persons of 18 years and over. All three films were rated 'R' (for restricted) in the United States. According to the terms of this rating, a viewer under the age of 17 'requires accompanying parent or adult guardian'.

Chapter 2

Texts in context

My examinations of *Basic Instinct*, *Bram Stoker's Dracula* and *Natural Born Killers* confront the historical contingency of the films' constitution and reception, by situating each in some of the many and variable contexts of its circulation and consumption. While issues of textual organisation remain pertinent to my present investigation, it has been greatly influenced by the significant, if rather halting, turn towards contextual issues made within film studies during the 1980s and 1990s.

The development of film scholarship in the 1950s, 1960s and 1970s saw the interpretation of film texts institutionalised as the dominant academic activity. There are a number of reasons for the rise to pre-eminence of textual analysis. These include the influence on film studies of more established academic disciplines such as literature, drama and art history; advances in viewing technology; and what David Bordwell has identified as 'the university's demand for teachable techniques, professional specialisation and rapid publication output'.[1] In the 1970s and 1980s, the centrality of the film text and its exegesis was both informed and reproduced by a number of highly influential theorisations of film spectatorship. These models drew on Althusserian Marxism, structuralism, semiotics and psychoanalysis of Freudian and Lacanian stripes to focus on the presumed operation of textual mechanisms on the individual viewer. They typically combined two totalising stereotypes of the film spectator: a controlling, voyeuristic male-gendered subject; and a passive dupe interpellated or positioned ideologically by the cinematic apparatus and the film text.[2] Such approaches – often labelled 'Screen theory' after the British film studies journal – thus advanced the notion of a 'dominated and dominating spectator', subjected by the text and cinematic apparatus, yet in paradoxical and illusory command of everything in 'his' field of vision.[3] Despite its avowed interest in processes of spectatorship, Screen theory's dominant paradigms tended to locate meaning as ultimately static, residing within the film text. They also implied that film audiences (and Hollywood cinema) were effectively homogeneous, asocial and trans-historical. The viewing subject was posited not as a person but as 'a conceptual "space"',[4] an invariant term 'inscribed' – that is, determined – by the internal workings of the film text. In conceptualising the spectator as essentially an effect of textual processes, occupying a single position fixed by a film's formal characteristics, these totalising models implied a uniformity of viewer response and meaning production, regardless of who was watching the film, or the conditions under which it was being viewed.[5] Investigations of spectatorship have moved on since the heyday of Screen theory in the 1970s, and some important studies have worked to bridge the distinct traditions of psychoanalytically informed film theory and audience research.[6] Nevertheless, Screen theory's exclusive focus on film texts and its neglect of actual audiences have persisted in some areas of the discipline. Thus, while post-structuralist thought has stressed the complexity and ambiguity of subjects and texts, its stress on the role of the reader–spectator still largely derives from close textual analysis.[7]

In reviewing this dominant text-centric tradition within film studies, it is important not to lose sight of the long history of audience investigations, even if much of this work has taken place outside the academy in projects sponsored by industries and governments[8], and that fraction within its confines has been pretty much marginalised. It was not until the 1980s that academic audience research became increasingly visible, initially within film history and British cultural studies. Around the same time, audiences' social experiences and pleasures were being partially acknowledged in star and genre studies. Work in these fields has located film texts industrially, intertextually and according to audience perspectives. In star studies, Richard Dyer's ground-breaking approach showed how a star image is constructed from filmic and nonfilmic texts, and from practices both industrial and quotidian, beyond the confines of any specific film.[9] Genre theorists such as Rick Altman and Steve Neale have focused in different ways on intertextual networks, interpretive communities, and audience knowledges and expectations in the operation of discursively produced generic conventions.[10] Studies of film stars and genres have thus opened up the prospect of approaching Hollywood as both an industrial institution and a popular entertainment. As such they offer possible prototypes of what Richard Maltby terms 'consumerist criticism', which addresses Hollywood as a system of production and consumption.[11] And yet, genre studies in particular have tended to assume audience investments rather than examining how, and indeed whether, they occur. (I return to a consideration of genre theory in chapter 4.) Despite this problem, the key point is that inquiries into film genres and stars can (at least potentially) cross some intra-disciplinary boundaries to combine analyses of specific film texts with considerations of economic and cultural contexts, and viewer dispositions and behaviours. It is just such a balanced scrutiny of popular film which I have attempted to realise in this book.

While work on stars and genres has often remained peripheral to the main currents of film studies, two other areas of inquiry have posed challenges to entirely text-centred theories of meaning and significance in film: cultural studies and cinema history. These approaches – to which I shall soon turn – have fed into new and still evolving research strategies which concern themselves with film audiences and conditions of reception. My methodology in this book draws on reception studies insofar as it offers an investigation of the social and historical settings in which films are viewed – a partial rather than comprehensive mapping of contexts, including elements of each film's 'discursive surround'.[12] Because of their historical slant, reception studies have often been unable to employ empirical audience research, reconstructing instead something of the range of probable meanings a film may have had at a particular location and moment in time. Nevertheless, there are clearly important overlaps between these two approaches in the ways that they may complicate and problematise critical interpretations derived from textual analysis alone. According to reception and audience studies, the text does not simply determine its own meaning. Rather, at least some meanings are relatively unstable and contingent – not set once and for all, but dependent upon the differing positions of those approaching the text and on the array of intertextual material surrounding it, as well as on its intrinsic properties.[13] Meanings and uses are thus generated in the interaction between text, audience and context. Viewers are conceived of as social subjects, and film consumption is understood as a social event, shaped by a range of local and variable factors, and anchored in the context of historically specific conditions.

So what exactly can empirical audience research add to a contextual understanding of a film's circulation? Without it, probable audience responses may be read off from reviews, promotional discourses and the like, yet these materials do not provide 'transparent', unmediated evidence, and any extrapolation from them can only be provisional.[14] Rather than assuming a fit between frameworks proposed through film marketing and journalism and the orientations of (prospective) viewers, I examine this nexus by asking how audiences negotiate such mechanisms of 'hype'. A number of specific uses of audience research will be demonstrated in the following chapters. Thinking more generally, there are four good reasons for undertaking this kind of work.

Firstly, to map out some of the complex relations between viewers, film texts and contexts. The implications of the turn towards audiences are set out clearly by Justin Lewis:

> As a form of literary or textual criticism, there is nothing wrong with an approach that treats the text as it likes, free from the specificities of the audience's cultural constraints. ... The problem comes when we infuse this literary endeavor with any wider historical or sociological purpose. ... if we are concerned with the meaning and significance of popular culture in contemporary society, with how cultural forms work ideologically or politically, then we need to understand cultural products (or 'texts') as they are understood by audiences.[15]

However, understanding how cultural forms work within contemporary society also requires an investigation of institutional contexts and commercial strategies and practices, as media consumption clearly does not happen in isolation from these operations. The object of study, then, is no longer the single discrete text but the film(s) as situated in specific contexts of production, circulation and reception.[16]

Secondly, audience research can query, and critique if necessary, some of the assumptions about audiences embedded in dominant traditions of textual analysis within film studies, including Screen theory.[17] I am equally motivated, however, by the need to retrieve audience study from the worst excesses of academic populism. Some of the work undertaken since 1980 has fallen into the trap of assuming that the agency of popular audiences is always productively 'oppositional'. In the words of Martin Allor, the risk here is that the researcher 'simply replaces one set of abstract totalities with another' – that is, the textually determined spectator position assumed in so many film analyses is abandoned for the equally monolithic notion of an automatically 'empowered' and 'progressive' viewer or media user.[18]

Thirdly, work on audiences can counter moral panics and some of the more dubious claims made about susceptible audiences and media 'effects'.[19] (One must beware a knee-jerk rejection of all and any concerns about media 'effects', however. I return to this issue in chapters 3 and 5.)

Fourthly, academic investigations of audiences can productively ask questions of the industry's own market research.[20] For example, my interest in cultural and social power relations entails a critical perspective on how industry-funded studies constitute, organise and hierarchise 'knowable' and commercially exploitable audiences (see chapters 4 and 5 in particular). Crucially, my use of audience research alongside contextual and textual analyses in a multidimensional framework enables me to (in Graham Murdock's words) 'analyze [some of] the underlying structures that provide the contexts and resources for audience activity and … demonstrate how they organize the making and taking of meaning in everyday life'.[21] In the process, I have drawn on cultural studies and film history, to which recent theoretical and empirical work on film audiences is heavily indebted, and on the political economy of popular cinema. It is to the first of these three critical traditions that I shall now turn.

The audience in cultural studies

The late 1970s and early 1980s saw the emergence within British cultural studies of a new interest in media audiences as agents in meaning production. Inquiries focused on the diverse social contexts of media use, the range of power relations – both institutional and social – articulated with and through media use, and the notion of reception as the terrain of ideological struggle and contestation.[22] These developments also entailed the growing recognition that 'audiences' are temporary collections of heterogeneous individuals, a notion which challenged the conception of media consumers as members of an undifferentiated, monolithic totality.[23]

The attention paid to active, diverse consumers, and the uses and pleasures they derive from engagement with media texts, called into question the pessimism with which scholars influenced by the criti-

cal theory of the Frankfurt School had viewed mass culture in the
1970s.[24] This shift away from ideas of popular culture as a straightforward vehicle for dominant ideology has been characterised by
Charlotte Brunsdon as a move 'from the "bad" text to the "good"
audience'.[25] In film studies, a similar if more gradual move took
place during the 1990s, questioning the legacy of Screen theory and
an associated and still prevalent suspicion of popular cinema. The
best work on media consumers does not, however, neglect issues of
cultural power and social or political hegemony in the rush to
embrace popular culture and its 'good' audiences.[26] An acknowledgement of the pleasures and uses derived by media consumers
should also entail a critical examination of their negotiations with
dominant discourses, institutional structures, textual mechanisms
and prevailing social relations, not a swing towards a naive and
unquestioning enthusiasm for their limitless creativity and autonomy. Thus, the complex processes of power in scenarios of media
consumption, at the interrelating levels of macro-structures (such as
social norms of behaviour or the operations of media institutions
and cultural producers) and micro-procedures (including interpersonal power relations), must not be forgotten.[27]

   This does not mean that the study of pleasure and popularity
should be rejected. As David Morley notes, these issues are vital to
an understanding of how commercial popular culture works: 'The
functioning of taste, and indeed of ideology, has to be understood as
a process in which the commercial world succeeds in producing
objects, programmes (and consumer goods) which do connect with
the lived desires of popular audiences.'[28] The point is that popular
culture's hegemonic operations cannot be divorced from the myriad
lived experiences which different individuals fashion from them.
Rather, the two fields interpenetrate. It will be my argument in the
course of this book that analyses of cultural consumption and use
must take into account the coexistence in everyday life of individual
agency along with the unevenly available resources for, and limits
on, such agency.

   My initial investigation of press responses to *Basic Instinct* uncovered a multiplicity of interpretive frames, rather than agreement on
a single reading of the film.[29] The diversity of meanings, uses and
(dis)pleasures was even more marked in viewer reactions revealed
through subsequent audience research. This begged the question:
how best to theorise and categorise the production of such divergent

orientations towards, and responses to, a film text? Much work on these issues remains indebted to Stuart Hall's seminal essay 'Encoding/Decoding', first published in 1973.[30] For Hall, whose exemplar is television news, the text is relatively, but not infinitely, open and polysemic. Certain 'preferred' meanings are 'encoded' into the text, but the way it is read, watched or 'decoded' is socially determined rather than simply and unproblematically predetermined by the text itself. Hall suggested three hypothetical positions from which the text may be decoded – dominant, negotiated and oppositional. A reading from the dominant position takes 'full and straight' the hegemonic or preferred interpretation as generated by political and institutional elites. This hegemonic viewpoint 'defines within its terms the mental horizon, the universe, of possible meanings'. It 'carries with it the stamp of legitimacy – it appears coterminous with what is "natural", "inevitable", "taken for granted" about the social order'.[31] The negotiated interpretation is more complex, containing 'a mixture of adaptive and oppositional elements'. Hall gives the example of a worker responding to calls for a wage freeze or limits on strike action. While s/he is likely to accept the broad hegemonic world view and its argument about the need for self-restraint in the interest of national economic wellbeing, the worker may still reserve the right to go on strike in reaction to local factors. Finally, the message may be decoded in a 'globally contrary way', that is according to an 'alternative frame of reference' or oppositional code. Hence, while the encoding of the preferred meaning limits the free play of interpretation and recognises the institutional power of the producers of texts – those with access to the media apparatus – that meaning is not necessarily taken up by the media consumer. The preferred meaning is thus 'never fully successful, but it is the exercise of power in the attempt to hegemonize the audience reading'.[32]

Hall's tripartite model has since been criticised for being simplistic and mechanistic. Janet Staiger, for example, questions the implication that 'media texts reproduce hegemonic ideology' and are thus never heterogeneous or contradictory.[33] Hall himself has since admitted that his theory assumes too close a fit between encoding and an unproblematic hegemonic message. He has also clarified the dominant and oppositional decoding positions as two ends of a spectrum, and suggested that the majority of readings fall into the 'negotiated space' in between.[34] Another criticism is that applications of the model often assume that consumers' responses can simply be read off once their class grouping has been ascertained.[35] The paradigm also fails to account for groups who may find a text irrelevant and who may be highly unlikely to consume it outside the research situation. And it is important to note that although Hall assumed a 'reactionary' text, oppositional readings of which would be 'progressive', in truth media users' resistance is not necessarily politically desirable. It may equally entail 'reactionary' responses to the preferred meaning of a 'progressive' text. One of the most damning criticisms is that the 'social' implicitly has a prophylactic function in the model, mitigating textual influence, and thus audiences effectively cease to be socially situated (their readings inflected by social conditions) when they take up the preferred reading of the text.[36] This is deeply problematic, as audiences' social locations may precisely encourage them to endorse a 'preferred reading', while still of course negotiating with it (see chapter 3). Finally, Hall overemphasises the rational dimension of response. As Graham Murdock puts it, 'the role of pleasure and desire in audience-text relations is marginalized by the way the central metaphor of code-breaking privileges cognitive operations'.[37] This is a widespread problem, which also affects work in reception studies and film analysis. In each of these critical traditions, emotional response and sensual, physical affect often remain under-examined.[38]

These problems notwithstanding, the significance of Hall's theory lies in its recognition of institutional and textual power, while avoiding textual determinism. It allows that a text may be viewed in different ways, and that 'resistance' on the part of an active reader/viewer is possible. But it stresses that the organisation and structuration of the text – how discourses are arranged in dominance – exerts pressure on the production of meaning. As David Morley later wrote: 'The point of the preferred reading model was to insist that readers are, of course, engaged in productive work, but under determinate conditions. Those determinate conditions are of course supplied both by the text, the producing institution and by the social history of the audience.'[39] These insights produce a conception of popular culture as the site of negotiation and struggles over meaning.

The encoding/decoding paradigm provided a crucial theoretical impetus for the boom in qualitative and interpretive empirical research into media audiences which has taken place since the late 1970s.[40] In practice, however, audience investigations within cultural studies and elsewhere have sometimes lost sight of the textual power recognised by Hall and so overstated media texts' 'openness' to diverse interpretations. John Corner has made a persuasive diagnosis of this problem, and offers an important reminder of the impact of textual characteristics on the production of meaning. He argues that much audience research has focused on higher levels of meaning production, particularly the third in his 'triple-decker' model of meanings (all of which are produced simultaneously during the act of reception). This is the level at which 'viewers and readers attach a generalized significance to what they have seen and heard, evaluating it … and locating it within a negotiated place in their knowledge or memory, where it may continue to do modifying work on other constituents of their consciousness (and, indeed, of their unconscious)'.[41] Corner contends that by concentrating on this third level, many audience investigations have underestimated the determinations upon meaning made by textual properties. Such properties operate most clearly at the two lower levels of meaning production: the 'primary signification' or denotation of a word, image, or sequence; and the connotative level of 'secondary, implicatory or associative signification', which takes account of larger textual structures and of the resources drawn on by viewers and readers. Corner suggests that a slippage has commonly occurred whereby arguments for the relative autonomy of media users at the third level of meaning production are assumed to hold for the two lower levels as well. However, because texts use 'systems of signification based on widespread social/national acceptance and having relatively low levels of ambiguity'[42] – particularly at the first, denotative level – they already limit the range of readings which audiences can make of them, and are thus never infinitely polysemic.[43] Such an understanding guards against the excesses of some 'demand-side' approaches to the media. Moreover, I would argue, it also serves to throw into relief the true significance of the contextually shaped interpretations and uses which consumers may actively produce from their encounters with media texts. Rather than being assumed as automatic, or, by implication, as stemming inevitably from texts which are almost infinitely polysemic in structure, readings and uses can then be seen to be negotiated from texts (and producing institutions) which have already set some limits on meaning. Such processes will be examined in detail in the following chapters.

The question remains: how should one address the interrelations between film consumption and the social patterning of audiences? In my case studies I debate the ways in which gendered, aged, and sexual identities do not simply inform but are also (re)produced through acts of viewing. Another, connected, way I approach audiences is via the notion of 'taste publics'. A taste public is not necessarily officially organised, but is a group sharing certain cultural repertoires, preferences and competences.[44] Work along this trajectory has been significantly influenced by the writings of the French sociologist Pierre Bourdieu.[45] He argues that 'cultural capital', or the symbolic resources and knowledges needed for cultural consumption, is both unequally distributed (via education and social environment) and value-laden, so that certain forms of consumption are legitimated and others derided. A hierarchy of cultural codes and practices is produced with those of dominant groups uppermost, and then naturalised through the arbitration of good or bad 'taste'. Thus variations in cultural behaviour become a means of distinguishing and categorising individuals, and of validating and reproducing power differentials in the process: 'the relationship of distinction is objectively inscribed within [the field of cultural goods] and is reactivated, intentionally or not, in each act of consumption'.[46] As it stands, Bourdieu's analysis of popular and elite tastes remains too heavily reliant on individuals' class origins and education for my purposes. An assessment of the positioning and subjectivity of film viewers must take account of complexities of cultural taste and behaviour which cannot simply be read off from class classifications. For instance, Bourdieu's model would have to be modified to take account of gendered taste hierarchies, or the accumulation of 'additional' cultural resources (above and beyond those accrued through family background and education) among, for example, media fans or members of social and political movements. Moreover, Bourdieu implies that class groupings are generally unitary and homogeneous, while in practice taste formations will not always match class, or any other conventional sociological categorisation, such as gender or age.[47] My own research addresses issues of gender, sexuality, age and (to a lesser extent) class, but also attempts to take account of variations in cultural competences and practices which operate across, and so subdivide, these identity groupings. For instance, in my discussion of *Bram Stoker's Dracula* in chapter 4, I draw on a modification of Bourdieu's paradigm made by Sarah Thornton, whose concept of 'subcultural capital' is in some ways more appropriate for the study of media-rich youth cultures.

So far I have considered viewer agency – the role of consumers in producing meanings and deriving pleasures and uses from media texts – and some of the (textual and structural) determinants which operate upon this; ideas of popular culture as a site of ideological negotiation; and the interactions of identity with media uses and tastes. The final strand of work within cultural studies which has shaped my audience research overlaps with these approaches in a number of ways. It addresses how media use is situated in the everyday lives of consumers.

I place my three chosen films in specific 'local' contexts, investigating the social and interpersonal relations at play in moments of film viewing. Janice Radway's book *Reading the Romance* is significant here for the importance it ascribes to the act of cultural consumption as a social event embedded in the rhythms and routines of daily life.[48] Again, the notion of the media text as exclusive site of meaning is questioned, but two further points arise. Firstly, the text is seen as situated within a particular social location, so that interpretations, pleasures and uses appear inextricably linked with questions of context. Secondly, a two-way relationship can be traced between, on the one hand, media users' subjectivities, social relations and 'lifeworlds',[49] and on the other, the cultural practices in which they are engaged. Thus media consumption is not simply and directly structured by pre-existing identities and local power relations, but rather both expresses and constructs them.

Radway has also outlined a way of rethinking media use to take account of the multiplicity of discourses to which the individual is exposed in everyday life. Her response to this, and to notions of nomadic subjectivity posited by post-structuralist thought, is an injunction to 'investigate the multitude of concrete connections which ever-changing, fluid subjects forge between ideological fragments, discourses, and practices'.[50] This echoes Stuart Hall's observation that 'we are not "viewers" with a single identity, ... all exposed to a single channel and type of "influence"'.[51] Radway's call to move beyond a focus on 'audiences' for a selected medium or genre shares some ground with Hermann Bausinger's study of the 'media ensemble' of overlapping forms and technologies (including television, radio and newspapers) integrated into the daily life of one particular family.[52] Her solution is to start not with specific instances of media use, but with an investigation of the habits and practices of everyday life. She proposes a collaborative ethnographic project: 'a collective mapping of the social terrain equal to the ambitious, majestic scope of our recent theories of subjectivity and intertextuality'.[53] However, this presents practical difficulties, as Radway herself admits. John Corner notes that this kind of research project 'is at risk of being confounded by its own empirical ambition'.[54] One obvious reason for the prevalence of simplifying conceptions of 'audiences' as bounded, locatable and observable, is that this facilitates empirical research. Furthermore, as Kim Christian Schroder has argued, a concern with ethnographies of everyday life may risk losing sight of the fact that ordinary people are repeatedly constituted as audiences for (rather than producers of) the mass media, through industrial and social processes, and that they often see themselves as such.[55] Singling out a single medium or text for study clearly does some violence to its embeddedness in the contexts of everyday life. However, one major advantage of this approach is that the researcher can immediately address the encounter between audience/consumer and text(s), all the while taking care to relate this as much as possible to specific social and inter-media contexts. A problem with Radway's suggestion is that the critical engagement with the audience/text interface may never arrive. I would argue that one can still attend to the play of contextual factors in and through the moment of media consumption, so that the 'social' and the 'everyday' – including the operations of institutional power – are addressed via this point of entry.

Some important overlaps exist between the work in cultural studies that I have been reviewing and roughly contemporaneous developments in film history. I consider next the implications for my project of film historians' examinations of audiences and conditions of reception. In the process I assess what this critical tradition can add to the perspectives and tools gleaned from cultural studies, particularly in terms of approaches to industrial, intertextual and discursive contexts.

Film history: industry, intertexts, reception

At much the same time that scholars in cultural studies were turning towards audience research, film history was becoming revitalised, in part through a new interest in issues of exhibition and reception. As Robert C. Allen observes, orthodox film history had for years offered little more than 'a succession of texts', a list of canonical films as material for textual analysis and exegesis.[56] The specific exhibition practices and viewing conditions experienced by the many different audiences watching these films were granted scant attention before the 1980s. Allen co-authored with Douglas Gomery an influential historiographical critique of the aims, assumptions and methods of traditional film history, which also provided a revisionist account of moments in the history of cinema in the United States.[57] The pair championed the investigation of the cinematic institution in its widest sense – economic, technological, cultural and social – through the study of not just films but also extra-filmic material such as company records, press reports and advertising. This commitment – which led Thomas Elsaesser to label their work 'New Film History, which should really be called New History of the Cinema'[58] – provides a precedent for my broad-based study of aspects of popular film culture in the 1990s.

The 1980s and early 1990s saw a flurry of 'New Historical' investigations into exhibition practices, audiences and production contexts, especially for the period 1895 to 1930. It is possible to locate a rough – but not always clear-cut – split between studies which explore production, distribution and exhibition with regard to the organisation of the industry, and those which ask how films were consumed by various audiences. The first approach includes Douglas Gomery's work on how the economics of the film industry interfaced with factors such as exhibition technology, cinema design, air conditioning and popcorn sales.[59] Gomery's achievement is to address cinemagoing as more than just the watching of films, and to show in detail how various inputs have shaped this experience over the century. A danger which arises here, however, is the implication that the industry unproblematically directs and controls passive viewers.[60] The best work in film history combines an awareness of industrial and institutional practices with, at the very least, an acknowledgement of the importance of audience perspectives, which may not always conform to the plans of producers, distributors and exhibitors.

Of course, serious practical problems attend any attempt to unearth evidence of the viewpoints of past cinemagoers. These difficulties have led some historians to examine, instead, the discursive practices and critical institutions which frame and attempt to regulate film reception. Looking beyond the confines of the single film, but faced with a general lack of empirical data about audiences, researchers have drawn heavily on the satellite texts circulating around films. These do not directly determine the meaning of any film text, but they may provide prospective viewers with background information and interpretive frames on which to draw when approaching and making sense of it. The 'primary' film text is thus conceived of as 'the referential centre of a wider range of intertextual expressions that help to delimit its meaning at any particular historical moment'.[61] Intertextual investigations have also played an important part in histories of 'reputation building'[62] – that is, of the discursive construction of, and shifts in, the critical standing of films and filmmakers. As in the cultural studies work reviewed above, investigations in this field are based on the understanding that a text's higher-level meanings are mutable rather than invariant, that they change over time and according to the contexts of reception. But here the contexts examined are more often than not institutional – industrial, journalistic or academic – rather than quotidian.[63]

A significant intervention in these debates, made from beyond the disciplinary boundaries of film history, is Tony Bennett and Janet Woollacott's study of intertextual relations, *Bond and Beyond*. Bennett and Woollacott investigated a 'considerable and accumulating set of texts' referring to the fictional spy and popular hero James Bond, across three decades.[64] They argue that a text can never be separated from the specific 'reading formation' within which it is activated. A reading formation is a product of social and ideological relations of reading (interpretation and use) constructed and contested through education, the media, and cultural taste.[65] The importance of Bennett and Woollacott's argument is, firstly, that it recognises something of the multitude of variable intertextual regimes and associations upon which media consumers may draw, and how these organise different reading strategies. Secondly, it highlights the artificial and partial nature of textual interpretations which attempt to isolate a cultural object for study as if it were in a vacuum. Insofar as they claim transparency, objectivity and hence 'correctness' for any single interpretation, such readings both disavow how the analyst's constitution of the text is derived from her/his own reading formation, and refuse the possibility of other, dissenting readings.[66] There is a risk that Bennett and Woollacott's work could be taken (erroneously) as a cue to abandon all analysis of textual structures, to dissolve the text entirely into its readings. However, rather than go this far, they argue (much as John Corner suggests) that meaning is not simply inherent within the text but is dependent upon both the internal organisation of the text and the specific reading formations and practices used by the individual reader/viewer to activate it.[67]

A contextual approach to meaning production has also been espoused by Janet Staiger. Her book, *Interpreting Films: Studies in the Historical Reception of American Cinema*, offers an 'historical explanation of the activities of interpretation' in a number of case studies, from the era of 'primitive' cinema to Woody Allen's *Zelig* (1983). Much as Bennett and Woollacott do, she rejects textually determined models of meaning production and refutes the assumption that a film text is a receptacle for a fixed, determinate meaning waiting to be 'uncovered' by the academic or critic. As she puts it: 'immanent meaning in a text is denied'.[68] Rather, audience response 'is a result of both textual and contextual determinants'.[69] Like the theorisations of taste publics discussed above, Staiger's argument rejects a conception of the viewer as *tabula rasa*, approaching the film free from any historical, social or cultural context. It calls attention not only to film-specific factors such as generic conventions and expectations, but also to a much wider sense of the viewer's social subjectivity and world view, drawing on discourses which operate beyond a narrow definition of the cinematic arena. Staiger outlines her context-activated model of reception thus: 'What we are interested in, then, is not the so-called correct reading of a particular film but the range of possible readings and reading processes at historical moments and their relation or lack of relation to groups of historical spectators. Such a project would result not in a history of objects but a history of meaning production.'[70] There are, however, limits to what reception studies, as defined by Staiger, can achieve. Faced with problems of evidence gathering, Staiger concentrates on the critical reception of films and eschews empirical audience research, which she regards with suspicion:

> Certainly in this case the notion of 'raw data' goes out the window. Any so-called evidence is so enmeshed in the first place within the processes of its existence that even its availability makes it suspect ... Marketing analyses, audience opinion polls, film reviews, interviews and letters to editors of periodicals are bound within an apparatus of perpetuating the pleasure of the cinematic institution. Even if we acknowledge mediation and distortion, these stumbling blocks can never be fully overcome.[71]

Staiger's conclusions here seem to me overstated and in contradiction of her initial premise. Certainly, any notion of audience research producing 'raw data' is indeed a chimera. It does not follow, however, that such investigations are worthless, only that they must be sufficiently self-reflexive to acknowledge their own imperfection and partiality. Any and all forms of evidence – whether textual or ethnographic, contemporary or retrospective – are a mediation of the moment of film reception, an experience which can only ever be retrieved through the operations of language. There is thus no 'pure' and pre-discursive source of evidence beyond the 'stumbling blocks' of mediation, representation and distortion.[72] Yet this is what Staiger's rejection of audience research implies. Moreover, the need for qualitative audience research is highlighted by the restricted nature of Staiger's own contextual investigations, which omit empirical details of everyday cinemagoing, and can ultimately only hypothesise about possible audience responses. The problems that exist in the gathering, mediation and retrieval of evidence – which I consider further in the next chapter – should not preclude scholars from utilising audience research. Taking a reception studies approach is an important first step towards tracing the circulation, meanings and uses made of films in popular culture. But there are limits to what it can achieve alone and instances where audience investigations would be needed to fill in the gaps left or even highlighted by this method.

There are notable overlaps between the film history investigations I have reviewed here (including historical reception studies) and work taking place under the banner of cultural studies. In drawing upon these two traditions, my present project should not be viewed as one unconcerned with textual structures and mechanisms. I reiterate this caution in part because there is a danger (within film studies in particular) of critical inquiry remaining corralled within two distinct and polarised camps: theory and history.[73] Within media and cultural studies, one might recast this schism as that between work centred on texts and on audiences. By contrast, I have attempted in this book to work across such boundaries: to redress a longstanding neglect of film audiences, but without losing sight of the operations of film texts. My intention has been to scrutinise some of the multiple uses to which selected films have been put, by the film industry as well as by audiences, and to trace how these texts' internal organisations are shaped by the former, and impact upon the activities of the latter.

So far, I have focused more on issues of reception than on the strategies of film producers and distributors. Accordingly, in the next section I turn my attention to the industrial contexts of my three chosen films, that is, the political economy of Hollywood in the 1990s.

Hollywood's dispersible texts

One common problem found in both historical investigations of reception contexts and empirical audience research is a tendency to bracket off or underplay issues of industrial activity and power. Yet these operations are crucial in influencing and in some ways organising (without fully fixing) film viewers' production of uses, meanings and pleasures. Any consideration of popular film culture must engage with economic practices if it is to arrive at a clear picture of the interrelated processes which constitute this circuit.[74] For my own purposes, an account of industrial procedures and power has to address mechanisms of production, marketing, distribution and exhibition. Concentrating most on marketing, my case studies attempt to investigate something of these operations alongside the social situations, dispositions and activities of specific viewers.[75] The industrial practices considered in this section shape what kind of films are made most readily available for mass audiences to watch, and the means by which potential viewers are made aware of these leisure opportunities. The success of such commercial strategies is by no means certain, however. Promotion is a contractual process, inviting audience members to invest in a film, in exchange for anticipated pleasures and uses. Whether, and exactly how, viewers do so depends upon their particular situations, competences and dispositions, and is investigated throughout the following chapters.

In an attempt to manage the inherent instability and insecurity of the market for popular film, producers and distributors routinely segment consumer populations according to perceived taste differentials. Market research and institutionalised systems of genres and stars enable the constitution and subdivision of 'knowable' audiences and the prediction of future demand based on 'established' preferences.[76] The film business, like other industries, has a stake in exploiting difference, insofar as its products can be successfully targeted at distinct niche markets. In this manner, the procedures of mass production and consumption do not simply erode difference in an ineluctable drift towards a homogenised culture, but operate according to a logic of managed plurality.[77] Nevertheless, attempts are also made to engineer film products which will sell successfully across different market segments. Assembling films as composite goods targeted at diverse audiences is not a new practice. At one level, all films combine different and overlapping textual elements – narrative, music, sound, performance, spectacle and display.[78] Moreover, generic hybridity, at its simplest and most standardised in the conventional double plot providing both romance and 'action', has a long tradition in Hollywood.[79] However, this mechanics of aggregation has in some ways intensified since the 1970s, driven by developments in economic organisation and procedures, including the shift to saturation release patterns, the growth in merchandising and cross-marketing, and the absorption or expansion of the major studios into horizontally integrated transnational entertainment conglomerates, selling film 'brands' across multimedia product lines.[80] While cross-promotion is hardly a new strategy, it has gained in significance and visibility in the decades since 1970 as 'synergy' (also known as 'tight diversification' or 'horizontal integration') has become the dominant mode of corporate organisation.[81] Crucially, synergy offers entertainment conglomerates scale economies, maximising the commercial exploitation of any single intellectual property across multiple outlets, and keeping overheads down by enabling the sharing of resources such as legal, management and marketing teams across different divisions. The massive earnings from successful film 'brands' also provide vital sources of operating capital to invest in developing new projects.[82]

The theatrically released feature film thus takes its place in an entertainment industry dominated by multimedia corporations such as Disney and AOL-Time Warner. The trend toward horizontal integration in business mergers and acquisitions forged new links between the major studios and other media operations such as television production companies, network and cable television channels, music and recording businesses, book, magazine and newspaper publishers, theme parks, and manufacturers of games, toys, and electronic hardware.[83] Such industrial organisation is in part an attempt to manage the economic risk of producing films for relatively unpredictable and volatile markets by generating multiple profit centres beyond the theatrical sector.[84] Proliferating release windows, from home video to pay-television to overseas markets,

have restored a degree of security to the majors by effectively providing 'second, third and fourth runs' for their films. As Martin Dale
notes, both tight diversification and vertical integration operate as
strategies to maximise returns and reduce risk:

> The high risk/low reward equation of the movies means that it is very
> difficult to establish a viable studio based on cinema alone. ... The true
> value of the film business is not the profits generated by the films, but
> the synergies that movies provide with other areas. These include tele-
> vision production, theme parks, consumer products, soundtracks,
> books, videogames and interactive entertainment. All of these areas
> have lower costs, lower risks and higher returns. Feature films provide
> the key to this magic kingdom. Following the same logic, a Major can
> stabilize its cash flow and control costs by controlling each section of
> the value chain. The heart of the Majors' business is software – the pro-
> duction of feature films – but the bulk of profits are earned further
> down the value chain in distribution and retail [theatrical exhibition
> and other delivery modes].[85]

While the logic of synergy has failed to eradicate commercial failure
from the system, it has enabled some box office disappointments
such as *Willow* (1988) and *Waterworld* (1995) to more than amor-
tise their costs through ancillary markets.[86] Moreover, in the context
of a tightly diversified and vertically integrated industry, the film
becomes 'only one ingredient in a multi-media package in which
each element is not only profit-earning in its own right, but serves as
publicity for every other part of the package'.[87]

As Thomas Schatz notes, this economic setting 'favours texts
strategically "open" to multiple readings'.[88] *Bram Stoker's Dracula*
and, to a lesser extent, *Basic Instinct* are clearly products of these
trends – examples of what I term the dispersible text. This is a package designed to achieve commercial, cultural and social reach, by
both facilitating and benefiting from promotional and conversa-
tional processes of fragmentation, elaboration and diffusion.[89] (*Natural Born Killers*, as will become apparent, is more of a niche
product, although it too was extended through a dynamic of dispersal.) The dispersible text is not unstructured or infinitely open to
interpretation, but its multiple address to a coalition of audience
fractions is readily amplified through advertising, publicity and merchandising.[90] My concept of the dispersible text builds on the work
of Barbara Klinger. According to Klinger, marketing, merchandising
and media 'hype' operate to pluralise a mainstream film by 'raiding'

the text for 'capitalizable' features that can circulate in their own right.[91] The dissemination of images, characters, songs, stars, ideas, and (re)interpretations of the film extends its presence in the social arena of potential viewers.[92]

Promotional operations of disaggregation and dilation do not simply work on the dispersible text as a finished film, but shape its assembly in the first place. Multiple bids to capture audiences are made intratextually, through each film's construction as a combination of attractions, as well as extratextually, via the advertising, publicity and ancillary products that the film generates. A constellation of satellite texts orbits the film, including not only licensed merchandising, but also media coverage arranged via symbiotic relations between distributors and television and press outlets. These satellites, from interviews with stars and personnel to promotional deals to soundtracks, commodify fragments of the dispersible text and canvas for interest from various audience groupings. Some such texts and forms may be consumed in their own right, their ancillary experiences enjoyed as more or less autonomous from the film. However, the logic of cross-promotion requires that they should also perform a promissory function, guiding potential viewers to the film, which will in turn send satisfied audiences away to purchase additional affiliated products.[93] (If the film proves successful at the American box office, its brand value can be subsequently exploited in overseas markets, video and television sectors, and via more licensed merchandising.) The successful dispersible text is thus at the hub of a triple movement: a centrifugal dynamic of aperture and extension via satellite texts, mirrored by a centripetal force which refers consumers from these texts to the film, and a further impetus to buy spin-off goods after leaving the cinema. These processes of dissemination, recruitment and ancillary consumption are anticipated and enabled by the particular construction of the dispersible text, and are commonly represented by the term 'hype'. In addition to their commercial function, such mechanisms multiply and complicate the promises, interpretations and invitations-to-view offered on behalf of the film.

The concept of the dispersible text thus attempts to take account of popular films' status as, simultaneously, both symbolic forms and commodities within a moving-image economy. Through the following case studies, I develop some points of contact between these two ways of envisaging films. As Graham Murdock writes: 'the economic determines in the first rather than the last instance, and ... it is therefore a necessary starting point for analysis but not a destination. Economic dynamics are crucial to critical inquiry because they establish some of the key contexts within which consumption takes place, but they do not negate the need for a full ... analysis of symbolic determinations.'[94]

Before I go any further I must make clear my own personal investment in this research. I admit to an interest in contemporary popular cinema – which in Britain largely means Hollywood – as both a consumer and an academic, and to an inclination to validate it as the object of critical investigation. In so doing, I am partly reacting against a vanguardist suspicion of popular forms and pleasures which still persists in some echelons of institutionalised film studies. However, I have attempted to ensure that this motivation does not lead to an uncritical celebration of the popular, but is harnessed to drive a fully critical engagement with the field. This requires a rigorous analysis of complicated and overlapping industrial, cultural, political and social procedures, negotiations and relations. As questions of sexuality are important to my investigation in chapter 3, I should make it clear that I am heterosexual. I am also white, middle class, and in my mid-thirties. While I am a regular consumer of Hollywood films, I would not count myself as a member of the horror or rock fan subcultures discussed in chapters 4 and 5.

Notes

1 David Bordwell, *Making Meaning: Inference and Rhetoric in the Interpretation of Cinema* (Cambridge, Mass. and London, Harvard University Press, 1989), p. 22.

2 See, for example, Jean-Louis Baudry, 'The Ideological effects of the basic cinematographic apparatus' (1970, trans. 1974), *Film Quarterly*, 28:22 (1974–5), 39–47, and 'The Apparatus: metapsychological approaches to the impression of reality in the cinema' (1975, trans. 1976), *Camera Obscura*, 12:1 (1976), 104–28; Laura Mulvey, 'Visual pleasure and narrative cinema', *Screen*, 16:3 (Autumn 1975), 6–18.

3 See Linda Williams, 'Introduction', in Williams (ed.), *Viewing Positions: Ways of Seeing Film* (New Brunswick, Rutgers University Press, 1995), p. 2.

4 Richard Maltby and Ian Craven, *Hollywood Cinema: An Introduction* (Oxford, Blackwell, 1995), p. 432. See also Mary Ann Doane, untitled, *Camera Obscura*, 20/21 (1989), 142.

5 For a critique of Screen theory's textual determinism, and of the gendered binary logic of its key psychoanalytic paradigms, see Jackie Stacey, *Star Gazing: Hollywood Cinema and Female Spectatorship* (London, Routledge, 1994), pp. 19–48.

6 I am thinking here in particular of Jackie Stacey's book, *Star Gazing*, to which I shall return.

7 For an overview of shifts in feminist film theory, see Lisa Taylor, 'From psychoanalytic feminism to popular feminism', in Joanne Hollows and Mark Jancovich (eds), *Approaches to Popular Film* (Manchester, Manchester University Press, 1995).

8 For general overviews of this work see Bruce A. Austin, *Immediate Seating: A Look at Movie Audiences* (Belmont, Wadsworth, 1989); Jostein Gripsrud, 'Film Audiences', in John Hill and Pamela Church Gibson (eds), *The Oxford Guide to Film Studies* (Oxford, Oxford University Press, 1998).

9 Richard Dyer, *Stars* (London, British Film Institute, 1979) and *Heavenly Bodies: Film Stars and Society* (Basingstoke, Macmillan, 1986). Dyer is also one of several scholars who have explored the appropriation of certain stars by particular, often marginalised, audiences such as gay men and lesbians. *Ibid*, pp. 141–94. See also Janet Staiger, *Interpreting Films: Studies in the Historical Reception of American Cinema* (Princeton, Princeton University Press, 1992), pp. 154–77.

10 See Rick Altman, *The American Film Musical* (Bloomington/London, Indiana University Press/BFI Publishing, 1987) and, more recently, his *Film/Genre* (London, British Film Institute, 1999); Steve Neale, 'Questions of Genre', *Screen*, 31:1 (1990), 45–66, and *Genre and Hollywood* (London, Routledge, 2000).

11 Maltby and Craven, *Hollywood Cinema*, pp. 8–9, 113–14.

12 Barbara Klinger, 'Film history terminable and interminable: recovering the past in reception studies', *Screen*, 38:2 (1997), 109. She has borrowed the phrase from Dana Polan. Klinger subdivides a 'total history' of popular film into the following categories: cinematic practices, intertextual zones, and social and historical contexts (such as law, economics, religion, and ideologies of class, gender and family).

13 For a further consideration of 'meaning' in audience–text relations, see p. 19 below.

14 See chapter 3 for a discussion of the epistemological status of data gathered through audience research techniques.

15 Justin Lewis, *The Ideological Octopus: An Exploration of Television and its Audience* (New York, Routledge, 1991), p. 47.

16 For studies which investigate media texts from the point of view of both producers and consumers, see Jostein Gripsrud, *The Dynasty Years: Hollywood Television and Critical Media Studies* (London,

Routledge, 1995); Janice Radway, *Reading the Romance: Women, Patriarchy, and Popular Literature* (Chapel Hill, University of North Carolina Press, 1984; rpt. London, Verso, 1987); Helen Taylor, *Scarlett's Women: Gone With The Wind and its Female Fans* (London, Virago, 1989).

17 See also Martin Barker with Thomas Austin, *From Antz to Titanic: Reinventing Film Analysis* (London, Pluto Press, 2000), pp. 2–31.

18 Martin Allor, 'Review' (of Ien Ang, *Desperately Seeking the Audience*, and James Lull, *Inside Family Viewing*), *Screen*, 34:1 (1993), 102. Jostein Gripsrud locates a further problem in many academic celebrations of popular culture and its audiences. For Gripsrud, such populist approaches are partly motivated by the desire of upwardly mobile entrants into academia for a 'symbolic homecoming' to their social origins in the working classes or non-academic middle classes. This longed-for reintegration as '"voices" for the people' is attempted through the validation of consumers of popular culture. In fact, he argues, while the academic enjoys a 'double access' to the codes and practices of both high and low culture, most of the consumers s/he champions are restricted to a 'single access' to low culture because of their more limited stock of cultural capital. However, in rejecting cultural hierarchies and saying that popular culture is no different from 'legitimate' high culture, populist academics deny their subject positions and the 'class privilege' of double access that they enjoy. Jostein Gripsrud, '"High culture" revisited', *Cultural Studies*, 3:2 (1989), 194–207.

19 On this point, see Martin Barker, 'Film audience research: making a virtue out of a necessity', *Iris*, 26 (1998), 131–47, especially 136–8.

20 For some commentators, academic audience research remains tainted by its methodological and epistemological similarities with market research. However, any such continuities should not be taken as grounds for simply ceding the territory of audience activity to industrial research. As Sonia Livingstone puts it: 'Can we not theorize audiences just because the term is also used by the media industry?'. Livingstone, 'Audience research at the crossroads: the "implied audience" in media and cultural theory', *European Journal of Cultural Studies*, 1:2 (1998), 197.

21 Graham Murdock, 'Critical inquiry and audience activity', in Brenda Dervin, Lawrence Grossberg, Barbara J. O'Keefe and Ellen Wartella (eds), *Rethinking Communication Volume 2: Paradigm Exemplars* (Newbury Park, London, New Delhi, Sage, 1989), p. 227. Structure is understood here, following Giddens, as 'always both constraining and enabling'. *Ibid.*, p. 227, quoting Giddens, *The Constitution of Society: Outline of the Theory of Structuration* (Cambridge, Polity, 1984), p. 25.

22 This work can be loosely divided into two broad, overlapping
    approaches. The first investigates the consumption and uses of specific
    texts. The second concerns the incorporation and use of media and
    communications technologies in everyday life.

23 See Rosalind Brunt, 'Engaging with the popular: audiences for mass
    culture and what to say about them', in Lawrence Grossberg, Cary
    Nelson and Paula A. Treichler (eds), *Cultural Studies* (London, Rout-
    ledge, 1992), pp. 69–80.

24 For perhaps the most influential Frankfurt School critique of the cul-
    ture industry, see Theodor Adorno and Max Horkheimer, 'The culture
    industry: enlightenment as mass deception', in *Dialectic of Enlighten-
    ment*, trans. John Cumming (London, Allen Lane, 1973).

25 Charlotte Brunsdon, 'Text and Audience', in Ellen Seiter, Hans
    Borchers, Gabriele Kreutzner and Eva-Maria Warth (eds), *Remote
    Control: Television, Audiences and Cultural Power* (London, Rut-
    ledge, 1989), p. 125.

26 John Fiske's work in the 1980s has been rightly accused of these traits.
    His recuperative populism overestimates the freedom of audiences
    and the 'progressive' potential of media consumption, and tends to
    disregard both textual and social influences upon the production of
    meaning and use, and the presence of 'reactionary' elements in popu-
    lar culture. See Fiske, 'British cultural studies and television', in Robert
    C. Allen (ed.), *Channels of Discourse: Television and Contemporary
    Criticism* (London, Methuen, 1987); *Understanding Popular Culture*
    (Boston, Unwin Hyman, 1989). Fiske is critiqued in Meaghan Morris,
    'Banality in cultural studies', *Discourse*, 10:2 (1988), 3–29.

27 See David Morley, 'Where the global meets the local: notes from the
    sitting room', *Screen*, 32:1 (1991), 5. See also Morley, 'Between the
    public and the private: the domestic uses of information and commu-
    nications technologies', in Jon Cruz and Justin Lewis (eds), *Viewing,
    Reading, Listening: Audiences and Cultural Reception* (Boulder, West-
    view Press, 1994), pp. 101–23.

28 David Morley, *Television, Audiences and Cultural Studies* (London,
    Routledge, 1992), pp. 35–6.

29 I conceive of 'frames' as interpretive structures that set particular texts
    or events within broader contexts, thus inserting 'the novel into famil-
    iar categories'. See Pippa Norris, 'Introduction: women, media, and
    politics', in Norris (ed.), *Women, Media, and Politics* (New York,
    Oxford University Press, 1997), p. 2.

30 Stuart Hall, 'Encoding/decoding', in Stuart Hall, Dorothy Hobson,
    Andrew Lowe and Paul Willis (eds), *Culture, Media Language: Work-
    ing Papers in Cultural Studies, 1972–79* (London, Hutchinson, 1980),
    pp. 128–38. For a consideration of the academic context, aims and

shortcomings of this model, see 'Reflections upon the encoding/ decoding model: an interview with Stuart Hall', in Cruz and Lewis, *Viewing, Reading, Listening*, pp. 253–74.

31 Hall, 'Encoding/decoding', p. 137.

32 Cruz and Lewis, 'Reflections upon the encoding/decoding model', p. 262.

33 Staiger, *Interpreting Films*, pp. 72–4. David Morley has also pointed out the possibility of a 'slide towards intentionality' in applications of the model. Morley, '"The Nationwide Audience" – a critical postscript', *Screen Education*, 39 (1981), 4.

34 Cruz and Lewis, *Viewing, Reading, Listening*, pp. 264–5.

35 See Staiger, *Interpreting Films*, p. 74; Martin Jordin and Rosalind Brunt, 'Constituting the television audience: a problem of method', in P. Drummond and R. Patterson (eds), *Television and its Audience* (London, British Film Institute, 1988), pp. 239–40; David Morley, *The 'Nationwide' Audience: Structure and Decoding* (London, British Film Institute, 1980); Morley, *Television, Audiences and Cultural Studies*, pp. 11–12, 159; and 'Changing paradigms in audience studies', in Seiter *et al.* (eds), *Remote Control*, p. 19.

36 See Martin Barker and Kate Brooks, *Knowing Audiences: Judge Dredd, its Friends, Fans and Foes* (Luton, University of Luton Press, 1998), pp. 93–5.

37 Murdock, 'Critical inquiry and audience activity', p. 237.

38 For critiques of the poverty of the cognitive model of spectator activity proposed by David Bordwell (in *Narration in the Fiction Film*: London,Methuen, 1985) and Kristin Thompson (in *Breaking the Glass Armor: Neo-Formalist Film Analysis*: Princeton, Princeton University Press, 1988) – specifically its stress on a narrow sense of comprehension which brackets off emotional response – see Barker with Austin, *From Antz to Titanic*, pp. 32–55; Geoffrey Nowell-Smith, 'How films mean, or from aesthetics to semiotics and half-way back again', in Christine Gledhill and Linda Williams (eds), *Reinventing Film Studies* (London, Arnold, 2000). As its title suggests, *Interpreting Films*, Janet Staiger's seminal work in reception studies, also privileges a rather narrow view of films' meanings and uses.

39 Morley, 'Changing Paradigms in Audience Studies', p. 19.

40 In its investigation of the concrete and social experience of informants, interpretive audience research usually employs qualitative techniques. These stand in opposition to the strong tradition of quantitative research in the social sciences, which utilises techniques such as standardised surveys and observation to produce statistical results. See Ien Ang, 'Wanted. Audiences. On the politics of empirical audience studies', in Seiter *et al.* (eds), *Remote Control*, pp. 96–115; Justin Lewis, 'What counts in cul-

tural studies', *Media, Culture and Society*, 19:1 (January 1997), 83–97.
Both interpretive and qualitative audience research are often referred to
as 'ethnographic'. This anthropological term means an attempt to
understand a specific culture 'from the native's point of view' through
extended observation 'in the field'. In cultural and media studies 'ethnographic' research rarely lives up to this definition, but the term has nevertheless become a general description of research into media use from
what Ien Ang calls 'the virtual standpoint of actual audiences'. Ien Ang,
Desperately Seeking the Audience (London, Routledge, 1991), p. 165. I
refer to my own work as audience research because, while it has been
influenced by ethnographic work, it draws on letters and questionnaires,
and does not aspire to the extended in-depth study characteristic of truly
ethnographic media research.

41 John Corner, 'Meaning, genre and context: The problematics of
    "public knowledge" in the new audience studies', in James Curran and
    Michael Gurevitch (eds), *Mass Media and Society* (London, Edward
    Arnold, 1991), p. 272.

42 *Ibid.*, p. 274.

43 The production of 'low-level' meanings in film texts has been exam-
    ined by the neoformalist or 'historical poetics' project most commonly
    associated with David Bordwell. For an attempt to move beyond the
    confines of a Bordwellian approach, see Barker with Austin, *From
    Antz to Titanic*.

44 See Jeffrey Sconce, 'Trashing the academy: taste, excess and the emerg-
    ing politics of cinematic style', *Screen*, 36:4 (1995), 375; Moores,
    Interpreting Audiences, pp. 30–1.

45 See Pierre Bourdieu, *Distinction: A Social Critique of the Judgement of
    Taste*, trans. Richard Nice (London, Routledge, 1984). Studies of taste
    publics have also drawn on reader-response theory. See Robert C.
    Allen, 'Reader-oriented criticism and television', in Allen (ed.), *Chan-
    nels of Discourse*; Stanley Fish, *Is There a Text In This Class? The
    Authority of Interpretive Communities* (Cambridge, Mass., Harvard
    University Press, 1980).

46 Bourdieu, *Distinction*, p. 226.

47 See John Corner, 'Media studies and the "knowledge problem"',
    Screen, 36:2 (1995), 278.

48 Radway, *Reading the Romance*. See also Hermann Bausinger, 'Media,
    technology and daily life', *Media, Culture, Society*, 6:4 (October
    1984), 343–51; Ann Gray, *Video Playtime: The Gendering of a Leisure
    Technology* (London, Routledge, 1992); David Morley, *Family Tele-
    vision: Cultural Power and Domestic Leisure* (London, Comedia,
    1986).

49 Graham Murdock, 'Critical inquiry and audience activity', quoted in

Morley, 'Where the global meets the local', 1.

50 Janice Radway, 'Reception study: ethnography and the problems of dispersed audiences and nomadic subjects', *Cultural Studies*, 2:3 (1988), 365.

51 Stuart Hall, 'Introduction', in Morley, *Family Television*, p. 10. See also *Ibid.*, pp. 41–3; Cruz and Lewis, *Viewing, Reading, Listening*, p. 256.

52 Bausinger, 'Media, technology and daily life', p. 349.

53 Radway, 'Reception study', pp. 367–8.

54 Corner, 'Meaning, genre and context', p. 280.

55 Kim Christian Schroder, 'Audience semiotics, interpretive communities and the "ethnographic turn" in media research', *Media Culture and Society*, 16:2 (1994), 337–47.

56 Robert C. Allen, 'From exhibition to reception: reflections on the audience in film history', *Screen*, 31:4 (1990), 347.

57 Robert Allen and Douglas Gomery, *Film History: Theory and Practice* (New York, McGraw-Hill, 1985).

58 Thomas Elsaesser, 'The new film history', *Sight and Sound*, 55:4 (1986), 246–51.

59 See Gomery, 'The coming of the talkies: invention, innovation, and diffusion', in Tino Balio (ed.), *The American Film Industry* (Madison, University of Wisconsin Press, 1976); *Shared Pleasures: A History of Movie Presentation in the United States* (London, British Film Institute, 1992); 'Warner Bros. innovates sound: a business history', in Gerald Mast (ed.), *The Movies in Our Midst* (Chicago, University of Chicago Press, 1982).

60 See Sue Harper, 'Review', *Screen*, 35:2 (1994), 200.

61 William Uricchio and Roberta E. Pearson, *Reframing Culture: The Case of the Vitagraph Quality Films* (Princeton, Princeton University Press, 1993), p. 206n.

62 Barbara Klinger, *Melodrama and Meaning: History, Culture and the Films of Douglas Sirk* (Bloomington, Indiana University Press, 1994), p. xiii.

63 See, for example, *Ibid.*; Robert E. Kapsis, *Hitchcock: The Making of a Reputation* (Chicago, University of Chicago Press, 1992).

64 Tony Bennett and Janet Woollacott, *Bond and Beyond: The Political Career of a Popular Hero* (London, Macmillan, 1987), p. 44.

65 *Ibid.*, p. 263. See also Tony Bennett, 'Texts in history: the determinations of readings and their texts', in Derek Attridge, Geoff Bennington and Robert Young (eds), *Post-structuralism and the Question of History* (Cambridge, Cambridge University Press, 1987), pp. 70–1.

66 An example of contrasting reading formations is provided by Meaghan Morris' exposition of the gulf between the viewer/text rela-

tions which hold for a mainstream cinema audience, and those of the textual analyst who participates in a very different activity, watching a video with remote control at the ready. Morris, 'Tooth and claw: tales of survival, and *Crocodile Dundee*', in her *The Pirate's Fiancee: Feminism, Reading, Postmoernism* (London, Verso, 1988), p. 256.

67 Bennett and Woollacott, *Bond and Beyond*, pp. 64–5.

68 Janet Staiger, 'Taboos and totems: cultural meanings of *The Silence of the Lambs*', in Jim Collins, Hilary Radner and Ava Preacher Collins (eds), *Film Theory Goes to the Movies* (New York, Routledge, 1993), p. 143.

69 Janet Staiger, 'The Handmaiden of villainy: methods and problems in studying the historical reception of film', *Wide Angle*, 8:1 (1986), 26.

70 *Ibid.*, 20, italics in original. See also Staiger, 'Taboos and totems'.

71 Staiger, 'The handmaiden of villainy', p. 21. See also *Interpreting Films*, pp. 79–80.

72 See also Stacey, *Star Gazing*, p. 56.

73 For an important attempt to end the 'division of labour' between theory and history, see Miriam Hansen, *Babel and Babylon: Spectatorship in American Silent Film* (Cambridge, Mass., Harvard University Press, 1991).

74 For an elaboration of the 'circuit of culture' (encompassing processes of production, consumption, regulation, representation, and identity) see Paul du Gay, Stuart Hall, Linda Janes, Hugh Mackay and Keith Negus, *Doing Cultural Studies: The Story of the Sony Walkman* (London /Milton Keynes, Sage/Open University, 1997). See also Richard Johnson, 'The story so far: and for the transformations', in D. Punter (ed.) *Introduction to Contemporary Cultural Studies* (London, Longman, 1986).

75 An analysis of the capitalistic organisation and deployment of labour in the processes of production, distribution and exhibition is beyond the scope of this book.

76 The industry's reliance upon market research has ballooned in the decades since World War Two. Increasingly, independent websites such as Harry Knowles' aint-it-cool-news.com are being scrutinised to monitor early word of mouth among 'avid' fan bases, while official sites for upcoming releases attempt to generate advance interest. On attempts to map audience habits and preferences in the 1930s and 1940s, see Susan Ohmer, 'The science of pleasure: George Gallup and audience research in Hollywood', in Melvyn Stokes and Richard Maltby (eds), *Identifying Hollywood's Audiences: Cultural Identity and the Movies* (London, British Film Institute, 1999); and her 'Measuring desire: George Gallup and audience research in Hollywood', *Journal of Film and Video*, 43:1–2 (1991), 3–28.

77 See, for example, the proliferation in the 1990s of partnership deals
    between the major transnational entertainment conglomerates and
    'local' content providers, television stations, theatre chains and inter-
    net companies. On partnership, see Tino Balio '"A major presence in
    all of the world's important markets": the globalization of Hollywood
    in the 1990s', in Steve Neale and Murray Smith (eds), *Contemporary
    Hollywood Cinema* (London, Routledge, 1998). On Hollywood's cus-
    tomisation of its products for international markets, see Toby Miller,
    'Hollywood abroad', in John Hill and Pamela Church Gibson (eds),
    The Oxford Guide to Film Studies (Oxford, Oxford University Press,
    1998); Martine Danan, 'Marketing the Hollywood blockbuster in
    France', *Journal of Popular Film and Television*, 22:3 (1995), 131–40.
78 Both academic analysis and 'serious' film reviewing have tended to
    privilege narrative over other filmic elements. For alternative accounts
    of classical Hollywood films as assemblages of component parts, see
    Maltby and Craven, *Hollywood Cinema*, p. 41; Elizabeth Cowie,
    'Storytelling: classical Hollywood cinema and classical narrative', in
    Neale and Smith (eds), *Contemporary Hollywood Cinema*.
79 Maltby, '"Sticks, hicks and flaps": classical Hollywood's generic con-
    ception of its audiences', in Stokes and Maltby (eds), *Identifying Hol-
    lywood's Audiences*; Altman, *Film/Genre*.
80 The terms 'merchandising' and 'tie-ins' overlap and are sometimes
    used interchangeably, but it is possible to draw a distinction between
    the two. Merchandising describes products based on a copyrighted
    film, its stars, characters and *mise-en-scène*. A tie-in is affiliated to a
    specific film, which it promotes, but the product is not actually derived
    from the film itself. Thus, a special edition Rambo knife is an example
    of merchandising, as is a Darth Vader action figure. Walls' *Star Wars*
    skinless sausages are, by contrast, a tie-in. See Janet Wasko, *Hollywood
    in the Information Age* (Cambridge, Polity Press, 1994), p. 197. On the
    post-*Star-Wars* boom in merchandising and promotions, especially
    those based on the 'toyetic' potential of extractable characters, props
    and settings, see *Ibid.*; Robert C. Allen, 'Home Alone together: Hol-
    lywood and the "family film"', in Stokes and Maltby (eds), *Identifying
    Hollywood's Audiences*; Tiiu Lukk, *Movie Marketing: Opening the Pic-
    ture and Giving it Legs* (Los Angeles, Silman-James Press, 1997), pp.
    253–74; Nevertheless, as Peter Kramer argues, the present state of
    Hollywood should be understood as in some ways 'an intensification
    of past structures … rather than as a radical break with them': Peter
    Kramer, 'The lure of the big picture: film, television and Hollywood',
    in John Hill and Martin McLoone (eds), *Big Picture, Small Screen: the
    Relations Between Film and Television* (Luton, University of Luton
    Press, 1996), p. 13.

81 Synergy originally referred to the strategy of cross-promotion between films and music recordings. Although the term only gained widespread use in the 1980s, synergistic connections between film and music go back to the 1910s. See Jeff Smith, *The Sounds of Commerce: Marketing Popular Film Music* (New York, Columbia University Press, 1998), p. 27.

82 *Ibid.*, pp. 187–8.

83 See Thomas Schatz, 'The new Hollywood', in Collins *et al.*, *Film Theory Goes to the Movies*, p. 29.

84 Some risks can be effectively devolved from film producers to their merchandising partners. For example, British publisher Dorling Kindersley made a licensing deal with Lucasfilm to sell books tied to *Star Wars: Episode 1*, but overestimated demand and was left at the end of 1999 with unsold books worth £14 million. See JoJo Moyes, '"Star Wars" failure leaves black hole where publisher's profits use to be', *The Independent*, 25 January 2000, 5; Cheryl Cole 'Making money from the toy story', *Investor's Week*, 31 March 2000, 24–5.

85 Martin Dale, *The Movie Game: The Film Business in Britain, Europe and America* (London, Cassell, 1997), pp. 25–6. During the 1980s, the Reagan administration effectively sanctioned the majors' large-scale re-entry into the theatre sector. See Wasko, *Hollywood in the Information Age*, pp. 177–80; Richard Trainor, 'Major powers', *Sight and Sound* 1987/8, 26–30. On the importance to the media corporations of distribution control, see Tino Balio, 'Adjusting to the new global economy: Hollywood in the 1990s', in Albert Moran (ed.), *Film Policy: International, National and Regional Perspectives* (New York, Routledge, 1996), pp. 27–34.

86 *Willow*, produced by George Lucas, cost $55 million. Despite advertising and promotional support from licensees worth millions of dollars, it grossed only $28 m at the American box office. However, it earned $42 m in overseas box office, another $33 m in video and television sales in the US and a further $22 m in these sectors abroad. See Wasko, *Hollywood in the Information Age*, pp. 197–8; Richard Maltby '"Nobody knows everything": post-classical historiographies and consolidated entertainment', in Neale and Smith (eds), *Contemporary Hollywood Cinema*, p. 44n, quoting figures from Nicholas Kent, *Naked Hollywood: Money Power and the Movies* (London, BBC Books, 1991), p. 60. *Waterworld* cost $175 m to produce, and grossed only $88 m in the US, but pulled in a further $167 m in overseas box office, plus further video earnings. Figures from imdb.com

87 Nicholas Garnham, *Capitalism and Communication: Global Culture and the Economics of Information* (London, Sage, 1990), p. 202.

88 Schatz, 'The new Hollywood', p. 34.

89 In focusing on recent industry practice, the 'universal' address of classical Hollywood should not simply be taken for granted. As Richard Maltby points out, the undifferentiated audience of the inter-war years was largely a useful rhetorical device, a trope for industry self-promotion. Nevertheless, some films of that era did succeed in selling across multiple audience fractions. See Maltby, 'Sticks, hicks and flaps', and '"A brief romantic interlude: Dick and Jane go to $3^1/_2$ seconds of the classical Hollywood cinema', in David Bordwell and Noel Carroll (eds), *Post-Theory: Reconstructing Film Studies* (Madison, University of Wisconsin Press, 1996), p. 443.

90 In terms of the commercial and cultural impact of their branded product ranges, some of the most successful dispersible texts are the 'family adventure films' at the centre of the *Star Wars, Batman* and *Jurassic Park* franchises. Perhaps the most celebrated example of a dispersible text selling across diverse taste formations is James Cameron's *Titanic* (1997). On family films in the 1980s and 1990s, see Allen, 'Home alone together'; Peter Kramer, 'Would you take your child to see this film? The cultural and social work of the family-adventure movie', in Neale and Smith (eds), *Contemporary Hollywood Cinema*. On *Star Wars*, see Schatz, 'The new Hollywood'; on *Batman*, see Eileen R. Meehan, '"Holy commodity fetish, Batman!" The political economy of a commercial intertext', in Roberta E. Pearson and William Uricchio (eds), *The Many Lives of the Batman: Critical Approaches to a Superhero and His Media* (New York and London, Routledge/British Film Institute, 1991); on *Jurassic Park*, see Constance Balides, 'Jurassic Post-Fordism: tall tales of economics in the theme park', *Screen*, 41:2 (2000), 139–60; on *Titanic*, see Peter Kramer, 'Women first: *Titanic* (1997), action-adventure films and Hollywood's female audience', *Historical Journal of Film, Radio and Television* 1998, 599–618.

91 Barbara Klinger, 'Digressions at the cinema: reception and mass culture', *Cinema Journal*, 28:4 (1989), 3–19. Compare Justin Wyatt's theory of a 'modular aesthetic' in post-classical Hollywood, whereby certain filmic elements (images, songs, sequences) are extracted for the purposes of marketing and merchandising. Wyatt, *High Concept: Movies and Marketing in Hollywood* (Austin, University of Texas Press, 1994).

92 For example, the British media advertising company Creative Partnership cut a special television trailer for Disney's animated feature *A Bug's Life* (1998) designed to extend the film's reach by appealing to a teenage and twenty-something audience perceived to be initially reluctant to watch such 'family-friendly' fare. The trailer comprised 'dark' and blackly comic moments from the film, accompanied by a cover of 'Ant Music' recorded by pop star Robbie Williams. Details

from a Creative Partnership presentation given to Hothouse film-making forum, Brighton, November 1999.

93 In the case of the *Pokémon* phenomenon of 1999–2000, the film occupied a less central position than usual in the product range, which included a video game, television cartoons, trading cards and toy figures.

94 Murdock, 'Critical inquiry and audience activity', pp. 229–30, Murdock is drawing here on Stuart Hall's 'The problem of ideology – Marxism without guarantees', in B. Matthews (ed.), *Marx: A Hundred Years On* (London, Lawrence and Wishart, 1983), p. 84.

Chapter 3

Basic Instinct: 'woman on top'?

In April 1992 the tabloid newspaper the *Daily Mirror* ran a centre-spread article anticipating the imminent British release of the Hollywood erotic thriller *Basic Instinct* (Paul Verhoeven, Carolco/Le Studio Canal +, United States, 1992). Dubbed 'controversial' because of its stormy reception in the United States, where allegations of misogyny and homophobia were accompanying a highly successful run at the box office, the film was rapidly becoming an object of gossip and dispute on the eastern side of the Atlantic as well.[1] While some publications accused *Basic Instinct* of pathologising women, the *Daily Mirror* celebrated its (anti)heroine as an assertive female role model, 'the champion of a new lust for sexual freedom' who spoke for the newspaper's women readers and their desires for social and sexual autonomy.[2] Here, the film was interpreted not as violent and sexually explicit escapism (a view widespread among commentators, both approving and disapproving) but rather as a highly topical manifestation of female aspirations. In the pages of the *Daily Mirror*, *Basic Instinct* was endowed with social validity, its reach extending beyond the cinema into the realm of everyday life. Other titles, from 'upmarket' broadsheet newspapers to the lesbian and gay press, chose to read *Basic Instinct* in very different ways – for instance, as an enjoyable fiction, an offensive 'male' fantasy, or a heterosexist assault on 'other' sexualities. The film text was further pluralised and extrapolated through the accretion of additional cultural debates – taken as an opportunity to discuss the 'excesses' of female emancipation, or the threat posed by 'politically correct' interventions into the world of entertainment. Simultaneously, marketing discourses sold the film as 'unmissable', highlighting star presences and generic elements, including sexual attractions, in a bid to lure multiple audience fractions to the film.

1 The *Daily Mirror* anticipates the release of *Basic Instinct*

Even in an era well used to the mechanisms of film 'hype' – aggressive marketing, engineered controversy, press sensationalism – *Basic Instinct* made a significant popular cultural impact in Britain. In terms of its wide media exposure, status in everyday talk and popular success, it lived up to its billing in trade paper *Screen International* as 'the "must-see" film of the summer'.[3] *Basic Instinct* attracted huge audiences, both for its cinema release and during its post-theatrical career. It topped the UK box office for 1992 and subsequently reached number two in the annual video rental chart, with a total of 3.4 million rentals, at an estimated value of £8.5 million.[4] This success, and the proliferation of discursive frameworks installed around the film by the *Daily Mirror* and other journalistic and promotional texts, pose a series of interrelating questions. What exactly were the commercial strategies employed by producers and distributors to maximise the audience for their film? How did such practices shape *Basic Instinct*'s particular generically inflected treatment of 'real world' issues such as gender roles and sexuality? How did prospective viewers respond to the flood of publicity? How do viewers mediate, utilise and make sense of a film like *Basic Instinct*, and the satellite texts circulating around it? In doing so (how) do they negotiate and assert their self-images? What mutual determinations between identities and media consumption could be observed? I explore here how the film was taken up and made use of by active and diverse viewers, and consider how these encounters were shaped by industrial, intertextual and social factors. Some similar interfaces between these mechanisms occur around other, less successful films, but in the case of a controversial and commercially significant film like *Basic Instinct* they are relatively overt and can be traced more clearly.

Selling *Basic Instinct*

Basic Instinct's advertising, publicity and distribution in Britain were the responsibility of Guild, the country's leading independent distributor at the time. British-owned, the company handled mostly mainstream American product.[5] Three of its most lucrative hits – *Total Recall* (Paul Verhoeven, United States, 1990), *Terminator 2: Judgement Day* (James Cameron, United States, 1991), and *Basic Instinct* – were 'event pictures' made by the high profile 'semi-independent' American producer Carolco.[6] Guild's marketing tactics were very similar to those pursued by the distribution arms of the Hollywood majors in Britain, and it was 'not afraid to outspend the majors on prints and advertising'.[7] This strategy should be seen in the context of Hollywood's ballooning expenditure on heavily advertised saturation releases to the growing multiplex sector, both in the United States and overseas. Since the 1970s, huge television-based advertising campaigns have become increasingly important in securing audience interest for shorter, more concentrated release periods.[8] Simultaneously, there has been a notable shift towards films containing elements that lend themselves to the quick sell demanded by television. As William Paul notes: 'It's not very easy to make an intimate drama look exciting in the context of a 30-sec spot, so questions of how to market the "product" necessarily come into play before the "product" is put into production.'[9] As the American majors became more involved in European distribution and exhibition sectors during the 1980s and 1990s, the practices of multiplexing, saturation release patterns, 'front-loading' the audience, and fast burn at the box office were gradually established in Britain and elsewhere.[10] With its mix of sex, violence, stars and glossy visuals, *Basic Instinct* was well suited to such conditions. For television and cinema trailers, these elements were edited together to the sound of a pumping dance tune. Moreover, the timing of its European release schedule allowed distributors to push the film on the back of its commercial success in the United States, building up its event status and differentiating it from less successful Hollywood rivals opening the same month, such as the erotic thriller *Final Analysis* (Phil Joanou, United States, 1992).[11]

Guild organised a very wide release for *Basic Instinct* in Britain, making more than 300 prints of the film available. To support this big opening, the company spent heavily on television and radio spots, press advertising, and posters. In addition, Guild secured editorial coverage in a number of publications.[12] The relationship between film distribution companies and the press is essentially symbiotic:

> Relations between media and ourselves is a constant see-saw. We need them for coverage; they need us for information. If they run a negative article from our perspective, we can't really leave them off future schedules as we will soon end up with no one to run features. Similarly, if we favour one newspaper over another for an interview, they can't afford to sever relations in case they miss the next opportunity for an interview, which may be around the corner.[13]

Basic Instinct was assembled and marketed as a dispersible text – a combination of attractions with a cross-gender appeal. This populist aim was apparent in the film's target audience, which Guild defined as: 'age 18–35, sex: male and female; class: B, C1 and C2'.[14] (In the event, women represented 44 per cent of *Basic Instinct's* cinema audience in the United Kingdom, and men 56 per cent.)[15] Guild's target audience was not perceived as a homogeneous or undifferentiated mass, but as an aggregation of several specific markets: both men and women, of different ages and class backgrounds, and with various cultural tastes. The film was intended to sell to these disparate sectors by offering a package of diverse textual elements, each appealing to one or more audience groupings.

Basic Instinct did not benefit from the 'multimedia reiteration'[16] deployed around heavily merchandised 'toy movie' blockbusters. The film was pluralised instead via the media space it was granted, an exposure solicited and facilitated by its intratextual organisation as a dispersible text.[17] John Ellis writes of a 'narrative image' as an idea or promise of a film that circulates via advertising, publicity and everyday conversation.[18] With the institutionalisation of the dispersible text, however, multiple promises are made about the same film. The polyvalent potential of *Basic Instinct's* generic mix, its double plot structure and its narrative indeterminacy were crucial to the bid for wide audience appeal. The film follows maverick San Francisco detective Nick 'Shooter' Curran (Michael Douglas) as he becomes sexually involved with glamorous murder suspect Catherine Tramell (Sharon Stone), a bisexual millionairess whose favoured weapon, it appears, is an ice pick. An open ending leaves the pair in an uneasy alliance and in bed together, neither having eradicated the other. Although lamented by some critics,[19] the refusal to resolve either the criminal plot or the sexual plot can be seen to defer judgement on which character is the most important vehicle for audience identification. The lack of certainty over the identity of the killer – who may or may not be Catherine – provided a talking point through which the film's presence in the everyday sphere could be further extended.[20]

Basic Instinct's established star, Michael Douglas, was expected to attract both male and female audiences, and members of several different taste publics. An idea of the breadth of his appeal is indicated by the press coverage he received, in publications ranging from specialist film titles through women's magazines and 'upmarket' men's monthlies, to the 'mass-market' tabloid press.[21] Douglas' casting provided a high marquee value and carried a number of good guy/bad guy associations based on previous films, from *Romancing the Stone* (Robert Zemeckis, United States, 1984) to *Fatal Attraction* (Adrian Lyne, United States, 1987).[22] The latter was an 'event film' much debated in the media for its treatment of adultery as a topical moral dilemma and its portrayal of the male adulterer as victimised by a vengeful woman.[23] When the best-selling tabloid newspaper *The Sun* called *Basic Instinct* '*Fatal Attraction* Part Two',[24] it was thus comparing not simply two Michael Douglas vehicles but two contentious 'adult' hits whose box office success was linked to their high media profiles as films 'everybody was talking about'.

Similarly, Douglas' co-star Sharon Stone was pitched to a number of markets, and was featured in women's magazines, 'male' titles, and publications as culturally diverse as the *Daily Mirror, Time Out* and *Vogue*.[25] Frequently interpreted as a sex symbol for heterosexual men, she was also read on occasions as a positive role model for the modern woman. The star and her role as the fictional Catherine Tramell were sometimes conflated in media coverage to form a composite figure, most commonly portrayed as sexually attractive to men, but often as also aggressive towards them.[26] (Stone was never represented in the media as sharing her character's bisexuality, but it became operative instead as a signifier of the actress' hyper-sexuality.) By contrast with Stone, coverage of Douglas tended to emphasise the difference between the star off-screen and the role of unhinged detective Nick Curran, with the gap bridged by Douglas' ability as an actor. Thus, they were represented as distinct types of actor: Douglas as a 'performer' who successfully 'impersonated' his characters, and Stone as a 'professional' who was more or less 'playing herself' through a process of 'personification'.[27]

In addition to the two stars, other attractions received media coverage in their own right, and so further extended the reach of the film. These included director Paul Verhoeven, named in popular auteurist discourse the 'sultan of shock';[28] the film's glossy look;[29] and Joe Eszterhas' $3 million script, dubbed the most expensive in history.[30] Some of the most important marketing hooks and media talking points were provided by explicit depictions of violence and sex in the film.[31] *Basic Instinct*'s 'controversial' subject matter included female aggression and various forms of sexual 'deviance', including bisexuality, lesbianism and bondage (Catherine ties her sexual partners to the bed with a silk scarf).[32] The sexual content was widely labelled in reports, reviews and interviews as excessive for a mainstream Hollywood star product, on the grounds of both its explicitness and its 'kinky' elements. It was figured synecdochically by the much-discussed exposure scene (a star-making moment for Stone) where murder suspect Catherine uncrosses her legs to reveal to detectives that she is wearing no underwear.[33] One of the most widely reproduced publicity stills for the film was of Catherine in the interrogation room with her legs crossed, prior to exposing her vagina.[34] Crucially, such 'soft porn' elements were offered in combination with markers of 'quality' – high production values, a relatively big budget (around $30 million),[35] a major star and name director, and a heavily promoted blanket release. The strategy for the assembly and marketing of *Basic Instinct* was thus in part a combination of product familiarity and differentiation. It offered as 'guarantees' of audience pleasure an established star presence (Douglas), a successful director, and the generic template of the femme fatale thriller. But it also promised the added attractions of sex scenes and violence (sexualised in scenes of 'rape' and murder during sex) unprecedented for a big budget production.[36] Thus *Screen International* labelled it a 'slick package of sex and violence', the popular film magazine *Empire* lauded its 'justifiably celebrated humping scenes' and the *Daily Mirror* called it 'probably the most sexually explicit and violent thriller you are ever likely to see in a public cinema'.[37] When Verhoeven submitted his first print of the film to the ratings board of the Motion Picture Association of America, he was told to trim three scenes in order to secure an 'R' rating (which allows viewers under the age of 17 to see a film accompanied by a parent or guardian). Verhoeven and Carolco were contractually required to deliver an 'R'-rated film as part of their deal with the American distributor TriStar. Without the cuts, *Basic Instinct* would have landed a 'NC17' rating (only to be seen by those over 17), which would have severely curtailed the film's commercial appeal and its advertising opportunities in the States.[38] The widely reported process of the film's repeated submissions for a rating garnered priceless media coverage. It also indicates the risks of making a big-budget film which sells in part on sex and violence. If one aim of the film was to cause a splash by going further than normal in its representations of sex and violence (both separately and in combination), the concomitant danger was of losing mass-market appeal. One

early manifestation of that risk came at the ratings stage, where Verhoeven and Carolco could have forfeited the chance to sell to the
relatively broad, mainstream audience implied by the 'R' category.

The multiple address of *Basic Instinct* was enhanced by its combination of disparate generic, canonical and populist elements. The
press pack circulated to journalists promoted the film as 'an erotic
psychological mystery' in the tradition of Hitchcock.[39] Elsewhere,
Basic Instinct was read as an upmarket transplantation of the
straight-to-video sex thriller, a contemporary film noir, a disguised
horror film, or a more than usually explicit big-screen mystery – 'like
Jagged Edge with sex'.[40] Whatever exact generic identity it might be
ascribed, *Basic Instinct* can be seen to 'piggyback' on developments
in popular culture and society more broadly – in particular, changes
in the sexual climate of the 1980s and early 1990s, which were both
mediated and fed by the increased sexualisation of the popular
media, including the growing home video market for heterosexual
'couples' pornography. As Linda Williams has observed, this production cycle recognised women as consumers of porn, and installed
female sexual subjectivity within hard-core, investigating 'the different nature of the woman's own desire and pleasure and ... the challenge of helping her to achieve them'.[41] This trend converged with
the adult thriller boom which had been precipitated by the surprise
success of *Jagged Edge* (Richard Marquand, United States, 1985,
and, like *Basic Instinct*, written by Eszterhas), to produce the
straight-to-video soft-core erotic thriller, of which *Basic Instinct* can
be regarded as a big-budget variant.[42] Stone's character, Catherine
Trammel, appears as a sexual pleasure-seeker, and as something of a
'post-feminist' heroine – an interpretation suggested in several
reviews. In such readings, to adapt Charlotte Brunsdon's formulation, Catherine is neither trapped in femininity nor rejects it, but
instead uses it to secure control in a move which derives from (and
distorts) 1970s feminism, even while disavowing its debt to this tradition.[43] This celebration of 'modern' womanhood was one of the
multiple and conflicting promises made on behalf of the film. The
invitation was made alongside the promotion of familiar male heterosexual pleasures centred on the sexualised display of the female
body. I will argue that, rather than remaining perfectly 'egalitarian',
this solicitation of divergent gendered viewing strategies was effectively hierarchised in some ways. Furthermore, such proliferating
invitations at times impacted on each other so that, for example,

some viewers' pleasures in the representation of Catherine as a confident 'new woman' were complicated and compromised by the simultaneous offer of (straight) male sexual pleasures.[44]

Guild's marketing campaign tailored different images of the film for audiences of differing cultural competences and preferences. These were targeted directly through advertising and indirectly through journalistic exposure. Canonical references to 'Hitchcockian elements' and film noir in the press pack were aimed at attracting critical approval and a 'sophisticated' upscale audience influenced by reviews.[45] Meanwhile, the film's sex, violence and stars were marketed to a wider audience, flagged in television spots, cinema trailers, press advertising, publicity photographs and poster art. The poster offered a range of information through its multiple generic codings. Film titles are concise and widely circulating sources of generic identity designed to cue audience expectations and intertextual connections (they may of course, as with *Bram Stoker's Dracula*, also carry codings of authorship). *Basic Instinct* conforms to a general trend for two-word titles in action, thriller, and comedy genres during the 1980s and 1990s. More specifically, the title carried probable intimations of violence and passion, which were consolidated by the visual details of the poster. The pairing of Stone (unbilled) with an apparently naked Douglas suggested a sexual element, while the ice pick motif in the title lettering recalled the iconography of the slasher film.[46] More overt gestures towards sex and violence converged in the tag-line 'Flesh seduces. Passion kills.' These same attractions – sex, violence and stars – were picked up in television reports and by all sectors of the press, but in particular by middle-market and tabloid newspapers. The latter outlets only ever mentioned two of Verhoeven's earlier films, the Hollywood hits *Robocop* (1987) and *Total Recall* (1990), and largely ignored references to Hitchcock and film noir. Mass-market publications labelled *Basic Instinct* a big-name shocker, a thriller, or a sex film, and were far more likely to concentrate on Douglas' star persona and on Stone as a new star in the making than on Verhoeven as an auteur.[47] By positioning *Basic Instinct* in such intertextual settings, both the film's distributor and the publications in question made assumptions about the cultural competences, repertoires and preferences of their different target audiences. As Pierre Bourdieu has suggested, such differences in cultural taste enforce social distinctions. Knowledge of, and interest in, film movements and directors typically indicates 'legitimate' taste, while knowledge of stars indicates 'ordinary', common taste.[48]

So far I have assessed the industrially motivated dispersal of various images and ideas of *Basic Instinct* through marketing and media coverage. The exposure of diverse attractions – including stars, director, generic elements and subject matter – sought to structure reception and maximise revenues by priming viewers to approach the film via one or more of multiple routes. This strategy appears to have been successful in attracting audiences to see the film: *Basic Instinct* provided Guild with more than half of the total gross for films handled by the company in 1992.[49] My commercial analysis cannot adequately explain how empirical audiences invested in and reacted to the film, however. Moreover, it is of little help in analysing 'unguided' responses to the film, both idiosyncratic and more clearly oppositional. The latter included lesbian and gay activists' accusations of homophobia. By campaigning against the film, they made an intervention into popular media discussions of it – in publications not usually disposed to consider the politics of representation – and joined more 'official' institutional sources to become visible and quotable as actors in the news story of the controversy forming around *Basic Instinct*.

Making an issue of it: discourses of protest and entertainment

Basic Instinct became an event film partly as a consequence of campaigns in the United States against its alleged homophobia. In addition to marketing-led hype and various reviewing practices, the media agenda surrounding the film's British release was significantly shaped by these demonstrations, so that *Basic Instinct* became widely framed in discourses of protest. Reports of the controversy surrounding the film began circulating in Britain in late 1991 and intensified after its American opening in March 1992, seven weeks before the British release. Complaints centred on the film's portrayal of not only femme fatale Catherine Tramell but also the three other significant female characters in the film. All four are either lesbian or bisexual; they are all also either suspected or confirmed murderers. *Basic Instinct* was interpreted by some as pathologising lesbians and bisexuals, and so offering the latest example of Hollywood's stereotyping of 'sexual deviants'. Protests were made in the United States by lesbian and gay lobby groups, sometimes allied under the 'queer' banner, including Queer Nation and the Gay and Lesbian Alliance Against Defamation (GLAAD).[50] (The most organised and visible interventions came from lesbian and gay organisations, but additional accusations of misogyny were made by women's groups. For instance, America's National Organisation for Women called *Basic Instinct* 'one of the most blatantly misogynistic films in recent memory'.)[51] Lesbian, gay and bisexual people campaigned for changes when the script became known, and disrupted shooting in San Francisco. Later, protestors claimed public space in several American cities, picketing cinemas in Los Angeles, Seattle, Chicago and New York. They leafleted cinemagoers and revealed the (probable) identity of the film's serial killer on placards and public address systems.[52] In the process, demonstrators also gained access to that public sphere constituted by the news media, both in the United States and Britain, to make accusations of homophobia against the film and against Hollywood in general.

Alberto Melucci's work on new social movements can usefully be applied to illuminate these interventions.[53] Melucci identifies forms of collective action in post-industrial societies organised beyond and beneath the institutions of the state and civil society, and operating at a distance from the world of 'official' politics. These independent groupings typically challenge dominant uses of symbolic resources such as stereotyping in the media, or state and industrial secrecy. They function as 'submerged' or 'subterranean' networks, significant in the everyday lives of their members but only visible in the public sphere during temporary mobilisations such as demonstrations. Individuals make emotional investments in the group and participate in the ongoing process of constructing a 'collective identity'.[54] Melucci is concerned with organisations such as peace and Green movements, women's and student groups, but his work is applicable to lesbian and gay organisations. Thus, while pressure groups such as GLAAD and Queer Nation in the United States and OutRage! in Britain operate on an everyday basis as submerged networks, they temporarily entered the public arena by campaigning against and commenting on *Basic Instinct*. In doing so, these groups 'translate[d] their actions into symbolic challenges to dominant codes', even though they did not always retain definitional power in the discursive framing of these actions by the news and entertainment media.[55]

Protestors and their supporters have characterised these actions as a way of capitalising on *Basic Instinct*'s media status as a major release to gain visibility for lesbian, gay and bisexual people and their concerns about negative stereotyping.[56] Meanwhile, the film's distributors reckoned the demonstrations added to its event status and box office take by increasing its public profile. 'Frankly, the protests are worth millions. You couldn't buy the advertising', a worker at TriStar, the distributor of the film in the United States, told the *Evening Standard*. This industry source was countered by a Queer Nation representative: 'The success of the movie [in the United States] wasn't unexpected. All the controversy helped to generate interest. But that was a trade-off we had to accept in order to make our point.'[57] This example shows the hegemonic flexibility of the industry, attempting to co-opt such salient negative readings of the film as further 'advertising' for it. But it also displays protestors' acceptance of this 'trade-off' as a price worth paying for their own use of the mainstream media, and their success in forcing charges to be aired by some outlets which routinely exclude them and their concerns.[58] Lesbian, gay and bisexual activists used *Basic Instinct* to make public statements not only about the alleged homophobia of Hollywood, but about their own self-identities, negotiations and struggles living in straight society, in which Hollywood plays a part.

It will become apparent, when I turn to audience research below, that media debates around allegations of homophobia and the film's explicit sex and violence encouraged some people to see *Basic Instinct* to find out for themselves what all the fuss was about, and to judge competing interpretations. Once they too have seen the film, viewers are 'socialised' into a transient collectivity formed around a shared visual event[59] and so become able to participate themselves in the debates over it. While some vocal lesbians, gays, bisexuals and feminists were highly critical of the film, it is important to note that these were never monolithic groupings, despite often being reported as such. The coalition opposing the film was always complex and fluid.[60] Indeed, some published debates over the rights and wrongs of *Basic Instinct* and the demonstrations it engendered foregrounded fissures within and between these heterogeneous groupings and temporary, shifting alliances.

American protests against *Basic Instinct* were mentioned in both news reports and film reviews in Britain, and thus achieved some success in forcing sexual political critiques of the film on to the media agenda. *Basic Instinct*'s consequent heightened status as a controversial popular cultural event certainly helped its box office performance, although the exact financial implications of the campaigns against it are impossible to quantify. Of course, the full range of audience reactions to the film extended beyond the boundaries of the media debate. As my research will show, some cinemagoers remained unaware of protests over the film and others drew pleasure from it in spite of protestors' warnings, but some were encouraged to think about and confront issues of representation. In addition to raising awareness and stimulating debate among some viewers, protests forced responses from industry personnel and reviewers, who frequently justified the film via Hollywood's professional ideology of entertainment. Moreover, in reacting to the protests, industry professionals and media commentators made public statements about their own positions towards not only the film but also those making these interventions. Such declarations often worked implicitly to assert social and sexual norms, and thus revealed some of the discursive processes by which heterosexuality is naturalised and reaffirmed. Protestors' accusations made an issue of *Basic Instinct* by forcing a public debate about its political implications. In pushing defenders of the film within the industry and the mainstream press to make explicit dominant notions of entertainment, they also made an issue of these usually tacit assumptions.

Hollywood's commercial imperative both encourages and attempts to regulate talk about film. The industry accommodates a limited proliferation of permissible viewing strategies, generally reckoned to maximise a film's audience appeal and revenue.[61] In the case of *Basic Instinct*, the film's textual organisation (including its generic mix, competing protagonists, and open ending) and marketing campaign encouraged its insertion into multiple interpretive frames. However, some efforts were also made to qualify the film's polysemy and the instability of its meanings. Industry representatives argued that it was up to audiences to decide how to interpret *Basic Instinct*, but within ideological constraints which excluded accusations of homophobia and misogyny. Responses by personnel who were forced to answer such charges often mobilised discourses of entertainment, not only to deny responsibility for any meanings ascribed to the film but also to evacuate meaning, to argue that the film 'meant' very little in itself.[62] Whether regarded as an industrial product or a work of artistic expression, *Basic Instinct* was always located in an implicitly discrete and apolitical arena of privatised leisure. From this point of view, it was ultimately nothing more than a pleasurable diversion for its audience, something not to be taken too seriously. This logic attempts a denial of the film's status as a symptom of power relations within society. For its defenders, *Basic Instinct* was a 'natural' organic whole, and certain 'political' acts of interpretation were unnatural, forced, and biased. For instance, a defensive remark by director Verhoeven in the British press pack indirectly acknowledged protestors' concerns, but represented them as a productive and false imposition upon the film: 'I don't think homosexuality or bisexuality should be made an issue in this film.'[63]

Interviewed in *Playboy*, Sharon Stone acknowledged that *Basic Instinct* provided 'a unique opportunity for the gay community to use a big media event as a way to be heard', but argued against protestors' 'political' readings of the film. By denying any connection between culture and 'reality' through a polarisation of fantasy and truth, she attempted to invalidate such critical interpretations: 'I don't think films are responsible for political issues unless they're being made specifically about a political issue. Films are there to inspire your fantasy. ... Journalism is responsible for telling the truth about the world.'[64] Her co-star Michael Douglas also defended the film as socially and politically irrelevant entertainment. Interviewed in the British men's monthly *GQ* he said: 'I ... reserve and demand the right to make two hours of entertainment without having to be the moral, social custodian of our society. I see this film as the equivalent of a smutty detective novel. It's well structured and well written, but I didn't read anything more into it.'[65] The implication that criticisms were based on inappropriate interpretations of the film and were essentially a fuss about nothing was summed up in the headline of a news story on the American opening in *Empire* magazine: 'It's only a movie'.[66]

The competing perspectives on *Basic Instinct* analysed thus far show popular culture as a site of ideological contestation. Protestors worked to win publicity and media exposure for their highly critical interpretations of the film, and of much Hollywood output. In trying to limit discussions to the success or failure of *Basic Instinct* as an entertainment and nothing more, defenders of the film attempted to side-step these concerns, and so to evade calls for 'socially responsible' filmmaking based on such reasoning. They ignored the lack of 'progressive' or 'ordinary' images of lesbians, gays and bisexuals (and, to a lesser extent, women) in Hollywood output beyond this single film – images which campaigners claimed were necessary to counterbalance Catherine Tramell and her deadly companions. Moreover, supporters of the film sometimes drew on discourses of entertainment to counter-charge lesbian and gay protestors with 'reading more' than was there to start with into a piece of well-made but insignificant popular fiction.

The organising discourse of 'political correctness' featured frequently in statements from *Basic Instinct*'s stars, director and distributors. 'Political correctness' is an unstable and multi-accentual term. In popular usage, however, its meaning is largely disparaging. Initially imported to Britain from the United States in the early 1990s, the phrase emerged as a label of contempt when used by conservative sections of the press to denounce anti-discriminatory practices and policies. It has become widely used as a derogatory term implying intolerant, oppressive and dogmatic behaviour, in particular the leftist 'policing' of culture and language.[67] Hostile readings of *Basic Instinct* in terms of the politics of its images, rather than its success or failure as an entertainment, were often characterised as 'politically correct', that is, as humourless, inimical to pleasure, and supportive of unreasonable censorship. For instance, Paul Brett, director of marketing at Guild, commented to *Empire*: 'The political correctness movement is frightening because it's censorship of the worst kind'.[68] Michael Douglas told *GQ* magazine: 'I've always supported gay rights. But this whole thing of being politically correct is really a bore. In movies somebody's got to be the villain and it can't always be the Italians.'[69] A feature in *Empire* opened with a defiant remark from Verhoeven, quoted with mock astonishment: '"Moviemaking is not about politically correct people," pronounces Paul Verhoeven ... "Fuck politically correct." Blimey.'[70]

Media commentators also raised concern over the threat to the freedom of artistic expression posed by 'politically correct' protests. The centre-right broadsheet the *Sunday Times* ran an article about the film's problems with the 'PC brigade' in America which reiterated suggestions of excessive zeal: 'Taken to a ludicrous extreme, the ultimate liberal consensus is interpreted as saying we can have no more negative images of minorities, full stop.'[71] *The Sun* newspaper acknowledged lesbian and gay criticisms of the film less directly. Its review commented: 'It's one of those movies you hate yourself for liking. It's soft-porn. It's anti-gay. It's violent. And they're the good points!'[72] Here, the film's 'anti-gay' stance becomes another of its attractions. Lesbians and gays are positioned as members of an 'out-group', marked as separate and different from an assumed hetero-sexual reader.[73] This otherness was often reinforced by signs of nationality. Thus several reports of American protests over *Basic Instinct* implied that these were only possible in a land of extremists and fanatics, and so would be doubly invalid as a response in Britain. (However, while 'politically correct America'[74] was located as the site of these campaigns, the film itself remained largely unmarked by its nation of origin, particularly in the tabloid press and popular film publications such as *Empire*. In contrast with elitist arguments which have typically characterised popular culture as American, *Basic Instinct* stood implicitly as part of an essentially Anglo-American stock of shared mass cultural resources, wherein the nation of origin of any single text is not noteworthy.) Reviewing *Basic Instinct*, *Empire*'s Barry McIlheney mounted a defence of audience pleasures endangered by the Orwellian image of the 'thought police':

> There is also, of course, the whole weight of the politically correct movement to take on board here, complete with the strenuous allega-tions of *Basic Instinct*'s general homophobia ... allegations which, frankly, fail to hold water on closer inspection. ... With the thought police closing in all the time, best enjoy this kind of mindless trash while you still have the chance.[75]

Frequently combined with discourses of entertainment, such rhetor-ical uses of the term 'politically correct' intend to contain argument and prohibit dissenting readings of *Basic Instinct* as unwelcome and dogmatic moves to force political considerations upon popular cul-ture.

My intention at this stage of the argument is not so much to offer my own judgement on *Basic Instinct*'s sexual politics as to consider what these processes of 'talk management' reveal about the interface between ideology and commerce. Hollywood's relationship to 'the social' is not transparent and unmediated, but is refracted via its eco-nomic imperatives, cultures of production, routinised practices and conventions. Its films do not provide straightforward indices of pop-ular demand and sentiment, despite claims made to this end on behalf of the star system and popular genres.[76] Nevertheless, Holly-wood's representations are clearly not autonomous from social for-mations and changes in their organisation: the relationship is, instead, mutually determining. In its own circumscribed and largely opportunistic way, Hollywood both responds to and contributes to social shifts such as emerging gay and lesbian lifestyles or the changes wrought by popular feminism since the 1970s – in part because they may offer the chance to develop and exploit new markets. *Basic Instinct* can be seen to take account of these changes in some ways, and to channel them via the generic model of the erotic thriller, thus achieving a particular mix of socio-cultural and generic verisimilitude.[77] But the film also trades in more familiar and normative representations of women as objects of sexual pleasure for straight male viewers. Furthermore, the promotional strategy for *Basic Instinct* could not accommodate perspectives that accused the film of homophobia and tried to persuade others of this. In other words, while the drive to maximise revenue through the provision of multiple 'points of entry' to popular film may override ideological coherence (in industry parlance 'how it plays' may be more important than 'what it says'), there is a risk of overstating this point. Hollywood's professional ideology holds that a film means very little apart from two hours of pleasure, and can be taken to mean almost anything, but its interpretations and uses are still to remain within certain ideological parameters. Thus marketing and journalistic texts attempt to organise and multiply 'preferred' viewing strategies and orientations, and to interdict others.

Competing readings of *Basic Instinct* raise issues of economic, cultural and social power. The agency of viewers and of lobby groups coexists alongside that of producers and distributors, but these agents remain unequal. Popular film texts and the marketing discourses around them bid for audiences with proliferating invitations. The textual structures of *Basic Instinct* encouraged this to a degree. But some interpretations remain too oppositional to be tolerated, and are consequently labelled aberrant – as happened with the furious responses to those publicly accusing *Basic Instinct* of homophobia and (to a lesser extent) misogyny.

Gendering *Basic Instinct* in the press

Press responses to *Basic Instinct*'s various attractions often characterised them as gender-specific. Media reports, both positive and hostile, frequently highlighted the film's sexual content as an implicitly heterosexual 'male' attraction, sometimes labelling this 'pornographic'.[78] Thus, while the *Evening Standard* lamented ingredients borrowed from 'pornographic videos',[79] a review in the feminist magazine *Harpies and Quines* commented: 'It's the "lesbianism" of *Playboy*, the male fantasy of a misguided woman who needs a proper screw, or bargain package of two women at once who get their kicks out of performing for a man.'[80] *Basic Instinct* was not always approached as a 'male' entertainment that rendered female pleasures problematic or impossible, however. The *Guardian* columnist Suzanne Moore praised the film's focus on a strong woman and its popularity among female audiences: 'What will really get women off in this film is not Catherine and Nick but Catherine herself. Her power, her danger and her lethal weapon – an icepick the size of which Michael Douglas could only dream about.'[81] The *Daily Mirror* article introduced at the start of this chapter constructed the significance of *Basic Instinct* via the topicality of Catherine under the headline 'WOMAN: THE SEXUAL TIGER'.[82] The film provided the opportunity to discuss women's sexual assertiveness and their novel status as consumers in a sexual marketplace offering 'sell-out male strip shows', the Femidom female contraceptive, and the soft-porn magazine *For Women*.[83] Catherine stood as a sign of changing sexual norms, a representative of the desiring new woman of the 1990s: [84] 'Men quiver at her dominance, sigh at her beauty and lust after her perfect body – but they know this athletic Amazon is a good boy's nightmare. ... women love her. She is a fantasy figure, the wildest, most perverse champion of a new lust for sexual freedom. And just one tiny bit of Catherine's sexual confidence is within every girl's reach.' [85]

While the *Daily Mirror* interpreted *Basic Instinct* as topical female-oriented (hetero)sexual entertainment, a more alarmist reading of Catherine was provided by the *Sunday Times*. It reported that violent crimes committed by women in Britain had increased by 350 per cent over the previous decade, and suggested that Hollywood films, including *Basic Instinct*, were reflections of a 'definite cultural shift': 'Women are not necessarily driven to, but are sometimes choosing to turn to crime'.[86] By framing *Basic Instinct* within a discourse which combined anxiety about female autonomy with fears about rising crime, the article offered prospective audiences an alternative viewing strategy with which to approach the film. *Basic Instinct* can, then, be termed a 'contested sign', in that there were clearly cultural negotiations taking place over what it meant.[87] Different publications speaking to different readerships characterised the film in various, often competing, ways.

The *Daily Mirror* and *Sunday Times* articles joined the expanding intertextual network around *Basic Instinct*, a constellation of diverse interpretations which extended the film's reach beyond the cinema into a broader social arena. Such surrounding texts and discourses may shape the 'horizons of expectation' which consumers bring to a film – that is, their cultural, social and aesthetic assumptions and expectations.[88] It is, however, necessary to avoid the supposition that media and promotional 'guides' are always followed by (potential) viewers, and so unproblematically determine their attitudes and reactions. My audience research shows that these texts provide information and set agendas and discursive frameworks which readers may select from, work within, ignore or reject.[89]

The audience research project

How did audiences (and those who chose not to see the film) react to *Basic Instinct*, and what factors shaped their responses? Which social events did the film become enmeshed in? What particular meanings, pleasures or displeasures were derived from it? What investments, if any, did viewers make in the figures of Nick and Catherine? Was the latter indeed the *Daily Mirror*'s 'champion of a new lust for sexual freedom'? What viewing strategies did straight men employ? How did people react to the discourses of protest and publicity around the film? How did the interpretations and social uses they made of *Basic Instinct* relate to those 'cued' by the film and by the satellite texts which framed it? And in what ways did viewers' responses exceed these 'invitations'?

To answer these and other questions, I will draw on empirical audience research. In 1994 I wrote to a dozen British magazines and newspapers, asking them to publish an invitation for readers to tell me their views on *Basic Instinct*, after which they would be sent a questionnaire. Five titles published my request: *Empire* magazine; the lesbian and gay newspaper *The Pink Paper*; *Gay Times* magazine; *The Guardian* (women's page); and the feminist monthly *Everywoman*. I wanted to access a broad range of respondents, of differing ethnicity, gender, sexual orientation, class and age profiles. Inevitably, the refusal of some publications to run my letter placed limits on this comparative approach, but I still garnered responses from men and women of various occupations, sexualities and ages. The questionnaire sample was entirely white, with the exception of one 'black Indian' respondent. The class and age spreads were ultimately not quite as wide as I had initially hoped because publications with large working-class and/or middle-aged and older readerships such as *TV Times*, *Radio Times*, the *Daily Mirror* and the *Daily Mail* declined to co-operate.[90] I received letters from 89 people, of whom 60 subsequently returned completed questionnaires. Of these, 34 were women and 26 men. A large majority of respondents were aged between 18 and 35 when they returned the questionnaire. Informants could have watched the film up to two years before responding, however: hence several watched the film when 'under age'.[91]

My research sample was thus based on self-selected readers of five specific publications who were sufficiently motivated to write to me expressing an opinion. Such a partial sample can have no pretensions of being either wholly (that is, statistically) representative or random. Nevertheless, some important suggestions about general patterns in film consumption can be derived from it. Although the size of the sample was quite small, it was large enough for the majority of informant statements to be repeated at least once. This partly mitigated the risk presented by over-reliance on exceptional data. The structure of the questionnaire was shaped by areas of interest developed through my research into marketing and press reception, and by the initial letters I received. A question on the first page asked respondents why they watched (or did not watch) the film, and what they thought of it. Along with the letters, this first section allowed me to assess what respondents wanted to say about *Basic Instinct* before they were steered towards specific lines of inquiry.[92] Obviously, I have selected from questionnaires and letters passages that appeared to me most interesting or significant. It is worth noting that in the pages that follow I have chosen to concentrate on viewers' engagements with particular aspects of the dispersible text, at the expense of others. For example, I pay more attention to sexual pleasures derived from *Basic Instinct* than those offered by its thriller plot.

The contingency of viewing

Wherever possible, I relate viewers' investments in and responses to *Basic Instinct* to their social situations and to specific conditions of reception. Before I embark upon this course, however, I want to address some of these local factors more directly by examining accounts in which watching *Basic Instinct* functions as part of a night out with a date, a meeting with friends, or simply to pass the time. What interests me in this section, then, is the contingency of the viewing scenario, the 'accidental' nature of some people's encounters with the film, and the range of social events in which *Basic Instinct* was embedded, or which demanded the (sometimes reluctant) viewing of the film. It is, of course, important to note that all viewings are influenced by the particularities of the reception context, not just those made out of politeness to friends, or to kill time. Ultimately, the significance and use of the film for any viewer cannot be detached from such considerations. This approach foregrounds the recognition that media use is 'constantly crossed through and influenced by non-media conditions and decisions',[93] and that 'film viewers' are never simply that. They always have ongoing social identities, habits and relationships that extend beyond the viewing experience, even while shaping and being (re)articulated through it.

Respondents wrote:

[I]t happened to be playing at the cinema on the particular night when my boyfriend and I had time to see a movie. We both wanted to see a movie, any movie, and my date chose *Basic Instinct*.
> (*14: Megan. School teacher, age 25, heterosexual.
> *Guardian* sample. Part one; Q4.)

In July 1992, my ex-husband and I spent the night in Calais before catching an early ferry back to Britain. ... The hotel we found wasn't particularly salubrious and so when we saw that *Basic Instinct* was on in a nearby cinema, it seemed like a good way to pass some time.
> (*15: anon. female. Public sector manager, age 31.
> *Guardian* sample. Letter.)

I saw *Basic Instinct* whilst staying the weekend with a close friend in Birmingham. ... I did not choose to watch it, nor did my husband. ... However, we had to defer to our friends' choice,
> (*58: Geraldine. Secretary and mother, age 46.
> *Empire* sample. Part one.)

People who had seen it at the pictures said it was an OK movie and there was nothing else at the video shop at the time worth a look; so I reluctantly suggested we should watch it.
> (*59: anon. female. Hairdresser, age 31. *Empire* sample. Letter.)

The overall effect of the commercial strategies of the film industry and its offshoots is to encourage the habitual viewing of films (on video and television, as well as at the cinema), over and above promoting the merits of any specific title. As David Morley puts it in relation to the cinema: 'Rather than selling individual films, cinema is best understood as having sold a habit, or a certain type of socialized experience.'[94] Joke Hermes' work on readers of women's magazines is also worth noting here, as it stresses the routine and relatively 'insignificant' nature of much of this activity. Hermes rightly points to a 'fallacy of meaningfulness' whereby academics assume an automatic significance in media use.[95] But in doing so, she fails to address fully why people might choose this particular pastime rather than any other to fill odd moments in their everyday life. Such a question raises issues of availability, word of mouth, title recognition, cost, familiarity, and portability. When applying similar considerations to a film like *Basic Instinct*, it becomes apparent that relatively 'meaningless' encounters with the film may still attest to its 'event status' in some ways. The film's commercial, cultural and social prominence made it more likely that undecided viewers would choose this film at the cinema or video shop, rather than one with a lower profile. In this respect, advertising and media exposure effectively established audience awareness of *Basic Instinct* as a leading 'brand name' in the marketplace, a position enhanced by its widespread availability.[96]

'Hype', talk and demand

Basic Instinct's considerable cultural and social presence was consolidated via a concerted marketing push, extensive journalistic exposure, saturation exhibition pattern and wide subsequent video release. Among respondents, these processes were frequently understood and represented by the term 'hype'. Many accounts registered an awareness of the film's existence and prime selling points derived from publicity, and developed through conversation and gossip. Even if disapproving at times, media coverage can effectively translate into diffuse social pressure to watch: the film becomes 'unmissable'. Only by watching *Basic Instinct* could one 'see what all the excitement was about' (*14). As informants put it: 'I felt everybody else had seen it except me' (*50); 'I could not give an opinion unless I saw it' (*39). Having seen the film, the viewer can voice her or his opinion to the peer group with authority.

'Hype' was often labelled mendacious: a promise which proved to be false. And for some viewers, the very mechanisms of extension surrounding the dispersible text may be a reason to avoid the film. In these instances, the pattern of (over-)exposure signals a lack of social and cultural 'value', both on the part of the film and its assumed audience.[97] For others, however, 'hype' contributed to the 'event' of queuing for and then watching *Basic Instinct*, an experience qualitatively different from that offered by 'smaller' films. In this account, the viewer's reactions are shaped by an atmosphere of shared anticipation, and the collective experience of seeing the film in the public space of the cinema:

> For only the third time since 1978 (when I had to queue through a whole screening of *Grease*) I had to queue for this film, even though it had been open for several weeks. The cinema was packed and there was an atmosphere of some hilarity. Perhaps the film's reputation was already spreading. Seeing *Basic Instinct* in these circumstances at the cinema has proved to be one of the best movie experiences I have ever had. The whole audience seemed to be wise to the clichés and hyped up sex scenes, and as a result we were all frequently reduced to hysterical laughter.
>
> (*17: Jacqueline. Teacher, age 26. *Guardian* sample. Letter.)

It is important to note that the mechanisms of advertising and publicity known as 'hype' do not entail the straightforward determination of audience wants and decisions. Rather, talk mediates these practices and influences their efficacy. Thus, any investigation of 'hype' must address a series of interpenetrating operations, including a commercially motivated marketing campaign; press coverage which is sometimes, but not always, symbiotic with this campaign; and everyday discussions among potential viewers.[98]

Basic Instinct's 'event' status as a controversial film which people were talking about encouraged several viewers to see it despite initial misgivings. Others rejected marketing appeals. One woman was 'warned off' by accusations of misogyny in the media. However, decisions about film viewing are not necessarily made on the basis of such criticisms alone. Thus, another deterrent for this respondent was the casting of Michael Douglas rather than Harrison Ford:

> The coverage of the film left me with the impression that it was a) not very good b) rather nasty and c) anti-women. I also don't particularly

like Michael Douglas as an actor – if it had starred, say, Harrison Ford,
I'd have been more tempted.

(*80: anon. female. No details given. *Guardian* sample. Letter.)

Cultural tastes, expectations of pleasure, and considerations of the
politics of representation coexist for the (prospective) viewer, and
do not always reinforce each other.

Basic Instinct was broadcast in a slightly edited form on British
terrestrial television in November 1994.[99] Cuts included the 'soften-
ing' of violence in the opening scene, where a man is stabbed to
death with an ice-pick by a woman during sex; showing less of 'what
appeared to have been a rape' perpetrated by Nick on Beth; and a
reduction in the number of uses of the word 'fuck' (of which the
Sunday Telegraph commentator Mary Kenny had counted 41 in the
original film).[100] The notorious exposure scene remained uncut. The
transmission led to a brief recapitulation of debates in the press over
the film's explicit nature.[101] It was followed by sixteen complaints to
the Broadcasting Standards Council over violence, sex and bad language. These were not upheld by the BSC, which accepted the
broadcaster's argument that 'as a result of the publicity surrounding
this film when it was first released, many viewers would not be sur-
prised at its content'.[102] The working assumption here appears to be
that one effect of media coverage of *Basic Instinct* around the time
of its theatrical release was to inform a large number of prospective
television viewers about the film, effectively 'warning off' many of
those most likely to be offended.

Gender and/in audience research

Basic Instinct was designed and positioned in the marketplace to sell
across audiences categorised via gender and sexuality, and these two
linked concepts were repeatedly mobilised as organisational discourses in different kinds of commentary and talk around the film.
Accordingly, two of the key axes around which I arranged my audience research sample were gender and sexuality. In some ways, this
subdivision could be seen to operate almost tautologically, producing the 'significance' of these factors. The researcher's own action of
discursively constituting gender as that which s/he claims to find
needs to be confronted here. Furthermore, gender should not always
be privileged as an analytical category at the expense of other, imbri-

cating elements of social experience and identity such as class, ethnicity, age and nationality.[103] An epistemological dilemma confronts any assumption that gender is an *a priori* characteristic of social life that fully precedes the moment of research. Gender, along with other facets of identity, is best viewed instead as always to an extent in process. Thus, gender (and sexuality) may be not only asserted but also partially rewritten through activities such as media consumption; the same is true of the act of responding to research inquiries. Gender can be termed an 'invention', in that, while it is grounded in the materiality of everyday life, it is also something fluid, the ongoing construction of which needs to be investigated rather than taken for granted as an inevitable 'natural' phenomenon. However, just as simplistic gender determinism should be avoided, so too should an implicit voluntarism which suggests that identities can be tried on and discarded more or less at will. Research into the interconnections between gender and media use needs to steer a course between these two poles, in part by attending to the social relations which regulate and reward 'appropriate' gendered behaviours. Such relations may well inform the diverse social events of media use and scenarios of audience research, as I will demonstrate in the following pages.

These observations necessitate caution on the part of the researcher, but they do not preclude the use of gender as a vector of analysis. It is, after all, a lived materiality reiterated and institutionalised through a range of social practices and power relations beyond those of audience research. Moreover, while it is important to remain aware of the complexities of identity constitution, explorations of the patterns of media use ultimately depend upon imperfect identity categorisations. David Morley notes: 'Without such generalizations, we risk floating in an endless realm of contextual specificity, a play of infinite difference, in which we are reluctant to make any generalization for fear of crudity.'[104] Nevertheless, a sensitivity to the processual nature of identity does require the analyst to take account of the research intervention as one practice through which identities, including those of gender, may be (re)produced. Such constructive processes are enacted by both informants and the researcher. In the present case, one way they operated was through my asking respondents to classify themselves as gender- and sexuality-identified, and then using this information as a prime means of categorisation for the analysis and interpretation of data. My questionnaire asked informants to describe themselves as either male or female, and to tick one of the following categories: 'heterosexual; lesbian; gay (male); bisexual; other (please specify)'. Some respondents openly challenged this taxonomy. For instance, Wim, a 33-year-old Dutch student, was self-identified as 'biologically male, gender mixed, sexuality gay or lesbian'.[105] I shall consider assertions of identity in some detail throughout my case studies.

It is crucial, then, that the researcher remains aware of her/his own intervention, in eliciting and organising audience statements, and so producing them as data. This is entailed in both the gathering and analysis of such material – two processes that are inextricably entwined. Ien Ang writes: 'it is only through the interpretative framework constructed by the researcher that understandings of the "empirical" come about'.[106] This argument has important implications for the epistemological status of the data produced. Self-reflexive audience researchers do not make unsubstantiable truth claims about the 'transparency' of their evidence. Instead, they make explicit their methodology and critical framework so that their 'findings' and their own roles as agents in the research scenario can be scrutinised and, if necessary, challenged by alternative interpretations.[107] I use the term 'audiencing' to refer to the discursive constitution of audiences and their activities – of which this book stands as an example.[108] When taken to extremes, self-reflexivity and self-criticism can hinder audience research, leading to a form of interpretive paralysis. As John Corner points out, some work has become obsessed with its own authorialism. Such self-consciousness can effectively displace interest in the topic of research.[109] It is nevertheless important to remain alive to the power relations structuring the research scenario, both those between the researcher and media users, and (if appropriate) among media users themselves.[110] A middle way needs to be navigated, avoiding both the naive positivism of treating audience research as a source of unmediated access to film viewing experiences, and a defeatism that too readily abandons empirical inquiry.

Female pleasures: identification, fantasy, desire

Basic Instinct shows Stone/Catherine inhabiting designer clothes, a sports car and a luxurious beach house. Her face and body are displayed in a variety of outfits, hairstyles and degrees of nakedness throughout the film and in associated publicity. According to my research, these images were a source of visual pleasure not only for some (straight and gay) male viewers, but for several women too. Catherine is not simply presented as a passive image or sex object, however. She has a high degree of autonomy within the narrative, and is portrayed as the active, desiring subject of sexual relations, initiating and controlling sex with Nick and (implicitly) her female lover Roxy. She is also economically and socially independent. A best-selling novelist with a $100 million inheritance, she (apparently) murders people to get her own way, and treats police inquiries with calm contempt. The film could be seen to foreground not just Catherine's body and wardrobe, then, but also her self-sufficiency, intelligence and aggression – characteristics which appealed to many women.[111]

Employing language reminiscent of the *Daily Mirror*, a student described Catherine as:

> A babe, rich, cool, – and what every woman wants to be … open minded, and dangerous – she always gets what she wants! MAD + BAD!
>
> (*23: Bronwen. Student, age 22, heterosexual.
> *Empire* sample. Q18a.)

This woman had seen the film three times at the cinema and bought the video. Part of her account appears as a 'confession' of a fantasy of becoming Stone/Catherine. By implication, the viewer's friend is transformed (also via similarity of hair colour) into Beth, Catherine's sometime lover:

> I went the first time with a girl who I found very attractive – I know this is sad, but as I've got blonde hair and she had brown, I imagined myself to be 'cool' like Sharon Stone.
>
> (*23: Bronwen. Part one.)

For this viewer and others, Catherine's attractiveness and 'cool' were tied to her material wealth. 'Cool' is loaded here with connotations of glamour. The sociologist Beverley Skeggs theorises the latter as 'a way of holding together sexuality and respectability', so avoiding the (classed) vulgarity of the 'tart'.[112] Glamour offers (straight) women the promise of confidence, desirability and subjectivity, but it is not easy to achieve in reality. It is associated with 'corporeal capital' but is also 'protected' by wealth and other markers of middle-class identity.[113] Skeggs suggests, furthermore, that this sense of female desirability and value typically requires confirmation through heterosexual male approval. As will become apparent, some women in my sample were not comfortable with this male surveillance and legitimation of ideal femininity, and felt that it compromised the pleasures that they found in *Basic Instinct*. For the moment, however, I shall concentrate upon women's investments in the representation of Catherine:

> [Catherine] had power – she was intelligent, successful, wealthy and incredibly beautiful – she oozed sex appeal and charisma. She intimidated men – she was dangerous. I found her very attractive. ... She does what many women only fantasize about. I admire her. ... After watching the film I craved sex.
>
> (*48: Kathryn. Computer operator, age 26, heterosexual.
> *Empire* sample. Q.19; Letter.)

> [T]he posters and the magazine ads really caught my eye, Sharon Stone looked great. ... I do remember thinking 'How Cool!' and trying to achieve the same arched eyebrows she sports in the photo!!
>
> (*22: anon. female. Student, age 21, heterosexual.
> *Empire* sample. Letter.)

The three accounts above reveal complex patterns of admiration and attraction towards *Basic Instinct*'s female protagonist. Exactly what parts do fantasy, desire and identification play in these women's relations with Stone/Catherine? Jackie Stacey's discussion of female spectatorship is useful here. Stacey questions the polarisation of desire and identification in film scholarship's applications of Freudian psychoanalysis. She proposes that the two processes are not rigidly opposed, but overlap to some degree. She argues instead for 'the eroticisation of some forms of identification',[114] drawing on Jessica Benjamin's theory of 'ideal love': 'The love of the ideal ... may express a desire to become more like that ideal, but this does not exclude the homoerotic pleasures of a love for that ideal.'[115] A similar interpenetration of identification and desire appears in some of my research findings. The first case above shows the viewer's fantasy of an ideal, cool self, and suggests a homoerotic pleasure in the star/character who inspires this longing for a 'better' self. A fantasy of transformation blurs the boundary between viewer and star ideal. In the third account, Stone/Catherine inspires an attempt to become more like her, pursued not just in fantasy but through fashioning arched eyebrows. In the second example, desire for the star/character is expressed more clearly, but there is also a pleasure in seeing

Catherine as a sexual and narrative agent who seeks both pleasure and control. Wanting to 'be' this ideal, who 'does what many women only fantasize about' is significant. Thus, desires to both 'have' and 'be' Stone/Catherine were important components of some (heterosexual) women's relations to *Basic Instinct*.

Several women commented positively on *Basic Instinct*'s representation of female sexual agency and pleasure. Catherine was seen as a sexual subject following her own desires, in both straight and (implicitly) lesbian sex, rather than as the sexual object of male desire. This was often taken to be a rare departure for a mainstream film. Moreover, for certain (bisexual and heterosexual) female viewers, Catherine embodied neither a 'male' sexual fantasy, nor a pathologisation of sexual 'deviance', but an advertisement for, or legitimation of, bisexuality and/or lesbianism. For example:

> [Lesbians and bisexuals were] made to look glamorous – I think it made it more appealing, I might be sad, but I wanted to give it a try – after the film.
>
> (*23: Bronwen. Q.18d.)

> The film helped to convince me that bisexualism is a 'natural' and 'normal' phenomenon. It suggests that sexual experimentalism is common.
>
> (*19: anon. female. Student, age 22, bisexual.
> *Everywoman* sample. Q.18d.)

The second account here appears to gesture towards the film's significance and social usefulness in helping this woman accept, assert and enjoy her own sexual identity as a bisexual. I shall consider similar processes with regard to heterosexual male teenagers below.

Catherine is suspected of the murders of at least four and possibly six men. Male respondents often side-stepped Catherine's narrative agency to focus on the interrogation scene and sexual 'numbers', so effectively repositioning her as an object of vision (see below, pp. 77–80). By contrast, several women took Catherine to be the film's multiple murderer and noted their enjoyment of the fact that she escapes punishing narrative closure. *Basic Instinct* was interpreted by some as a cautionary tale addressed to men demonstrating women's strength. For instance:

> Women can be dangerous without being insane. Push us too far and we could all become like Catherine! ... I hope Catherine was the murderer

because she was ruthlessly killing men for their money and knew exactly what she was doing. ... [women] should be rational and intelligent like most male film serial killers.

(*19: anon. female. Part one; Q.22.)

Thus, for several female respondents, Catherine was, at least in part, the 'champion of a new lust for sexual freedom', even if defined more widely by some than the *Daily Mirror* would have it. But she also spoke to their dreams of, and demands for, broader social and financial empowerment.

Women's reactions often appeared complex and ambivalent, rather than consistently positive or negative. Several accounts indicated a duality of response: a simultaneous investment in, and detachment from, the film. Responses may change over time and according to the contexts of reception (and of recall).[116] Some women may have enjoyed the film as a 'holiday' from their habitual scrutiny of female representations, but then returned to a more sceptical perspective at a later moment, and/or when asked to write to me.[117]

In the following account, the portrayal of Stone/Catherine allows the viewer to make a pleasurable connection, even while she notes its failure to adhere to standards of empirical realism:

[Catherine was] a very strong figure. I found the way she was so in control of her life very inspiring. However, I did think (although not on the first viewing) that she was a little unrealistic – two degrees, aged 30-ish, beautiful, multi millionairess, etc. I really enjoyed the film the first time. I came out thinking that it was a really good film all round. I didn't get it out on video until about a year later for a video party, but I admit that it was purely to laugh at the sex scenes which we all agreed were completely untrue to life.

(*40: Rebecca. Student, age 19, heterosexual. *Empire* sample. Letter.)

In this particular case, the informant's ambivalence about the film – simultaneously investing in and ridiculing it – also suggests the multiple subjectivities and viewing positions that any viewer can occupy at one moment.[118] At the video party her pleasures in the film seem to be overwritten by a public disavowal of a 'serious' relation to it, along with a possible articulation of sexual 'maturity': the 'experienced' viewer has no need to seek sexual knowledge in sex scenes, and so laughs at them, finding them ridiculous. Thus, rather than existing as complete prior to media consumption, identity is at least partly constructed through it.

The appearance and behaviour of Douglas/Nick was a major cause of dissatisfaction, even among women who enjoyed much of the film. The casting of Douglas as a presumed sex object – inviting a straight female gaze at the male body – was a crucial aspect of *Basic Instinct*'s address to women. He proved popular with a few female respondents, most of whom were aged over 30, but several women ridiculed him as 'old ugly chops' and an 'overweight, sexless old man' with a 'horrible body'. (I discuss a male perspective on this female appraisal of the male form below.) Dissatisfaction with Nick centred in particular on his 'rape' of Beth and the open ending in which Catherine has sex with Nick, and reaches for, but refrains from using, an ice pick under the bed. Some women imagined alternative conclusions in which Nick – variously regarded as a 'frustrated rapist', an 'amoral, obnoxious, prick' and a 'lusty little twerp' – was killed by Catherine. For instance:

> Hopefully she will use the ice pick under the bed again!
>
> (*19: anon. female. Q.20.)

> I think that the male lead would eventually have been killed at the novelist's convenience later. (I often extend a story in my mind when I am not satisfied with the ending!)
>
> (*63: Ann. Age 57, no other details given. *Guardian* sample. Letter.)

These fantasy re-writings attest not only to the active, imaginative practices of viewers, but also to the significance of the structure of the dispersible film text, in that its two protagonists and refusal of closure facilitated such productivity. Nevertheless, as I have suggested, certain interpretations of, and responses to, the film (such as the boycott campaign) were so problematic for industry representatives that efforts were made to mark them as 'unjustified' and 'excessive'. Furthermore, as will become evident, while the film can be seen to offer certain 'female' pleasures, it elicited very different responses from straight male viewers. The largely positive audience accounts discussed so far are significant because they indicate not unconditional enjoyment of all aspects of *Basic Instinct* but processes of negotiation, both in responding to the film, and formulating and writing opinions retrospectively. Each individual makes investments in certain (pleasurable, memorable, relevant) elements, which are appropriated and incorporated, at least temporarily, into their 'lifeworld', while passing over, temporarily blocking out or rejecting outright other elements.

'A very male film'

Central to *Basic Instinct*'s assembly, and amplified through its marketing campaign and media exposure, was a multiple address to men and women. However, for some women, *Basic Instinct* was gendered as an (implicitly heterosexual) 'male' entertainment. In making such criticisms, these women also asserted their identities *as* women, articulating their various senses of self in opposition to the film's perceived 'maleness':

> It was so pornographic – weak plot, hetero-lesbian scenes, close-up shots of women's vaginas, sadistic-masochistic representations of death/sex – need I go on?
>
> (*21: Arwen. Part one)

> The portrayal of women as sexually violent ... – this is a lie and a distortion of what is actually happening in society. This was a very white, male heterosexual film.
>
> (*3: Barbara. Rape counsellor, age 48, lesbian.
> Unknown sample. Q.23.)

> [I] mostly agreed with the [lesbian, gay and bisexual] protests – more so after seeing the film. We're not psychopaths, criminals, murderers, perverts and we don't want to be viewed/treated as such.
> (*9: Helen. Student, age 26, lesbian. *Pink Paper* sample. Q.14.)

Other informants explicitly countered suggestions that *Basic Instinct* showed women in positions of power:

> Over 2^1/$_2$ years later, I still feel very strongly about the thoroughly degrading depiction of people, especially women, in the film. It continues to bother me, as many of my female friends perceived the Sharon Stone character as turning the tables of violation on men, but I see this as an illusion. This film is just as biased against women as any that exploits them.
>
> (*14: Megan. Q.27.)

> I was cross about the 'woman on top' bit. Liberated woman – taking control. Like hell – more 'Tits oot for the lads'.
>
> (*58: Geraldine. Part one)

This woman and others accused the film of double standards regarding nudity:

> I hope they don't make a sequel. But if they do, the roles should be

reversed so we see, e.g. Keanu Reeves crossing and uncrossing his legs with no knickers on!!

(*39: Rachel. Student, age 19, heterosexual. *Empire* sample.)

Some respondents found pleasures in watching *Basic Instinct* but also noted the 'male' attractions on offer. The next woman watched the film on video with her boyfriend:

I decided to watch it, as I hadn't seen it before. He had already seen it, but was prepared to watch it again to see Sharon Stone 'take her kit off'. I saw it for all the American things which attract my interest. He saw it for the nude woman scenes. He didn't mention just how many sex scenes there were, probably in case I said no. I liked seeing all the rich places Catherine lived in. I didn't like Sharon's sex scenes as I'm envious of her great body, which my boyfriend ogled.

(*25: Deborah. Trainee teacher, age 19, heterosexual. *Empire* sample. Q.4; Q.5; Q.10)

This account grants an insight into inter-personal dynamics and the gendered micro-politics of media use. Deborah's response to the film is partly shaped by her perception of her boyfriend's enjoyment of the sight of Stone/Catherine's body, and by implication, the judgement of her own body as 'inadequate' in comparison. In this context, the film offers the female viewer touristic images and a luxurious *mise–en-scène* which are pleasurable partly through their distance from the everyday. But it also presents an impossibly 'perfect' image of corporeal femininity. Deborah effectively internalises a masculine scrutiny of her own body here.[119] In this case, one of the costs of watching *Basic Instinct* is a reminder of the power of masculinity, its surveillance and selective authorisation of femininity. Masculinity thus operates with what Beverley Skeggs calls 'the power to impose standards, make evaluations and confirm validity' on women, through both textual mediations of ideal femininities, and local practices such as that involving Deborah and her boyfriend.[120]

A similar disparity between male and female viewing practices was noted in the following account:

It's erotic and so I watch it now with groups or just men on their own that I fancy – also as the woman is always in control – but I think men always just want to see S. Stone's tits!

(*23: Bronwen. Part one.)

The multiple viewing strategies cued by *Basic Instinct* collide here. When watched with men 'that I fancy', it offers Bronwen some of the sexual pleasures of 'couples' soft porn. It also offers two further invitations, which appear to be mutually contradictory. Bronwen has the chance to enjoy Catherine as a figure of female empowerment, but her pleasures in this representation of autonomy and control are not unalloyed. Like the different investments made by Deborah, they coexist uncomfortably alongside an awareness of straight male scrutiny of the female body. The account again points to an objectifying male way of looking at the female star. This repositions the woman on screen from sexual and narrative agent (which Bronwen so enjoys) to mere spectacle – a mode of engagement to which I shall return.[121]

Female audiences were far from uniform in their reactions to *Basic Instinct*. Many different, even conflicting, views were espoused across the research sample. But in all cases, viewers' readings of the film involved some negotiation of pleasurable and/or unpleasurable elements, and of their own self-identities, aspirations, desires and social positions. It is important to note that positive reactions to a film pronounced misogynistic in some quarters do not involve women subscribing to the 'false consciousness' of patriarchy. These viewers actively inhabit and make use of the film to derive their own meanings and pleasures from it. Such manoeuvres show women manipulating, investing in and utilising a largely male-produced text. In so doing, they employ what Michel de Certeau calls the tactics of 'making do', enjoying the compensatory pleasures of the relatively disempowered.[122] Thus 'the weak make use of the strong' through productive practices of consumption.

Audiences must not, however, be envisaged as autonomous from textual operations, from the operations of marketing and journalism, or from the specific locations and wider socio-cultural contexts in which they encounter the film text. Some women's interpretations and uses of *Basic Instinct* were actively encouraged by promotional and journalistic discourses. Moreover, viewers do not escape or overturn the (often gendered) structures and processes that limit access to the means of production in the culture industries, nor those that naturalise and reproduce male ways of looking at women as sexual objects. But these women do integrate *Basic Instinct* into their everyday lives. Through such acts of assimilation, the film is activated, interpreted and (re)shaped in relation to viewers' individual perspectives. Thus, some women made the film work to question patriarchal values, viewing it as a pleasurable fantasy of female assertion and/or as a warning to men of female power. However, as I have

suggested, women's pleasures in the film were on occasions complicated and compromised by their perceptions of very different
straight male viewing strategies, which coexisted alongside and
impacted upon their own perspectives. Viewers responding nega-
tively to *Basic Instinct* also drew on their own lifeworlds and cir-
cumstances to make sense of it. For instance, the rape counsellor
measured the film against her knowledge and experience, and found
it a grotesque distortion of sexual power relations. In this example
and other 'oppositional' readings of *Basic Instinct*, there was a
refusal of (primary and secondary) textual invitations to invest in
and enjoy the film. Instead, reference was made to (professional)
experience, in relation to which the film appeared as a misleading
'male heterosexual' fiction.

Remaining for many women a 'man's film', *Basic Instinct* nevertheless made sufficient concessions to attract a significant female
audience.[123] Ultimately, the primary goal of the film's producers and
distributors was commercial success facilitated by cross-gender
appeal, not narrow ideological coherence. This success was built on
the multiple promises of the dispersible text, amplified through marketing and journalistic discourses. Popular cinema works by inviting
(rather than simply determining) the production of multiple meanings and genuine pleasures by varied and heterogeneous audiences.
For decades this ability to speak and sell to different constituencies
has helped secure and consolidate Hollywood's economic dominance and its presence in the everyday lives of its viewers. The
'inclusive' audience address of Hollywood also forms a part of its
professional ideology of entertainment. As such it is mythified in the
industry's self-promotion, and needs to be critically scrutinised. For
all those people whom a Hollywood film (and its advertising campaign) explicitly addresses, others may feel tacitly marginalised or
excluded. Moreover, viewers in both of these categories may derive
their own pleasures and interpretations beyond those anticipated or
cued through textual structures and marketing procedures.

'Desperate to see it': straight males watching *Basic Instinct*

Occupying the normative, unmarked identity category of western culture, straight (white) men have tended to remain a given, beyond
scrutiny in much empirical work on media audiences.[124] Furthermore,
text-based analyses have often assumed that popular culture texts

inculcate and reinforce patriarchal and heterosexist attitudes and stereotypes among their male readers and viewers in a relatively straightforward way. (In certain cases such texts may be recuperated by critical 'reading against the grain', but these remain by implication exceptional.) Under both approaches, little time is spent on examining the complexities of how actual heterosexual male media users engage with popular texts. In the rest of this chapter I attempt to address some of these under-examined processes by interrogating male (hetero)sexual viewing strategies, and associated knowledges and pleasures derived from watching *Basic Instinct*.[125] In the process, I explore some ways in which real straight male viewers negotiated the film's images of women and men. My primary purpose in examining such viewing practices is to try to understand how they are produced. I assess the uses to which *Basic Instinct* was put by male adolescents in particular; the discursive and social contexts in which they viewed it; and the role played by advertising, media coverage and gossip in the formation of expectations of, and orientations towards, the film.

I have discussed how women's perceptions of Stone/Catherine ranged from an empowering figure to an oppressive 'male' sexual fantasy. The accounts of heterosexual male respondents also varied, but a number of them afforded primacy to the sight of the female body. These accounts typically suppressed the narrative agency of Catherine in favour of positioning her as sexual object. For some straight males, *Basic Instinct*'s appeal lay in sexual and pornographic elements offered in combination with markers of cultural prestige such as high production values, major stars and a 'quality' thriller plot. These additional features presented pleasures hitherto absent from their experience of porn films, and may have also provided alibis for their enjoyment of its sexual attractions that could be mobilised in certain situations. The following informants deployed viewing protocols based on their previous consumption of screen pornography in general and/or erotic thrillers in particular:

> I adore a little scene or two of tits and arse. Usually you have to sit through some B type film, XXXX rated to get a glimpse of a nipple. For me this was a new experience. A major film, good story and the sexy scenes. A joy.
>
>   (*73: Tony. No details given. *Empire* sample. Letter.)

> I found myself, like most hot-blooded heterosexual males titillated by the lesbian sub-plot and the infamous 'flash' by Ms Stone. I actually

enjoyed the film almost guiltily in fact due to its a) gratuitous sex b) gratuitous violence. Overall I would say it was a perfect example of its genre: the 'Erotic Thriller'.

(*75: Mick. No details given. *Empire* sample. Letter.)

Paul Willemen has argued that, due to pornography's direct address, 'there is no way the viewer can fade into the diegesis or, alternatively, shove the responsibility of the discourse onto the author'.[126] However, both of these (qualified) alibis – and the 'non-pornographic' attractions that underpin them – are prompted by the aesthetic aspirations of soft-core pornography. They might also be derived from *Basic Instinct*: the first through the partial integration of sex scenes into the thriller narrative (a less than secure insertion, from which they were extracted by publicity and gossip); the second through the media attention accorded, and stylistic signature accredited to, Verhoeven as popular auteur. While the above informants do not appear overly concerned about employing such alibis in their letters to me, there is apparent in the second account an awareness of possible disapproval of 'gratuitous' sex and violence – on the part of both a generalised public and the researcher as addressee – which makes the film a guilty pleasure.

Linda Williams has defined film pornography as the 'representation of living, moving bodies engaged in explicit, usually unfaked, sexual acts with a primary intent of arousing viewers'.[127] Central to Williams' work on pornography, and to my use of the term, is the understanding that this genre offers pleasures in and of (sexual) knowledge. Thus, pornography 'seeks knowledge of the pleasures of sex'.[128] *Basic Instinct* can be seen to offer a soft-core replication of certain pornographic scenarios, including the oscillation Williams locates in the primitive stag film between 'the impossible direct relation between a spectator and the exhibitionist object he watches in close-up and the ideal voyeurism of a spectator who observes a sexual event in which a surrogate male acts for him'.[129] The first viewing pleasure is provided by Stone/Catherine's 'flash' in the interrogation scene, a genital show offering a glimpse of the secrets of the female body, what Williams terms 'the wonders of the unseen world'.[130] The second is provided in the (simulated) sexual events between Catherine and Johnny Boz (her first victim), Nick and his sometime lover Beth, and Catherine and Nick. A third pleasure, although somewhat less explicit, is that of the 'lesbian sub-plot' between Catherine and her female lover Roxy. The first two pleasures in particular were raised repeatedly in straight men's accounts of *Basic Instinct*. These typically located Catherine as a sexualised object of vision, reduced in the everyday language of heterosexual males to body parts such as 'tits and arse' or 'a great leg'. Objectifying perspectives on Catherine thus contained any threat that this assertive and autonomous woman may have posed to men (a threat located and celebrated by some commentators and female respondents). Recuperative male viewings often saw Catherine's bisexuality as titillating, or appeared to elide it entirely, effectively rewriting her as a heterosexual. In these instances, viewer agency and productivity is not necessarily progressive, as some work on media audiences has tended to imply.

Informants stressed the pleasures of looking at the female body both in isolated close-up (the interrogation scene) and in (sexual) motion. Stone/Catherine's was not the only body viewed in this way. One viewer compared the bodies of three women in the film, foregrounding them as its prime attractions:

> The reason I watched [was] Sharon Stone, but after viewing the film I found Jeanne Tripplehorn [Beth] far more sexy and with a better figure than Sharon Stone. At the beginning of the film the violent love scene involving a sumptuously built blonde (whose body doesn't quite resemble any one of three main suspects) who was that body double?
> (* 72: Basil. No details given. *Empire* sample. Letter.)[131]

This account privileges sights of the female body over narrative developments such as the murder of Johnny Boz in the opening scene, or Nick's 'rape' of Beth. (Her semi-clothed body is 'on display' in a scene which moves from kissing and foreplay to the 'rape'.)[132] I would suggest that the female body could also be consumed as an enjoyable sexualised spectacle at moments when it was not unclothed or engaged in sexual activity, if the viewer watches with what I shall call an appraising gaze. Such objectifying ways of looking at women have become naturalised in everyday heterosexual male culture.[133] It is, then, vital that any single film text is not regarded as an isolated source of 'sexist' ideology, but that the film and its viewer(s) are situated according to prevailing social and cultural conditions, including the range of (dominant and marginal) viewing strategies and interpretive frames which shape the text's reception. In short, viewing practices do not simply emanate from a particular text, but are also learned and reproduced (and negotiated, reworked, even resisted) through the social and discursive contexts in which audiences and films take their places.[134] The film is not without a certain textual power, however. When watched for male heterosexual pleasures, *Basic Instinct* effectively reinforces certain viewer dispositions, including that of the appraising gaze – something that does not automatically hold true for all other films.

Much of the material I make use of in this section is drawn from letters responding to my request in *Empire* film magazine, written by males who did not return the questionnaires I subsequently sent them. A large proportion of these men appear to have had a relatively limited education, and are probably working class. (This is an informed speculation made from language used and the lack of completed questionnaires, suggesting that these respondents had less cultural resources and less inclination to answer a relatively lengthy questionnaire.) Care must be taken, however, not to stereotype working-class males as more likely to have 'pornographic' tastes than members of the middle classes. It may be simply that the former are more honest about these predilections, and that middle-class men are in this instance more reticent about their sexual desires and pleasures – perhaps because of a greater awareness of popular feminist discourse and of social expectations to modify their behaviour accordingly, or perhaps because of a tendency (and ability) to defend 'private' pleasures more tenaciously in the face of enquiries from a stranger, a tendency often disguised as class reserve and 'politeness'.

The male reactions to the film's construction of femininity with which I am concerned here contrasted with those of several female commentators and respondents, who viewed Stone/Catherine as a positive representation of a financially independent and sexually desiring woman. If men often wrote about moments of sexual display and activity as the highlights of the film, women were more likely to stress their enjoyment of the narrative, which they saw as driven by the femme fatale. For several female informants, *Basic Instinct* was an enjoyable (and erotic) celebration of female agency and desire, and a warning to men about women's power. However, rather than the male flight from Stone/Catherine suggested by some female journalists and respondents, my research uncovered male viewing practices which derived sexual pleasures from the film by approaching her as a sexual object. How might I make sense of these responses? Lynne Segal writes of 'the solace men seek from pornography' as a compensatory mythology, when faced with (even limited) social change in the wake of second-wave feminism. In symbolising male power over women, pornography provides reassurance 'in these times of intensified struggle around gender and increasing insecurity about masculinity and male sexuality'.[135] I would make a similar suggestion about some pornographic engagements with *Basic Instinct*. Catherine's sexual agency and murderous habits complicate but do not preclude these investments. (Some men may have approached Catherine as a dominatrix figure, but this perspective was not mentioned in my research sample.) Certainly, a dynamic of female assertion and countervailing male sexual aggression can be located in the actions of *Basic Instinct*'s competing but sexually involved protagonists. There is little overt evidence of Nick's appeal to male viewers as an embodiment of 'penile potency' (in Segal's phrase), an image of male supremacy in the face of the perceived social demands of women. But such an impulse may be evident indirectly in some of those straight male responses that return Catherine to the position of sexualised object of desire, denying her sexual and narrative agency. This viewing strategy was by no means the only one invited by the structure of the film text and the diverse interpretive frames mobilised in promotional and journalistic discourses, or employed by viewers of the film. Nevertheless, it was the most widely available, and so might be termed the dominant or normative strategy in many social contexts of reception.

My audience analysis has tended to reinforce a gendered dichotomy between (largely heterosexual) 'male' and 'female' engagements with *Basic Instinct*. It is, therefore, instructive to note, first, that there were positive and negative responses to the film among both men and women, and, secondly, that some straight couples approached the film as (potentially at least) addressed to both genders. In the following case, the (apparently shared) intention was to consume *Basic Instinct* as 'couples' soft porn:

Like everyone else we went to see it for the SEX!

After the movie was over we came to the opinion that as a thriller the movie would have worked just as well without its over-hyped sex scenes which we thought were 'very mechanical' and not in the least erotic, the scene between M. Douglas and J. Tripplehorn [Beth] was more like a 'rape'.

(The sex scenes in *The Piano* were much more erotic.)
     (*36: anon. male. Unemployed, age 33. *Empire* sample. Letter.)

The woman in this couple described *Basic Instinct*'s portrayal of sex as 'boring' and 'not caring'. (*37: anon. female. Housewife and mother, age 25.) The (hetero)sexual partners in *The Piano* appear to have been far more successful as surrogates acting for, and arousing desire in, this watching couple than do the combinations of Nick, Catherine and Beth in *Basic Instinct*.[136] Nick's 'rape' of Beth in particular undermined the notion of consensual heterosexual coupling on screen and, by extension, between these viewers.[137]

Adolescent males

I now want to consider male teenagers' consumption of the film, investigating the social relations in play at moments of viewing. The film is approached as embedded within particular social locations, so that questions of context and of textual interpretations, pleasures and uses are inextricably linked. Among 'under age' males, the social act of viewing *Basic Instinct*, with its tally of sex and violence, endowed status or 'cool' in the peer group. This sixth-former watched the film on video with a male friend:

> I saw *Basic Instinct* for many reasons: – everyone was talking about it and I wanted to see what all the fuss was about. To see how far they pushed the boundaries of sex and violence. To tell all my mates how 'cool' I was for seeing it! To see if in the infamous interrogation scene, you really do see her private area.

> I was about 15 years old when I saw it. All my friends and I were crazy about Sharon Stone and all the hype surrounding it (because of the explicit sex scenes, it has to be said!) We were all desperate to see it. Since we were under age we tried many scams to get hold of a copy of it. Eventually I got around to renting it, one morning … I thought it was a really entertaining trash thriller. Unlike most films of this genre or tackiness which promise lots of sex, but don't deliver the goods (so to speak) *Basic Instinct* gave what the viewer wanted.

> The script was so awful, it was funny and it brought up many interesting topics of discussion – such as 'What does it all mean' and 'Did they really DO IT' (!)
> (*46: Paul. No details given. *Empire* sample. Part one; letter.)

A key motive here for seeing the film is sexual curiosity about, and pleasure taken in the sight of, the female body – motives shared in some ways with Douglas' character. *Basic Instinct* constitutes an important source of information about 'doing it' for this teenage viewer. Gossip and expectation centre on Stone/Catherine – notably the intimate knowledge and scopic pleasures provided by seeing 'her private area', and the question of whether sex really took place as a profilmic act.[138] These private, individual motives coexist simultaneously with the negotiation of social relations in the peer group and a public presentation of self as 'in the know' about the film and its illicit pleasures.

Media consumption is not simply shaped by pre-existing identities, but rather both expresses and (re)constructs identity.[139] As Liesbet van Zoonen notes, identity is never fixed, stable or 'true', but is always to some extent in process: '[B]eing a "woman" or a "man" does not come easily and requires continuous work. ... Media reception is one of the practices in which the construction of (gender) identity takes place.'[140] This observation applies not just to the media encounter but also to the kind of discussions mentioned by the above respondent, and to the written accounts sent to me. In these activities, 'masculinity is actively produced and sustained through talk', as David Buckingham has put it.[141] In the above case, the consumption of sexualised images of women not only produces private pleasures, but is also part of an attempted public articulation of an 'adult' heterosexual male identity. (This gendered and sexual identity is of course overlaid with other factors such as class, age and ethnicity, and will not hold consistently across all social situations.) The example of Paul and others like it suggest the fragility of adolescent male identities. An insecurity can be traced in the ongoing efforts made to fix a stable, 'cool' identity and, in the process, to claim status in the peer group. I find Harry Brod's concept of 'fratriarchy' useful here.[142] It foregrounds gaps between the public face of male power and individual male anxieties, and highlights the 'sibling rivalry' among straight men, transactions worked out around self-image and social hierarchies like that suggested in Paul's account. Moreover, the act of viewing *Basic Instinct* can be seen not simply as an attempt to find pleasure and to claim an 'adult' identity, but, simultaneously, as a sign of immaturity. Being 'desperate to see it' can mean more than enjoyable anticipation. It also suggests the desperation of the sexually inexperienced male who consumes pornography as a substitute for 'real' sex. Paul's stress on the attractions of the 'peepshow' – the sexualised display of the female body – could be seen in part as an attempt to evade the challenge of recognising (straight) female sexual desire and attendant male 'performance anxiety', particularly acute for a sexual novice.[143]

It should be emphasised here that informants' accounts cannot be regarded as granting transparent, unmediated access to their opinions or feelings. Close attention has to be paid not only to the content of statements but also to the use of language, which is both constructed according to specific repertoires and constructive of social relations and identity.[144] As Ien Ang has cautioned: 'What people say or write about their experiences, preferences, habits, etc., cannot be taken entirely at face value … we must search for what is behind the explicitly written, for the presuppositions and accepted attitudes concealed within them. In other words, [informants'] letters must be regarded as texts.'[145] Approaching viewers' statements as texts does not entail disbelieving them, but it requires situating these texts according to the contexts of their production.[146] In other words, one must acknowledge that the process of 'audiencing' is shaped by the particularities of 'an actual social relationship' between informants and researcher.[147] An obligation to recognise the motivations and power relations which shape the research scenario attends this understanding. As Meaghan Morris notes, the 'understanding' and 'encouraging' researcher may share some aspects of the researched culture, 'but in the process of interrogation and analysis is momentarily located outside it'.[148] Concerns about the essential inequality of any dialogue between researcher and informants remind me of some of the ethical dilemmas I used to face when working as a journalist. Both practices can involve extracting information from people placed in a socially subordinate position by dint of one's relatively powerful identity as professional researcher/interviewer. They also call for the selection, editing and critical decoding after the fact of spoken or written responses. This power relationship is not so problematic, however, that it requires the abandonment of audience research. The dynamics of audiencing in the present project were complex and variable rather than fixed throughout. Thus, while I stood in a powerful position relative to informants whose statements I categorised and analysed, I had initially depended upon them to accept or write off for, then fill in and return, my questionnaires.[149] Furthermore, respondents had their own reasons for choosing to participate in my research, which I have not always uncovered.

My inquiry offered all informants a space in which to speak, to have their pleasures, investments, or anger taken seriously. For adolescents, the research project was often taken as a chance to share the excitement of seeing a violent and sexually explicit film when 'under age'. For some, it also provided a further opportunity to occupy and project an 'adult' identity, beyond the act of viewing the film itself. For instance, a 14–year-old female wrote:

> it was on Sky, my parents were out, I was babysitting my younger brother – and I wasn't supposed to watch it. I watched it simply because I love films and prepared to watch anything once. Yes, it was an '18' certificate – but who cares? The sex scenes, were, well loud, the swearing not at all shocking (to me anyway).
>
> (*42: anon. female. *Empire* sample. Letter.)

In the following account, the informant appears unfazed and 'cool' about both the film's sex and its violence. This is not a fictional or dishonest statement, but it does show the respondent displaying his own viewing history and knowledge, and presenting a normative image of 'unshockable' masculinity which may mirror that under-taken for the benefit of his peer group:

> I was 16 at the time (I am now 18) and to tell the truth it did not shock me. Having seen *Reservoir Dogs* eight or nine times and Marlon Brando's performance in *Last Tango in Paris*, I have to confess that the 'action' in *Basic Instinct* was what I would consider par for the course in today's movie terms.
>
> (*28: James. Taking year off before university.
> *Empire* sample. Letter.)

Research into (male) teenage viewing practices has suggested that video classification functions as 'an index of desirability', with 18-rated videos at the summit, operating as both a forbidden pleasure and 'something "to test yourself out on"'.[150] For adolescents of both genders, *Basic Instinct* had an 'adult' status as a forbidden text. Through the social event of viewing, such a status could be imparted to its viewers, so long as they remained (apparently) unshockable. However, while Paul, quoted above, focused enthusiastically on het-erosexual desire for the female body (perhaps too enthusiastically to be really 'cool'),[151] he admitted to discomfort at the film's depiction of 'nasty' violence. This appeared to be an 'adult' pleasure that he was not expecting, particularly in the opening scene, which shifts from heterosexual sex to the woman's bloody stabbing to death of her male partner:

You are witnessing this beautiful sex scene, then you are experiencing the most disgusting bit of bloodshed in a long time. The violence was really nasty – Hard to watch.

(*46: Paul. Questionnaire.)

There is clearly a problem for the male viewer here in adjusting to the relocation of woman from sexual object to assailant during this scene.[152] I consider Paul's responses to the portrayal of male sexual violence in the film below.

Home video

For straight male viewers of various ages, watching such a sexually explicit film in a crowded cinema, in the presence of women as well as other men, could be a source of discomfort and embarrassment:

I would be lying if I said that an unclothed Miss Stone wasn't a factor in me seeing the film, but I always find that watching sex or erotic scenes in the same room as a hundred or so other people is, for me, just plain uncomfortable. ... That, of course is watching the film in a crowded ODEON MULTIPLEX, watching the film at home is another kettle of fish.

(*76: Sean. Student. *Empire* sample. Letter.)[153]

Watching *Basic Instinct* on home video, either alone or in select groupings, could avoid such problems. It also offered the possibility of repeated playback of 'highlight' sequences of violence, and, in particular, of sex. This mode of viewing – the replay of sexual scenes with the tacit but I think quite plausible implication of masturbation – clearly relocates *Basic Instinct* as a soft porn erotic thriller on video, a production cycle from which the film derives.

Basic Instinct was most commonly viewed on video among the adolescent age group in my sample. A further advantage of the video format could lie in the avoidance of age restrictions at cinema screenings. For teenagers of both genders, watching *Basic Instinct* on video typically entailed finding a 'private' space to escape the threat of parental interference. This resulted in the spatial and/or temporal separation of teenage viewing from parental presence in the home. For instance, one male informant bought the video unseen at the age of 16 and watched it after his parents had gone to bed:

I'm 17 years old, and my parents would not have been too happy that
I'd bought such a film!

                       (*57: David. Student. *Empire* sample. Letter.)

Another respondent watched *Basic Instinct* on video in his bedroom
between three and five in the morning, at the age of 14. In his
account, there is a confession of the 'desperation' of the sexually
inexperienced:

> I want to help you with your studies. But I won't give my address
> because you know what parents are like! 'I hope you didn't watch filth
> like that' etc. Well, I got out *Basic Instinct* last year from my local
> v[ideo] shop. I've got a video in my room so I stayed up until 5:00 am
> and watched it with earphones on desperate heah! Well that's all about
> the hype. You hear everyone talking about it and you see pics of Sharon
> and you just have to watch it. I'm sure you felt the same at 14!
>
>   (*71: Shane. *Empire* sample. Letter.)

Shane appears aware that the lengths to which he went to in order
to watch the film free from parental surveillance could be easily
mocked. Anticipating this, he tries to regulate the interpretation of
his remarks made by myself (the addressee) and, by extension, to
control this imagined reader's construction of an identity for him (as
the author of the account).[154] Thus, as Jackie Stacey argues, a 'tria-
logic' relationship can be traced between respondent, imagined
reader and that 'imagined other's fantasy of the [respondent's]
self'.[155] In an attempt to intervene in this assumed (mocking and/or
disapproving) production of an identity for him, Shane stresses com-
monality with the addressee and asserts, pretty accurately, that the
'mature' researcher was once like him, a sexually inexperienced
straight male teenager consuming sexual images as a substitute for
the 'real thing'. Shane's suggestion temporarily closed the gap
between researcher and researched, and proved an unexpected
source of (empathetic and somewhat nostalgic) pleasure: I recognised in him a part of my younger self.[156] Although an awareness of
this similarity does not erase the power relations structuring the
research exercise, it can partially offset the process of 'othering' constituted by the act of research. It also forced me to examine my own
reaction to the film text, which I had hitherto failed to acknowledge.
This included (hetero)sexual pleasures derived from the spectacle of
Stone/Catherine's body, not dissimilar from those experienced by
some of the 'others' I have been discussing here.[157]

Masculinities

So far, I have shown how some straight male viewers derived sexual knowledges and pleasures from watching *Basic Instinct*. In addition, my analysis has suggested that the social act of viewing can be a means of establishing identity and status in the adolescent peer group. I have argued that an assessment of male teenagers' reasons for utilising the video of *Basic Instinct* can contribute to an understanding of how adolescents learn to behave as heterosexual men through the consumption of images of women. In the process, textually mediated images of femininity and masculinity interact with local negotiations of straight male identity and broader, socially embedded discourses of gender.

Analysing viewers' accounts as texts enables the researcher to uncover revealing blanks in these stories of film viewing. For example, Michael Douglas' naked body remained a structuring absence in the vast majority of male responses. The problem of the male body on display is that it may imply homoerotic desire, or the presence of a female audience inclined to look at men and evaluate them physically, much as men do to women. Shane provided a rare exception to this revealing silence in his energetic refutation of any possible pleasure in looking at the male star naked: 'M. Douglas' ass turned me off my popcorn.' The figure of Douglas/Nick operated more commonly as a surrogate for some male viewers, through his drive to investigate the (sexual) secrets of Catherine. However, Paul's account manifested not a monolithic acceptance of the film's construction of what it is to be male, but rather a series of negotiations of a particular masculinity represented as antisocial and violent as well as sexually active. Thus, while this viewer shared Nick's curiosity about and desire for Catherine, enjoying vicarious pleasures in the 'sexual event' between them, he criticised Nick's treatment of Beth:

> [Nick was] A real stupid gullible bastard with no will power. A real 'fuck up'.

> [Beth was] a very intelligent sensible woman who gets treated badly by shitheads like Michael Douglas.
>
> (*46: Paul. Q.18f; Q.18b.)

The first comment here appears to refer to Nick's sexual attraction to Catherine, which he follows against the warnings of his partner,

Gus. (It may or may not also refer to Nick's killing of innocent citizens in the film's backstory, or his consumption of alcohol, which is coded as problematic.) The second statement appears to be a reference to Nick's 'rape' of Beth. The convergence of surrogate sexual agent and abject violent 'fuck up' in the figure of Nick raises questions about investment and identification. Is the viewer complicit in Nick's violence against women, as well as in his lust for them? Another teenager, James, called Nick 'an obscene, uncaring, selfish man who is someway meant to be "the hero"' (*28: Q17f). These two cases suggest one way in which straight male viewers negotiated their way through the film, both in the act of viewing and in the process of forming and writing responses retrospectively. They picked and chose elements, focusing on some (what might be called 'good sex') and filtering out others (such as violence and 'bad sex'). Splitting images of 'bad sex' off from the spectrum of 'legitimate' male (hetero)sexual activity may be necessary for some men to enjoy the portrayal of 'good sex' as exciting and arousing, but also as ultimately consensual and 'non-violent'. The violence inherent in Nick's sexuality is negotiated in the cases of Paul and James through attempts to divorce it from the heterosexual desire the viewer shares with the character, and to expel it as 'sickening' and 'obscene'. Other straight male informants appeared to negotiate the film's construction of a sexually aggressive masculinity by attempting to evade it. The textual moment when this construction is most clearly apparent, Nick's 'rape' of Beth, was markedly absent from many accounts.[158]

The above cases demand a flexible and mobile model of identification, rather than the total and unquestioning absorption into voyeuristic and sadistic pleasures proposed by some paradigms of 'male' spectatorship. Murray Smith has queried dominant models of identification, in part by uncoupling two processes which have often been conflated by theorists: 'alignment' ('the way a film gives us access to the actions, thoughts, and feelings of characters') and 'allegiance' ('the way a film attempts to marshal our sympathies for or against the various characters').[159] Smith argues that alignment and positive allegiance are conventionally paired through the organisation of many films, but that this connection is not inevitable. In the case of *Basic Instinct* then, the film 'aligns' the viewer with Nick (and also, if rather less frequently, with Catherine), but this is not always accompanied by textual operations which prompt positive viewer allegiance. Instead,

Basic Instinct cues viewer sympathy for Nick (and Catherine) at certain moments and antipathy at others. In Smith's terms, both Nick and Catherine are 'alloys' combining 'morally "base" and "precious" qualities'.[160] It is not easy to be clear about the film's moral commentary upon its characters, because it refuses two key norms of the conventional 'moral structure' which Smith locates in classical Hollywood cinema: a moral centre (grounded in a benchmark character) and moral resolution.[161] *Basic Instinct* lacks a clear set of values or 'cotext'.[162] Instead, it can be called an 'agonistic' film – 'in which the struggle between opposing forces is conceived as a sort of game'[163] – or, better still, an example of what Richard Maltby calls the 'antinomian text'.[164] Maltby uses this term to describe a certain kind of film produced in Hollywood in the 1930s and 1940s, which was sufficiently ambiguous in its treatment of sexual subject matter to accommodate 'sophisticated' and 'innocent' audiences simultaneously.[165] Like Maltby's antinomian texts, the lack of a clear moral commentary in *Basic Instinct* is to a great extent commercially motivated, inviting multiple perspectives on, and investments in, competing characters, in order to maximise the film's audience.[166] This is not to argue that elements of the film were never evaluated according to norms and standards that might be called 'moral'. After all, this is just the kind of process in which Paul and James, and a number of reviewers and commentators, participated. Textual operations such as those inviting 'allegiance' are clearly not 'guaranteed', but work in conjunction with the orientations, knowledges and value systems of specific viewers as social subjects. To recall Corner's 'triple-decker' model of meaning production, there can be little dispute about the primary (denotative) aspects of Nick's forced sex with Beth (including her evident response, which combines signs of pleasure, discomfort and alarm). But the secondary (implicatory) and tertiary levels of signification (the latter involving generalised significances, which may be accorded 'a negotiated place in [a viewer's] knowledge or memory')[167] are much more open to difference and disagreement. Whether one takes Nick's 'side' in this narrative event (and whether one calls it a 'rape' or not) is clearly variable, and is informed both by 'internal' factors such as character action, music and dialogue, and by a host of interrelating 'external' understandings, values and dispositions, which are socially produced and will be shaped in part by factors such as age, sexual history, sexuality, gender, and conditions of viewing.

Conclusions

Some heterosexual male informants found *Basic Instinct* a violent and exploitative example of the objectification of women. However, at the risk of appearing to reproduce a certain gendered stereotype, I have chosen to concentrate here on a category of response which, although widely recognised, is more assumed than examined in studies of film and mass media – that of male (hetero)sexual viewing strategies which locate woman precisely as object. These objectifying looks, with their pleasures, subtleties and uses, are socially embedded in a range of everyday situations including (but not limited to) those of watching film, video and television. It is tempting but erroneous to assume that the men employing such strategies passively imbibe heterosexist and patriarchal ideologies from popular culture texts in a straightforward, monolithic and ultimately uninteresting and unimportant way. Rather, they actively inhabit, live out and engage with elements of such ideologies via the dominant, everyday norms and practices of masculine identity and behaviour, which shape the decoding as well as the encoding of films such as *Basic Instinct*. Thus an undercover return to a hypodermic transmission model which 'explains' straight male pleasures and interpretations must be avoided. This model has long since been abandoned for other groups of media users such as heterosexual and lesbian women and gay men. Heterosexual men too actively negotiate their self-images along with the meanings of the texts they consume. The fact that the outcomes of such negotiations may often be politically conservative is no reason for ignoring – and may indeed be a reason for attending to – the processes through which they come about. In the case of *Basic Instinct* this can mean eliding Catherine's narrative autonomy to position her as a female sexual spectacle, or grappling with the film's construction of a masculinity which is violent and unstable but driven by an all too recognisable heterosexual desire. Or it can mean deriving visual pleasures and knowledges from female bodily display, along with the kudos of seeing an 'adult' film 'under age'; or encountering costs such as the perceived social disapproval of the 'pervert', or the embarrassment of watching sex scenes in a public cinema.

Such pleasures and significances are not simply 'read off' from the film text, in which fixed meanings inhere. While *Basic Instinct*'s relatively 'open' organisation as a dispersible text clearly invites multiple and conflicting approaches to, and uses of, the film, these emerge from the interfaces between text, viewers and contexts. A range of interpretive frames was proposed by promotional and journalistic satellite texts in circulation around the film. The exact details and diversity of such intertexts will of course vary from film to film, but they will, in conjunction with the 'internal' mechanisms of the film text, solicit some viewing strategies and responses more vigorously than others. In the case of *Basic Instinct*, prospective viewers were promised various attractions, including those of 'couples' soft porn, the 'peepshow' pleasures of sexualised female display, a thriller plot, star presences, a 'postfeminist' assertion of female empowerment and sexual subjectivity, and even bisexual and lesbian pleasures. That such a diversity of sometimes contradictory approaches and uses could be proposed on behalf of, and productively derived from, the same film, attests to the multivocality and flexibility of the dispersible text. As Richard Maltby points out, Hollywood's 'commercial aesthetic' is 'too opportunistic to prize coherence, organic unity or even the absence of contradiction among its primary virtues'.[168] Nevertheless, these various invitations-to-view were in effect hierarchised, in terms of both where they appeared (in mass readership or niche publications, for example) and how they drew upon and were supported by, wider discourses. To use Stuart Hall's familiar phrase, they were – to an extent – 'structured in dominance' rather than arranged entirely equitably.

Basic Instinct was designed and marketed to sell across genders and diverse sexualities, but, in sexual terms, its multiple appeals worked more within than against dominant discourses. The film's target audience was both diversified and stratified through its textual structures and promotional strategies. Straight male viewers were invited by these mechanisms to deploy what I have called an appraising gaze at the sexualised female body. By contrast, heterosexual women were invited to invest in Catherine Tramell as a sexual and narrative agent, and (less successfully) to enjoy the (far less foregrounded) sight of Douglas' male body. In addition, lesbian or bisexual pleasures in female sexual display could be derived from the film, but people occupying these identities constituted a far less significant market than straight audiences.[169] My point is that such 'alternative' and subordinated viewpoints, while certainly possible, are not only less widely endorsed in mainstream Anglo-American cultures, but in this case were also offered leaner pickings by the film, compared to

the more familiar heterosexual male pleasures taken in the objectification of women. It was this socially dominant viewing strategy that
was cued most effectively by the film and much of its promotion and
reviews, thus rewarding the many male viewers who approached
Basic Instinct with such a framework to hand. In addition, as I have
shown, attempts were made to invalidate unwanted interpretations
such as accusations of misogyny and homophobia.

The most assiduously courted audiences for the film were straight
men and women. While the former were more likely to find their
habitual sexualised viewing strategies legitimated by the phenomenon of *Basic Instinct*, some (straight and bisexual) women at least
could enjoy it as a narrative of female empowerment, and/or as
delivering sexual pleasures. In mixed-gender viewing groups, however, the pleasures of some women were on occasions mitigated by
awareness of a male scrutiny of female bodies in the film, and
accompanying feelings of their own physical inadequacy. I am not
suggesting that the phenomenon of *Basic Instinct* does nothing but
mirror and reproduce dominant ideology. The film's (generically
mediated) gestures towards female autonomy, bisexuality and lesbianism, as picked up and amplified through certain commentaries
and viewing strategies, could be seen to both acknowledge and contribute to social and cultural shifts such as the increasing recognition
of 'other' sexualities and of women's subjectivity and aspirations.
Nevertheless, the film could also be viewed as co-opting such trap-
pings to update a more familiar sexualisation of women for straight
male enjoyment, or even as part of a backlash against such developments. Thus, if 'marginal' interpretive frames can be seen to actively
rework wider social and cultural contexts, the same is also true of
more conservative avenues of approach to the film. All of these
viewing strategies, with their varying degrees of social endorsement,
feed into the ongoing flux of society and culture.

The diversity of audience responses which I have uncovered
evinces a large degree of instability and contingency in the production of higher-category meanings, uses and significances from popular film. In the words of Barbara Klinger, investigating film reception
thus 'provides a sense, not of *the* ideology the text had in a historical context, but its *many* ideologies'.[170] But this awareness must be
balanced by a sense of the operations of social and cultural power –
through the functioning at textual and contextual levels of (often
gendered) norms, conventions and practices such as those discussed

here. The more radical fringes of reception theory risk missing these operations in their abiding concentration on variety and contingency.

What I have undertaken in this chapter is, among other things, an examination of 'media effects'. In using this contentious term, I intend to extend its meaning, moving away from some of the problematic assumptions about more or less direct textual influence on 'susceptible' audiences that have attended the screen violence debate.[171] I want to hold on to the notion that media consumption, including watching films (on television and video as well as at the cinema) informs and impacts upon our daily lives – but in complex and contextually shaped ways. It does this in part by offering explanatory frameworks that may be applied to the social world: models of speech, dress, behaviour and convention. Such 'effects' are always constituted according to the particularity of the social settings in which texts are encountered, and so exceed, for example, the simplistic logics of 'glamorising violence' which circulate in some common-sense knowledges and indictments of popular screen media. Nevertheless – and while viewers and readers will usually be well aware of their fictive status – popular fictions still play a significant role in shaping how people understand and make sense of their own experiences, validating some but not others.[172] In the case of *Basic Instinct*, the film and some of its satellite texts effectively sanction a socially embedded heterosexual male viewing strategy which holds women as objects of an appraising gaze, while also offering less well established pleasures for (some) female audiences. The film does not simply originate, but rather recruits, commodifies, reproduces and reworks certain discourses and practices already in existence – from straight male (and, potentially at least, couples') pleasures in soft porn, to 'postfeminist' assertion.[173] Hollywood trades in 'real world' discourses, all the while mediating them via its own operating practices, generic templates, and conventional systems of stardom, spectacle and narrative. The dimensions of its 'effects' cannot be accurately drawn without acknowledgement of the orientations and agency of its different viewers, and the significance of its varied contexts of reception, at both micro- and macro-social levels. These factors may lend support to one viewing strategy over another. John Corner describes this dynamic very well: 'cultural power and ideological reproduction work as much, if not more, through the social factors bearing upon interpretive action as they do through that which might be thought to be "carried" by, or "inscribed" within, media texts themselves. Failure to attend properly to this has often lead to … an overly simplistic play-off between textual power and reader freedom.'[174] Like Corner, I want to move beyond the limits of a binary logic here – to argue that audience activity and 'effects' or influences can and do commonly coexist, and that contextual considerations provide the key to breaking down this either/or thinking.[175] In specific contexts, audience activity does not necessarily provide a counter-dynamic to textual mechanisms, but often operates to reinforce media influence.[176] A clear instance of this is when heterosexual male teenagers secure access to *Basic Instinct* and negotiate the viewing experience by selecting and rejecting certain moments and textual strands, while in the process practising and reproducing the 'appraising gaze' at the female body which is socially sanctioned in their culture.

Whether viewers located in *Basic Instinct* pleasures and meanings which had been promised through marketing and/or journalistic texts, found ones which had been overlooked or explicitly refuted in these 'guides', or rejected (elements of) the film, they engaged with *Basic Instinct* in complicated and subtle ways. However, under an integrated approach to popular cinema, audience activities cannot be divorced from the particularities of social contexts, at local and more general levels, or from the operations of 'colonizing organizations'[177] in the production, marketing and critical reception of films. These procedures work to organise and regulate interpretations, pleasures and uses with varying degrees of success. The 'textual power' of the film and its various incarnations in the popular media should be neither underestimated nor overstated. Although never fully determining how *Basic Instinct* was approached and utilised, the structure of the film text and the constellation of satellite texts around it opened up (limited) space for proliferating but hierarchised interpretations and uses, including, for example, very different male and female responses to the character of Catherine. Viewers' diverse practices coexisted alongside, and interpenetrated with, these industrial and cultural mechanisms. Thus reception is shaped by the operations of institutional and textual power and by the specificities of individual media use, which are in turn structured by social factors such as gender, sexuality, class, age, and specific socio-cultural contexts. The functioning of cultural power is best understood, then, as a matrix through which film texts, audiences, industrial mechanisms, and discursive and social contexts interact. These are the overlapping determinants of popular film's significance, meaning and use, which a multi-dimensional examination of film culture attempts to address.

Notes

1 On American protests against the film, see Chris Holmlund, '"Cruisin' for a bruisin": Hollywood's deadly (lesbian) dolls', *Cinema Journal*, 34:1 (1994), 34–6.
2 Fiona McIntosh, 'Woman: the sexual tiger', *Daily Mirror*, 27 April 1992, 16–17.
3 Patricia Dobson, 'Basic Instinct', *Screen International*, 3–9 April 1992, 18.
4 'Top 10 video rental titles, 1992', *British Film Institute Film and Television Handbook 1994* (London, British Film Institute, 1993), p. 63. *Basic Instinct*'s terrestrial television premiere on ITV in November 1994 was watched by 7.35 million viewers. While this figure is relatively low compared to the most successful annual film broadcasts (the top 20 films screened on British terrestrial television in 1994 attracted more than 11 million viewers each), it highlights the size of television audiences for films. 'Top 10 films and TV movies', *Broadcast*, 9 December 1994, 19. 'Top 20 feature films shown on terrestrial TV in 1994', *British Film Institute Film and Television Handbook 1996* (London, British Film Institute, 1995), p. 58.
5 Guild was sold to the French media and textiles group Chargeurs in late 1992.
6 Following cashflow problems and the commercial flop of *Cutthroat Island* (Renny Harlin, United States, 1995) Carolco filed for bankruptcy in 1995. See Martin Dale, *The Movie Game: The Film Business in Britain, Europe and America* (London, Cassell, 1997), pp. 85–6.
7 *British Film Institute Film and Television Handbook 1993* (London, British Film Institute, 1992), p. 42.
8 The 'fast burn' of even big hits at the box office enables quicker payback of production loans or reinvestment of capital, while soaring advertising budgets serve to defend the market against new competitors by raising the price of entry. See Nicholas Garnham, *Capitalism and Communication: Global Culture and the Economics of Information* (London, Sage, 1990), pp. 200–1.
9 William Paul, 'The K-mart audience at the mall movies', *Film History*, 6 (1994), p. 497.
10 Work on the first British multiplex began in 1985. By the end of 1995, there were 79 sites, accounting for 706 screens, or 28 per cent of the

United Kingdom total. Growth continued through the decade, and by 1998 167 multiplex sites housed 1,488 screens, or 58 per cent of the UK total. *British Film Institute Film and Television Handbook 1997* (London, 1996), p. 34, and *2000* (London, British Film Institute, 1999), pp. 30–1. On the Hollywood studios' influence and interventions in the British exhibition sector, and their dominance of the multiplex end of the market in particular, see Sarah Street, *British National Cinema* (London and New York, Routledge, 1997), pp. 17–18.

11 See Simon Banner, 'Hype, gore and a hit film that appeals to Basic Instincts', *Evening Standard*, 27 March 1992, 17; Geoff Brown, 'Body count at maximum', *The Times*, Life and Times, 7 May 1992, 3; Laurence Earle, 'Rushes', *The Independent*, 8 May 1992, 18. On release patterns, see Garnham, *Capitalism and Communication*, p. 203. American box office performance is not necessarily an accurate indication of subsequent overseas success, however. See Janet Wasko, *Hollywood in the Information Age: Beyond the Silver Screen* (London, Polity Press, 1994) p. 232.

12 Guild Film Distribution Ltd., Marketing and Publicity Department, letter to the author, 10 July 1992.

13 Jon Anderson, director of advertising and publicity at Columbia TriStar Films (UK), letter to the author, 19 July 1993. According to Philip Thomas, then editor of the British film monthly *Empire*, breakdowns in symbiosis do occur from time to time – for example, in disputes over who will be the magazine's cover star. Philip Thomas, telephone interview, 5 May 1995.

14 Guild Film Distribution Ltd., Marketing and Publicity Department, letter to the author.

15 Cinema Advertising Association, CAVIAR Film Profiles, May 1997. 54 per cent of the audience were from classes ABC1, and 46 per cent were from classes C2DE. Class codings are as follows: A = Upper Middle Class; B = Middle Class; C1 = Lower Middle Class; C2 = Skilled Working Class; D = Working Class; E = Lowest Level of Subsistence.

16 Thomas Schatz, 'The new Hollywood', in Jim Collins, Hilary Radner and Ava Preacher Collins (eds), *Film Theory Goes to the Movies* (New York, Routledge, 1993), p. 33.

17 Merchandising for *Basic Instinct* in Britain was limited to a music soundtrack by Jerry Goldsmith, on the Varese Sarabande recording label, and a novelisation of the film by Richard Osborne, published in paperback by Signet, an imprint owned by Penguin.

18 John Ellis, *Visible Fictions: Cinema: Television: Video* (London, Routledge and Kegan Paul, 1982), pp. 31–2.

19 See Philip French, 'Hot for an ice pick', *The Observer*, 10 May 1992,

52; Alexander Walker, 'Trashy thrills and basest instincts', *Evening Standard*, 7 May 1992, 28; Derek Malcolm, 'From panters to painters', *The Guardian*, 7 May 1992, 29; Kim Newman, 'Basic Instinct', *Sight and Sound*, 2:1 (NS) (May 1992), 45.

20 A rather different strategy capitalises upon a plot twist or revelation, to which advertising calls attention, but without divulging too many details. Employed for films such as *The Usual Suspects* (Bryan Singer, United States, 1995), *The Crying Game* (Neil Jordan, United Kingdom, 1992) and *The Sixth Sense* (M. Night Shyamalan, United States, 1999), this strictly regulated dispersal of textual information extends each film's social reach by recruiting reviewers and, subsequently, viewers into a privileged group who know the secret, and who are relied upon to talk about the film without giving too much away. Thanks to Matt Hills on this point.

21 See for example Jenny Cooney, 'Naked Hollywood', *Empire*, 36 (June 1992), 54–60; Gil Gibson, 'Saint Michael?' *For Women*, Summer 1992, 34–7; Roberta Grant, 'Michael Douglas cuts it close', *GQ*, May 1992, 94–9; Nancy Griffin, 'The sympathetic sinner', *Premiere*, April 1992, 84–96; Michael Hellicar, 'Michael Douglas: killer instinct', *Daily Star*, series of three articles, 18–20 May 1992; James Law, 'I've always been interested in lust', *Woman's Own*, 27 April 1992, 52–3. Some of this coverage was arranged by Guild.

22 David Thomson notes Douglas' 'rare ability to be strong and weak at the same time' in many performances, and this may indeed be one source of his popularity. David Thomson, *A Biographical Dictionary of Film* (London, Andre Deutsch, 1994), p. 207.

23 See Chris Holmlund, 'Reading character with a vengeance: the *Fatal Attraction* phenomenon', *The Velvet Light Trap*, 27 (1991), 25–36.

24 Peter Cox, 'Douglas earns his strips', *The Sun*, 8 May 1992, 15. The two films were packaged together in a boxed set video to buy, in November 1993.

25 See Hilary Bonner, 'Killer instinct', *Daily Mirror*, 11 May 1992, 9; Alex McGregor, 'Sharon Stone', *Time Out*, 22–9 April 1992, 20; Rick Sky, 'The hottest property since Monroe', *Daily Mirror*, 25 March 1992, 16–17; Shane Watson, 'Stoned love', *Vogue*, June 1992, 138–9; 'Instinct for controversy', *Options*, June 1992, 127. Stone's highest-profile role before *Basic Instinct* had been a supporting part in Verhoeven's *Total Recall*, starring Arnold Schwarzenegger.

26 This association was played upon in a retrospective of Stone's career, 'Know any beautiful blondes?' *Empire*, 51 (September 1993), 92–3; and in 'Prowess', an advertisement for Gap clothing, *Vanity Fair*, June 1992, 8–9. See also Bonner, 'Killer instinct'.

27 There were rumours of Douglas being admitted to a clinic for 'sex

addiction' after making the film. In this instance, the star's 'real' personality was seen to have collapsed into his fictional role. Nevertheless – and possibly as a deliberate attempt to counter these rumours – Douglas was typically normalised in the press through references to his happy home life and professional status as a powerful and ambitious actor–producer. See Cooney, 'Naked Hollywood'; Grant, 'Michael Douglas cuts it close'; Griffin, 'The sympathetic sinner'; Hellicar, 'Michael Douglas: killer instinct'. On Douglas' personal life, see John Parker, *Michael Douglas: Acting on Instinct* (London, 1994), pp. 241–53, abridged in 'My name is Mike, I'm a sex addict', *Daily Mail*, 18 October 1994, 28–30. On 'personification' and 'impersonation', see Barry King, 'Articulating stardom', *Screen*, 26:5 (1985), 27–50. On 'professionals' and 'performers', see Christine Geraghty, 'Re-examining stardom: questions of texts, bodies and performance', in Christine Gledhill and Linda Williams (eds), *Reinventing Film Studies* (London, Arnold, 2000), pp. 183–201.

28 Griffin, 'The sympathetic sinner', p. 86. See also Cooney, 'Naked Hollywood'; Alex McGregor, 'Sex crimes', *Time Out*, 22–9 April 1992, 19–21; Lisa Sewards, 'How I took screen sex to the limit', *Daily Express*, 7 May 1992, 23–4.

29 On designer clothes in the film see Geoff Broome, Costume drama', *International Collections*, Summer 1992, 78–81. On clothes and lighting, see Patricia Dobson, 'Basic Instinct', *Screen International*, 3–9 April 1992, 18.

30 See Claudia Eller, 'Eszterhas script picks up record $3–mil from Carolco', *Variety*, 27 June 1990, 10, 14; Martin A. Grove, 'Hollywood report', *Hollywood Reporter*, 24 August 1990, 10; Jeanie Kasindorf, 'The millionaire boys club', *Empire*, 19 (January 1991), 54–7; Nigel Andrews, 'Injuries inflicted on basic intelligence', *Financial Times*, 7 May 1992, 21; Banner, 'Hype, gore and a hit film', 17; Brown, 'Body count at maximum', 3.

31 On the film's graphic violence, see Cox, 'Douglas earns his strips'; Dobson, 'Basic Instinct'; Malcolm, 'From panters to painters', 29; Barry McIlheney, 'Basic Instinct', *Empire*, 36 (June 1992), 20; Walker, 'Trashy thrills and basest instincts'. On gossip about sex and violence, see below.

32 In marked contrast to heterosexual acts, sex between women was hinted at but never shown in the film. Some commentators saw *Basic Instinct* as an initiator of a fashion cycle of titillating images of 'lipstick lesbianism' or 'lesbian chic' in heterosexual popular culture. See 'Woman to woman', *For Women*, Summer 1992, 7; Diane Hamer and Belinda Budge, 'Introduction', in Hamer and Budge (eds), *The Good the Bad and the Gorgeous: Popular Culture's Romance with Lesbianism* (London, Pandora, 1994), pp. 1–14.

33 See for example Andrews, 'Injuries inflicted on basic intelligence'; Baz Bamigboye, 'Full frontal attraction', *Daily Mail*, 1 September 1990, 7; Banner, 'Hype, gore and a hit film'; Brown, 'Body count at maximum'; McIlheney, 'Basic Instinct'; Adam Mars-Jones, 'Mad, bad and dangerous to know', *The Independent*, 8 May 1992, p. 18; Pauline McLeod, 'Pretty suspect', *Daily Mirror*, 8 May 1992, 22; Sewards, 'How I took screen sex to the limit'. The scene was parodied in the sex thriller spoof *Fatal Instinct*, and featured in a regular series on 'classic' screen moments in *Empire*, and in the magazine's list of '100 most gob-smacking movie moments'. 'Games are fun … ', *Empire*, 51 (September 1993), 130; *Empire*, 85 (July 1996), 93.

34 This still also appeared on the front cover of Melvyn Stokes and Richard Maltby (eds), *Identifying Hollywood's Audiences: Cultural Identity and the Movies* (London, British Film Institute, 1999). Academic publications may thus trade on such a recognisable – and sexualised – image.

35 Figures from Imdb.com

36 While I interpreted Nick's aggressive sex with Beth as rape, not all press and audience accounts did so. I have placed the word in quotation marks here to indicate its contested status. For references to sex, violence and a combination of the two, see for example McIlheney, 'Basic Instinct': 'with Verhoeven … going just about as far with a pair of mainstream Hollywood performers as it is permissible to go'; McLeod, 'Pretty suspect'. See also 'Sharon strips for action', *Daily Mail*, 15 February 1991, 23; 'Lust, human nature and basic instinct, by Douglas', *Evening Standard*, 21 April 1992, 3; Simon Barnett, 'Basic Instinct', *Northern Star*, 14–21 May 1992, 21; Cooney, 'Naked Hollywood'; Grant, 'Divide and conquer'; McGregor, 'Sex crimes'; Sewards, 'How I took screen sex to the limit; Hellicar, 'Sexy Sharon got nude scenes down to basics'.

37 Dobson, 'Basic Instinct'; McIlheney, 'Basic Instinct'; McLeod, 'Pretty suspect'.

38 See Steven Cohan, 'Censorship and narrative indeterminacy in *Basic Instinct*: "You won't learn anything from me I don't want you to know"', in Steve Neale and Murray Smith (eds), *Contemporary Hollywood Cinema* (London, Routledge, 1998), pp. 264–7. Several of these cuts were restored for the European release.

39 Guild Film Distribution Ltd., *Basic Instinct: Production Notes and Biographies* (1992), p. 2. For reworkings of the erotic mystery label, see Cox, 'Douglas earns his strips'; McLeod, 'Pretty suspect'.

40 See Walker, 'Trashy thrills and basest instincts'; Newman, 'Basic Instinct'; Linda Ruth Williams, 'Erotic thrillers and rude women', *Sight and Sound*, 3:7 (NS) (July 1993), 12–14. See French, 'Hot for an

ice pick'; Malcolm, 'From panters to painters'. Gregory Solman, 'The Bs of Summer', *Film Comment*, 29:4 (July–August 1993), 13. Steve Grant, 'Divide and conquer', *Time Out*, 22–6 April 1992, 21. These generic labels clearly overlap to varying extents. For more on generic classification, see chapter 4.

41 Linda Williams, *Hard Core: Power, Pleasure and the 'Frenzy of the Visible'* (Berkeley, University of California Press, 1989), p. 233.

42 On *Jagged Edge*, see Robert E. Kapsis, *Hitchcock: The Making of a Reputation* (Chicago, University of Chicago Press, 1992), pp. 176–7.

43 Charlotte Brunsdon, 'Post-feminism and shopping films', in her *Screen Tastes: Soap Opera to Satellite Dishes* (London, Routledge, 1997,) pp. 81–102. Brunsdon is discussing *Working Girl* (Mike Nichols, United States, 1988) and *Pretty Woman* (Gary Marshall, United States, 1990). Catherine could also be said to be 'post-feminist' in that the implications of her success – social, sexual and economic – are that equality has been achieved and women no longer need feminism; that it has become irrelevant; that apolitical individualism, not collective political action, is what women should now rely on.

44 Thanks to Charlotte Adcock on this point.

45 *Basic Instinct: Production Notes and Biographies*, p. 2. These references were indeed picked up in reviews for trade papers, the 'serious' film magazine *Sight and Sound*, and 'up-market' broadsheet newspapers. However, they were often cited as benchmarks against which *Basic Instinct* fell short. See Andrews, 'Injuries inflicted on basic intelligence'; Gareth Davis, 'Back to basics', *The Pink Paper*, 10 May 1992, 13; Mars-Jones, 'Mad, bad and dangerous to know'; J. Hoberman, 'Fantastic projections', *Sight and Sound*, 2:1 (NS) (May 1992), 4; Malcolm 'From panters to painters', p.29. On how references to Hitchcock's work have been used to promote and critically evaluate horrors and thrillers since the 1970s, see Kapsis, *Hitchcock*, pp. 158–215.

46 This motif also appeared in the cover art of video thriller *Fear Inside* (Leon Ichaso, United States, 1992).

47 A rare exception is 'middle-market' newspaper the *Daily Express*, which carried an interview with the director. Sewards, 'How I took screen sex to the limit'.

48 See Pierre Bourdieu, *Distinction: A Social Critique of the Judgement of Taste*, trans. Richard Nice (London, Routledge & Kegan Paul, 1984), pp. 26–7.

49 Guild distributed 12 films in 1992, and was the fourth largest distributor in the UK with 11 per cent of the market. 'UK distributor market share total', *Screen International*, Friday 29 January 1993, 15.

50 For chronologies of these protests, see 'The making of *Basic Instinct*', in Cooney, 'Naked Hollywood', *Empire*, 36 (June 1992), 60; Grant,

'Divide and conquer'; Charles Lyons, 'The paradox of protest, American film, 1980–1992', in Francis Couvares (ed.), *Movie Censorship and American Culture* (Washington and London, Smithsonian Institute Press, 1996), pp. 291–300. See also 'Empire goes to the Oscars', *Empire*, 35 (May 1992), 70–1. For a review of protests and press responses in the United States, see Holmlund, '"Cruisin' for a bruisin"', 34–6.

51 Reported in Cooney, 'Naked Hollywood', 56. A *Daily Express* interview with Verhoeven noted attacks on *Basic Instinct* by 'women's rights activists in America', but made no mention of lesbian and gay protests. Sewards, 'How I took screen sex to the limit'.

52 On the differing tactics of GLAAD (education and persuasion) and Queer Nation (disruption) in the American campaigns against *Basic Instinct*, see Angela Galvin, '*Basic Instinct*: damning dykes', in Hamer and Budge (eds), *The Good the Bad and the Gorgeous*, p. 220, and Lyons, 'The paradox of protest'.

53 Alberto Melucci, *Nomads of the Present: Social Movements and Individual Needs in Contemporary Society*, eds J. Keane, P. Mier (London, Hutchinson Radius, 1989).

54 *Ibid.*, pp. 34–5.

55 *Ibid.*, p. 12. Thanks to Charlotte Adcock on this point. On links between identity politics, resistance and popular culture, see Judith Halberstam, 'Imagined violence/queer violence: representation, rage and resistance', *Social Text*, 37 (1993), 190–5.

56 See Earle, 'Rushes'.

57 Banner, 'Hype, gore and a hit film'. See also 'It's only a movie', *Empire*, 35 (May 1992), 6.

58 For further coverage of the American boycott, see 'Film', *Gay Times*, May 1992, 69; Irene Coffey, 'Basic Instinct', *Spare Rib*, June 1992, 20.

59 See Claus-Dieter Rath, 'Live/life: television as a generator of events in everyday life', in Phillip Drummond and Richard Paterson (eds), *Television and its Audience* (London, British Film Institute, 1988), pp. 36–7.

60 Judith Halberstam suggests that 'the protests were led by gay men, … and many lesbians involved in the protests changed their minds after actually viewing the film'. Halberstam, 'Imagined violence/queer violence', 196.

61 See Barbara Klinger, 'Digressions at the cinema: reception and mass culture', *Cinema Journal* 28:4, 16–17; Richard Maltby and Ian Craven, *Hollywood Cinema: An Introduction* (Oxford, Blackwell, 1995), pp. 42–3, 438–9. The cancellation of preview screenings, and 'front-loading' the audience through saturation advertising and large-scale openings are different attempts to limit the damaging effects that

unwelcome talk – whether poor reviews or negative word of mouth – can have on a film's box office. See Schatz, 'The new Hollywood', p. 19.

62 There are historical precedents for such a strategy. A policy of 'deniability' centred on the production of ambiguous 'antinomian texts' was institutionalised in Hollywood during the 1930s, in order to both maximise commercial potential and accommodate the strictures of the Production Code. See Richard Maltby, '"A brief romantic interlude": Dick and Jane go to $3^{1}/_{2}$ seconds of the classical Hollywood cinema', in David Bordwell and Noel Carroll (eds), *Post-Theory: Reconstructing Film Studies* (Madison, University of Wisconsin Press, 1996), pp. 434–59; Ruth Vasey, *The World According to Hollywood, 1918–1939* (Exeter, University of Exeter Press, 1997).

63 *Basic Instinct: Production Notes and Biographies*, p. 4.

64 '*Playboy* Interview: Sharon Stone', *Playboy*, 39:12 (December 1992), 73, cited in Holmlund, '"Crusin' for a bruisin'"', 50–1n.

65 Grant, 'Michael Douglas cuts it close'. The *Daily Mail*'s film critic commented similarly: 'Gay rights protestors hate the movie but it is well-crafted rubbish, unfit to be taken seriously.' Shaun Usher, 'Following the instinct to make a fast buck, basically', *Daily Mail*, 8 May 1992.

66 'It's only a movie'.

67 See Ann Karpf, 'The unbearable rightness of being PC', *The Guardian*, 24 September 1992, 34. For a range of interpretations, see Sarah Dunant (ed.), *War of the Words: the Political Correctness Debate* (London, Virago, 1994).

68 'It's only a movie'.

69 Grant, 'Michael Douglas cuts it close'.

70 Cooney, 'Naked Hollywood'.

71 Susan Ellicott, 'Total recoil', the *Sunday Times*, 22 March 1992, section 4, 1.

72 Cox, 'Douglas earns his strips'.

73 On 'out-groups', see Teun van Dijk, *Racism and the Press* (London, Routledge, 1991), pp. 141–7; 207–8.

74 'Too hot to handle', the *Sunday Times*, 26 January 1992, section 6, 13.

75 McIlheney, 'Basic Instinct'. The popular film magazine *Premiere* reported similarly: 'Douglas is hoping that *Basic Instinct* will give people some unbridled fun during these constricted times.' Griffin, 'The sympathetic sinner'.

76 For example, Peter Kramer's work demonstrates how, as late as the 1990s, Hollywood executives ignored market research which indicated that many women felt marginalised by the relative down-grading of 'female-oriented' genres such as musicals and romantic comedies in favour of the violent, 'male-oriented' action pictures, which domi-

nated production strategies from the 1970s to the 1990s. Peter Kramer, 'A powerful cinemagoing force? Hollywood and female audiences since the 1960s', in Stokes and Maltby (eds), *Identifying Hollywood's Audiences*, pp. 93–108.

77 On genre films and the balance between these two types of verisimilitude, see Steve Neale, *Genre and Hollywood* (London, Routledge, 2000) pp. 31–5. As Christine Gledhill points out, socio-cultural verisimilitude is constantly contested and subject to change. Gledhill, 'Rethinking genre', in Gledhill and Linda Williams (eds), *Reinventing Film Studies* (London, Arnold, 2000) p. 236.

78 See, for example, Winsome Hines, 'Basic Instinct', *The Voice*, 12 May 1992, 25; Mars-Jones, 'Mad, bad and dangerous to know'; Usher, 'Following the instinct to make a fast buck, basically', 30.

79 Walker, 'Trashy thrills and basest instincts'.

80 Lucinda Broadbent, 'Basic Instinct', *Harpies and Quines*, August–September 1992, 33–4. See also Galvin, '*Basic Instinct*: damning dykes', p. 231; Coffey, 'Basic Instinct'.

81 Suzanne Moore, untitled, *The Guardian*, 7 May 1992, 34.

82 McIntosh, 'Woman: the sexual tiger'.

83 While this catalogue of explicit discussions of sex in 'female' popular culture referred to sexualised images of men, nowhere in the article was Douglas/Nick presented as a sex object for female consumption. Contrast Gibson, 'Saint Michael?'; Law, 'I've always been interested in lust'.

84 Catherine's specific ethnic and class identity were naturalised in the *Daily Mirror*, so that this image of a white, wealthy middle-class American was proposed as a universal vehicle for female wish-fulfilment. Although her bisexuality – a mark of difference – was noted, it did not prevent her from standing for the aspirations of heterosexual women. Indeed, it is unclear how lesbian or bisexual reader–viewers were expected to approach the film. Elsewhere, several reviewers accused the film of eradicating Catherine's bisexuality and repositioning her as a heterosexual. See Simon Barnett, 'Basic Instinct', *Northern Star*, 14–21 May 1992, 21; Broadbent, 'Basic Instinct'; Hoberman, 'Fantastic projections'.

85 The following day, the *Daily Mirror* complicated its celebration of the female 'sexual tiger' by publishing a feature detailing male flight from the new woman to a submissive, nurturing femininity, under the intriguing headline 'We want Doris Day'. Fiona McIntosh, 'We want Doris Day', *Daily Mirror*, 28 April 1992, 16–17. By contrast, a feature on Stone run a month previously had presented her as a far less problematic object for straight male sexual gratification. Sky, 'The hottest property since Monroe'. In this way the newspaper, much like the film,

can be seen to be multivocal, offering multiple possible avenues of access to its users. Thanks to Charlotte Adcock on this point.

86 Margarette Driscoll, 'All for love', the *Sunday Times*, 7 June 1992, section 5: 1.

87 See Janet Staiger, *Interpreting Films: Studies in the Historical Reception of American Cinema* (Princeton, Princeton University Press, 1992), p. 6. See also V. N. Volosinov, *Marxism and the Philosophy of Language*, 1929, trans. Ladislav Matejka and I.R. Titunik (New York, Seminar Press, 1973).

88 See Hans Robert Jauss, *Toward an Aesthetic of Reception*, trans. Timothy Bahti (Brighton, Harvester Press, 1982). As Susan Suleiman argues, Jauss' implication of a homogeneous public with a single horizon of expectation needs to be replaced with a notion of 'different horizons of expectations co-existing among different publics'. And, as Janet Staiger points out, horizons of expectation can be extended beyond the strictly fictional to take into account political, scientific and other discourses. Susan R. Suleiman, 'Introduction: varieties of audience-oriented criticism', in Suleiman and Inge Crosman (eds), *The Reader in the Text* (Princeton, Princeton University Press, 1980), p. 37; Janet Staiger, 'The handmaiden of villainy: methods and problems in studying the historical reception of a film', *Wide Angle*, 8:1 (1986), 22.

89 In the words of Allen and Gomery, critical discourse on popular cinema has an 'agenda-setting' function, not telling audiences what to think so much as 'what to think about'. Robert C. Allen and Douglas Gomery, *Film History: Theory and Practice* (New York, McGraw-Hill, 1985), p. 90, cited in Mark Jancovich, 'Genre and the audience: genre classifications and cultural distinctions in the mediation of *The Silence of the Lambs*', in Melvyn Stokes and Richard Maltby (eds), *Hollywood Spectatorship: Changing Perceptions of Cinema Audiences* (London, British Film Institute, forthcoming 2001).

90 The lesbian magazine *Diva*, London listings magazine *Time Out*, and style and music monthly *The Face* also declined to publish my request.

91 Cinema Advertising Association figures show that 77 per cent of *Basic Instinct*'s cinema audience in the UK was under 35. They list 0 per cent as under 18. For further information about the questionnaire sample, see appendix 3.

92 The questionnaire is reproduced in full at appendix 2.

93 Hermann Bausinger, 'Media, technology and daily life', *Media, Culture, Society*, 6:4 (1984), 349.

94 David Morley, *Television, Audiences and Cultural Studies* (London, Routledge, 1992), p. 158.

95 Joke Hermes, *Reading Women's Magazines: An Analysis of Everyday Media Use* (Cambridge, Polity Press, 1995), p. 16.

96 For whatever reasons *Basic Instinct* was watched in the first place, it
    had sufficient impact on the respondents quoted here for them to take
    the trouble to write to me. It is in general more difficult for audience
    researchers to gain access to people who do not feel much at all about
    the specified media form or text. This has been one reason for the pre-
    dominance of fan studies within audience research.

97 Thanks to Matt Hills on this point. I return to this issue in chapter 4.

98 Although a film's marketing campaign and media exposure are at their
    greatest intensity shortly before and during its theatrical release, for
    some viewers the impact of 'hype' does not result in the purchase of a
    cinema ticket, but feeds through into a later demand to watch the film
    on video or television. Perceptions of the social-cultural impact of the
    initial cinema release may also spur demand in these post-theatrical
    markets.

99 ITV, 16 November 1994, 10.30pm. The film was first carried by Sky
    satellite television's Movie Channel on 23 October 1993, at 10pm.

100 Broadcasting Standards Council, *Complaints Bulletin*, 50 (28 March
    1995), p. 18. Mary Kenny, 'The rape of the movie-goer', the *Sunday
    Telegraph*, 10 May 1992, 20.

101 See Andrew Culf, '"Too cautious" ITV aims to confound critics with
    £176m autumn season', *The Guardian*, 20 July 1994, 7; 'Knickers to
    Sharon ban', *The Sun*, 15 November 1994, 9; Elaine Lipworth, 'Lady
    thriller', *TV Times*, 12–18 November 1994, 22–3; Suzanne Moore,
    'Furthermoore', *The Guardian*, 22 July 1994, G2, 6; Richard Wallace,
    'CENSORED Sharon is too sexy for viewers say ITV', *Daily Mirror*,
    20 July 1994, 3; Pauline Wallin, 'ITV Goes Basic', *Today*, 20 July
    1994, p. 13; Derek Winnert, 'Film', *Radio Times*, 12–18 November
    1994, 66.

102 *Complaints Bulletin*, p. 18.

103 On this problem see Liz Stanley, 'Women have servants and men never
    eat: issues in reading gender, using the case study of Mass-Observa-
    tion's 1937 day-diaries', *Women's History Review*, 4:1 (1995),
    85–102; Ien Ang and Joke Hermes, 'Gender and/in media consump-
    tion', in James Curran and Michael Gurevitch (eds), *Mass Media and
    Society* (London, Edward Arnold, 1991), pp. 307–28.

104 Morley, *Television, Audiences and Cultural Studies*, pp. 161–2.

105 Other informants refused the identity category of 'white European'
    proposed in the questionnaire, and overwrote it with their own asser-
    tions of Englishness or Britishness.

106 Ien Ang, 'Wanted. Audiences', p. 105.

107 See Jackie Stacey, *Star Gazing: Hollywood Cinema and Female Spec-
    tatorship* (London, Routledge, 1994), p. 72.

108 For a different use of the term 'audiencing' to refer to 'the process in

which audiences selectively produce meanings and pleasures from texts', see John Fiske and Robert Dawson 'Audiencing violence: watching homeless men watch *Die Hard*', in James Hay, Lawrence Grossberg and Ellen Wartella (eds), *The Audience and Its Landscape* (Boulder, Westview Press, 1996), pp. 297–316.

109 John Corner, 'Media Studies and the "Knowledge Problem"', *Screen*, 36:2 (1995) 152.

110 On research as voyeurism, surveillance, and attempted control of the audience, see Valerie Walkerdine, 'Video replay: families, films and fantasy', in Victor Burgin, James Donald and Cora Kaplan (eds), *Formations of Fantasy* (London, Methuen, 1986), p. 167; Tania Modleski, *Feminism Without Women: Culture and Criticism in a 'Postfeminist' Age* (New York, Routledge, 1991), pp. 38–9.

111 Thus, for some women, Stone/Catherine combined the gendered functions polarised in Laura Mulvey's influential model of classical Hollywood's 'division of labour' into passive female and active male roles. Laura Mulvey, 'Visual pleasure and narrative cinema', *Screen*, 16:3 (Autumn 1975) 6–18.

112 Beverley Skeggs, *Formations of Class and Gender* (London, Sage, 1997), p. 110. Skeggs' research centres on how working-class women negotiate class and gender identities. Unfortunately, my project offers only limited information about informants' occupations, and does not facilitate a detailed investigation of class.

113 *Ibid.*

114 Stacey, *Star Gazing*, p. 175.

115 *Ibid.*, p. 174. See also Jessica Benjamin, *The Bonds of Love* (New York, Pantheon, 1988).

116 Distancing techniques may have been partly encouraged by the questionnaire, which could be taken to invite a 'critical' stance; they also may have operated as partial 'retreats' from accounts which were overly revealing or confessional.

117 Tamsin Wilton discusses how watching a film can allow her to temporarily escape the 'obligations' of a lesbian identity in 'On not being Lady Macbeth: some troubled thoughts on lesbian spectatorship', in Wilton (ed.), *Immortal Invisible: Lesbians and the Moving Image* (London, Routledge, 1995).

118 On this point, see Stuart Hall, 'Introduction', in David Morley, *Family Television: Cultural Power and Domestic Leisure* (London, Comedia, 1986), p. 10.

119 Compare this comment by the female film reviewer in the *Today* newspaper: 'Stone has the kind of perfect body that makes one rush home to turn out the lights.' Sue Heal, 'Douglas follows his instinct in full frontal assault', *Today*, 8 May 1992, 21, 24.

120 Skeggs, *Formations of Class and Gender*, p. 112.

121 This tendency to focus on – here, sexual – attractions and moments of display over narrative developments throws into question the centrality accorded to narrative in some psychoanalytic and neo-formalist approaches to film, and challenges the narrow sense of 'interpretation' prevalent in some critical approaches to reception.

122 Michel de Certeau, *The Practice of Everyday Life* (Berkeley, University of California Press, 1984), pp. xix–xx, 18, 29–42.

123 By contrast, Verhoeven and Eszterhas' subsequent film, the commercial flop *Showgirls* (1995) again contained 'pornographic' elements apparently aimed at a heterosexual male audience, but appeared to offer few or no concessions to women.

124 On whiteness as a normative category, see Richard Dyer, *White* (London, Routledge, 1997); on whiteness and audience response, see John Gabriel, 'What do you do when minority means you? *Falling Down* and the construction of "whiteness"', *Screen*, 37:2 (1996), 129–51.

125 I received six questionnaires from gay men, but have chosen to concentrate here on straight male viewers of the film.

126 Paul Willemen, 'Letter to John', *Screen*, 21:2 (1980) 59.

127 Williams, *Hard Core*, p. 30.

128 *Ibid.*, p. 31.

129 *Ibid.*, p. 80.

130 *Ibid.*, pp. 59, 80.

131 The opening scene was shot using Stone, not a body double, according to Verhoeven, quoted in Douglas Thompson, *Sharon Stone: Basic Ambition* (London, Warner Books, 1995), p. 124.

132 More women than men in the sample interpreted Nick's aggressive sex with Beth as rape. In the film, Beth protests relatively mildly. As the 'rape' is not mentioned by Basil, it is impossible to say whether or not he derived pleasure from it.

133 As Marcia Pally argues, a knee-jerk rejection of objectification *per se* should be queried: 'It cannot be a goal of feminism to eliminate moments during the day when a heterosexual man considers a woman, or women as a class, to be sexually desirable. ... It is a feminist goal for women to recognize the objects of *their* desire.' Nevertheless, such a way of envisaging women is, of course, entirely inappropriate in certain contexts. One might add to Pally's second point the aim of women to be recognised by men as desiring subjects. Marcia Pally, 'Out of sight and out of harm's way', *Index on Censorship*, 1 (1993), 6, cited in Brian McNair, *Mediated Sex: Pornography and Postmodern Culture* (London, Arnold, 1996), p. 95. Italics in original.

134 Carol Clover notes that 'There is no single "right reading" of pornography'. I would stress, however, that some readings may be more

socially and culturally sanctioned than others. Carol Clover, 'Intro-duction', in Pamela Church Gibson and Roma Gibson (eds), *Dirty Looks: Women, Pornography, Power* (London, British Film Institute, 1993), p. 4.

135 Lynne Segal, *Slow Motion: Changing Masculinities, Changing Men* (London, Virago, 1990), p. 229. As Segal makes clear, to note male resentments and feelings of insecurity is in no sense to ignore the mate-rial and gendered power that men, and heterosexual men in partic-ular, still enjoy in contemporary society.

136 Compared to *Basic Instinct*, *The Piano* is clearly more covert about its sexual pleasures, which may pass under the alibis of good taste and 'serious' intent.

137 A 'good sex'/'bad sex' distinction also maps on to *The Piano* which again portrays consensual and (attempted) non-consensual sex.

138 In hard-core pornography, the 'meat shot' answers this question, pro-viding 'irrefutable visual evidence of penetration'. Linda Williams, 'Pornographies on/scene or diff'rent strokes for diff'rent folks', in Lynne Segal and Mary McIntosh (eds), *Sex Exposed* (London, Virago, 1992), p. 241.

139 Ang and Hermes 'Gender and/in media consumption', p. 319.

140 Liesbet van Zoonen, *Feminist Media Studies* (London, Sage, 1994), p. 123.

141 David Buckingham, 'Boys' talk: television and the policing of mas-culinity', in Buckingham (ed.), *Reading Audiences: Young People and the Media* (Manchester, Manchester University Press, 1993), p. 97. Other respondents used my research as an opportunity to display their knowledge as film buffs.

142 Harry Brod, 'Pornography and the alienation of male sexuality', in Jeff Hearn and David Morgan (eds), *Men, Masculinities and Social Theory* (London, Unwin Hyman, 1990), pp. 132–4.

143 Film director Michael Cristofer makes an intriguing comment on the 'problem' with *Showgirls*, which might also apply to some viewers watching *Basic Instinct*: 'Any studio with any brains knows that movies that come on strong with nudity, like *Showgirls*, are threatening to the young male audience – which is their primary target. It places a huge responsibility on their shoulders to know more about sex than they do.' 'Sex sells, says Hollywood', *The Observer* magazine, 16 July 2000, 23.

144 David Buckingham, 'What are words worth? Interpreting children's talk about television', *Cultural Studies*, 5:2 (May 1991), 229–30.

145 Ien Ang, *Watching Dallas: Soap Opera and the Melodramatic Imagi-nation* (London, Routledge, 1980), p. 11.

146 Stacey, *Star Gazing*, p. 76.

147 Janice Radway, '"The hegemony of specificity" and the impasse in audience research: cultural studies and the problem of ethnography', in James Hay, Lawrence Grossberg and Ellen Wartella (eds), *The Audience and its Landscape* (Boulder, Westview Press, 1996), p. 240.

148 Meaghan Morris, 'Banality in cultural studies', *Discourse*, 10:2 (1988), 16. Morris is writing about Fiske, 'British cultural studies and television' in Robert C. Allen (ed.), *Channels of Discourse: Television and Contemporary Criticism* (London, Routledge, 1987).

149 Whether or not my initial requests for viewer responses were published, and the form these requests sometimes took, were also decisions beyond my control, taken by publications staff. The unequal power relationship of researcher and researched was reversed when I requested information from industry executives, on whose co-operation and goodwill I had to rely, and who largely controlled the content and duration of interviews and written replies. This dependence was exacerbated by my lack of 'official' authority as a mere postgraduate researcher.

150 Julian Wood, 'Repeatable pleasures: notes on young people's use of video', in Buckingham (ed.), *Reading Audiences*, p. 188.

151 Paul's use of quotation marks around the word may signal a (retrospective) recognition of his younger self's failure to fully achieve 'cool'.

152 It seems to me that this shocking shift owes something to (and reworks in a very different direction) the unexpected murder of Marion shortly after the sexualised display of her body in *Psycho* (Alfred Hitchcock, United States, 1960). As I have argued above, most male informants tended to dwell on the pleasures of watching the eroticised female body, rather than on the consequences of witnessing female violence towards men. On the 'destabilizing effect' of narrative surprise in *Psycho*'s shower scene, see Linda Williams, 'Discipline and fun: *Psycho* and postmodern cinema', in Christine Geraghty and Linda Williams (eds), *Reinventing Film Studies* (London, Arnold, 2000), p. 355.

153 The use of the formulations 'Ms' and 'Miss Stone' by a number of men could indicate respect for the actress/character, attempted politeness, or the adoption of a rather facetious and exaggeratedly polite tone used, for example, to discuss sex in the common register of *Empire* magazine.

154 Compare the following: 'The media makes out that Sharon keeps her legs open for longer than 10 seconds. I myself, was very disappointed at the fact that she only keeps her legs open for 2 seconds. ... This letter makes me out to be a complete pervert but I'm not.' (*74: Jason. No details given. *Empire* sample. Letter.)

155 Jackie Stacey, 'Hollywood memories', *Screen*, 35:4 (1994), 326. Stacey is drawing on theorisations of dialogics by Volosinov and Bakhtin.

156 There are also, of course, voyeuristic pleasures to be had in audience research. See Walkerdine, 'Video replay'.

157 In making these remarks, I remain aware of the dangers of romanticising straight male experience. But this risk should not prevent any attempt to properly interrogate the social and cultural practices discussed here.

158 Clearly, an admission of enjoying male sexual aggression and 'rape' breaks a social taboo and so would risk disapproval on the part of the addressee. A further problematisation of identification between male adolescents and Douglas' character could stem from the significant age gap between such viewers and the actor.

159 Murray Smith, *Engaging Characters: Fiction, Emotion and the Cinema* (Oxford, Clarendon Press, 1995), p. 6.

160 *Ibid.*, p. 209.

161 *Ibid.*, pp. 213–14.

162 'The co-text is the set of values, beliefs, and so forth which form the backdrop to the events of the narrative – the context within the text, as it were.' *Ibid.*, p. 194. While internally produced, the 'co-text' will draw on some 'external' norms available beyond the film.

163 *Ibid.*, p. 198.

164 Maltby, '"A brief romantic interlude"', p. 447.

165 *Ibid.*, pp. 443, 447.

166 The film's lack of a clear moral 'message' was lamented in many reviews, but applauded as generically appropriate in some others. For disapproving commentaries, see: 'A slick mix of decadence and murder', *Hello!*, 202 (May 1992), 27; Usher, 'Following the instinct to make a fast buck, basically'.

167 John Corner, 'Meaning, genre and context: the problematics of "public knowledge" in the new audience studies', in James Curran and Michael Gurevitch (eds), *Mass Media and Society* (London, Edward Arnold, 1991), p. 272.

168 Maltby and Craven, *Hollywood Cinema*, pp. 27, 35.

169 American film critic J. Hoberman located a nod to gay male subculture in the San Francisco bar used as a location for some scenes. 'Fantastic projections'.

170 Barbara Klinger, 'Film history terminable and interminable: recovering the past in reception studies', *Screen*, 38:2 (1997), 110. Italics in original.

171 See Martin Barker and Julian Petley (eds), *Ill Effects: the Media/Violence Debate (London, Routledge, 1997)* for a series of debates in this area. I return to the subject of screen violence in chapter 5.

172 See also Jenny Kitzinger, 'A sociology of media power: key issues in audience reception research', in Greg Philo (ed), *Message Received:*

Glasgow Media Group Research 1993–1998 (Harlow, Longman), pp. 16–17. She shows how the representation of a false accusation of male rape in *Disclosure* (Barry Levinson, United States, 1994) confirms some young men's pre-existing concerns. *Ibid.*, p. 6. The underestimation of audience competences in recognising fictional forms and conventions remains a problem in much work on audiences and 'effects', including, for example, Greg Philo's emotive but logically problematic investigation of children talking about *Pulp Fiction* (Quentin Tarantino, United States, 1994). Philo, 'Children and film/video/TV violence', in *Message Received*, pp. 35–53.

173 James Curran makes a similar observation about the 'selective reinforcement' and realignment of popular attitudes by the media in the process of generating moral panics. James Curran, 'Rethinking mass communications', in James Curran, David Morley and Valerie Walkerdine (eds), *Cultural Studies and Communications* (London, Arnold, 1996), pp. 150–1.

174 Corner, 'Meaning, genre and context', p. 271.

175 See also Kitzinger, 'A sociology of media power', pp. 13–14.

176 *Ibid.*, p. 19.

177 de Certeau, *The Practice of Everyday Life*, p. 31.

Chapter 4

Bram Stoker's Dracula: 'Gone With the Wind plus fangs'

Bram Stoker's Dracula (Francis Ford Coppola, Columbia Pictures, United States, 1992) is a particularly overt example of contemporary Hollywood's 'commercial aesthetic' of aggregation.[1] The film is a combination of diverse textual components subsequently disaggregated and promoted through marketing, media exposure and merchandising. These procedures mobilised a series of sometimes conflicting promises about the film: different audience fractions were invited to see it for different reasons. It was variously advertised, reviewed and consumed as the latest creation of an auteur, a star vehicle (for any of four stars), a reworking of a popular myth, an adaptation of a literary 'classic', as horror, art film or romance, or as a mixture of these genres. In other words, Bram Stoker's Dracula was organised as a dispersible text, designed and positioned to 'touch base with all the sectors of the audience'.[2] The industrially motivated hybridity and ultimate commercial success of the film foreground issues of genre, taste, and the discursive categorisation of audiences.[3] In this chapter I interrogate how such formulations are produced, and how distinctions are made between audiences in three imbricating fields of activity: industrial practices, publicity and media commentary, and the behaviours of film viewers. In the process, I shall reconsider some assumptions of orthodox genre theory as it has developed in film studies.

The procedures of film assembly and marketing target audiences by anticipating patterns of consumption and 'piggybacking' on established tastes, including those for stars, story properties, music, and visual styles. (These 'presold' elements are derived not just from film but from other popular media, in a parasitic practice dating back as far as the earliest years of 'silent' cinema.) The production and advertisement of generically identifiable films constitutes one such attempt to manage demand, minimise risk and secure a stable market by promising 'guaranteed' pleasures.[4] Genre typologies also facilitate the segmentation and classification of film audiences according to perceived spending habits, and the standardisation of product via a system of regulated difference.[5] For genres to function successfully, the industry not only has to 'institutionalise … expectations, which it will be able to fulfil',[6] but audiences have to play – and pay – their part in such 'contractual' propositions. In this way, generic regimes operate in the circuit of production, distribution and consumption by mediating between industry and audiences. However, as my research will demonstrate, there is no guaranteed fit between business intent and consumer response, despite the tacit assumptions to this effect which underpin many studies of film genres.[7]

Hollywood's markets ultimately remain beyond absolute control, despite the industry's best efforts to regulate – that is, to predict, incite, and exploit – consumer demand. In this case study I concentrate on taste conflicts fought out over the generic classification of *Bram Stoker's Dracula* and its corresponding assumed audiences, which were variously championed and disparaged by industry representatives, published reviewers and observers, and viewers. I track two conflicting tendencies in the marketing of the film: firstly, the commercial aim of disseminating it across multiple taste formations, and secondly, the hierarchisation of textual components, and the audiences for which they bid, according to their perceived economic significance. These procedures of dispersal and stratification were mediated, complicated and sometimes contested by the actions of commentators and individual viewers.

Back in 1984, Alan Williams asserted that: 'Genre studies' notion of the film audience will not stand up to examination: audiences are not uniform masses, reacting with uniformity and consistency'.[8] Despite two significant interventions, to which I shall soon turn, Williams' reproach remains apposite. Audiences' participation in the genre system is too often taken for granted, rather than subjected to sustained scrutiny.[9] One of my aims is to address this blind spot by demonstrating how film viewers make use of ideas of genre, in part to construct their own discursive distinctions between audience groups. Rather than argue that genre is an invalid or redundant concept, I investigate its usages for a range of different agents variously engaged in the processes of formulating cultural and social categorisations. I consider the contingent and fluid nature of genres as collective understandings, and the power relations that structure the demarcation and circulation of genre taxonomies. In taking this approach, I am building on James Naremore's concept of the 'genre function'.[10] This foregrounds the discursive productivity of critical acts of genre naming, and the difficulty of defining a genre based on verifiable internal textual qualities.[11] Naremore also offers a diachronic model, showing how generic discourses can be appropriated and reworked across time and according to critical and industrial imperatives. Rick Altman has developed a similar line of inquiry in his seminal analysis of 'genrification' – that is, the ongoing discursive construction and reconstruction of film genres. Altman shows how genres are always in process and subject to the interventions of producers, critics (both popular and academic) and (potentially) audiences.[12] However, Naremore focuses exclusively on institutional factors in the naming and policing of genres, and Altman's work on audience engagements with ideas of genre remains largely speculative. By contrast, I investigate both how genre headings, canons and hierarchies are mobilised through commercial procedures, and how they are reproduced or rewritten not only by press commentators, but also by individual viewers. In the process, I trace continuities and differences in the deployment of genre categories across these three sectors, and map the differentiation of audiences enacted through generic taxonomies. The restoration of the audience thus enables a fuller understanding of the role which genre plays in the production, distribution and consumption of popular film, not least by facilitating a comparison between industrial, critical and 'ground-level' perspectives on audiences for particular genres.

Differentiating *Bram Stoker's Dracula* from previous versions of the vampire myth

Bram Stoker's Dracula was the first release in a short-lived Hollywood production cycle of big-budget 'classic' costume horrors which included *Mary Shelley's Frankenstein* (Kenneth Branagh, United States, 1994) and *Mary Reilly* (Stephen Frears, United States, 1996) – a reinterpretation of Robert Louis Stevenson's *The Strange Case of Dr Jekyll and Mr Hyde*. *Bram Stoker's Dracula* was made for Columbia Pictures while the other two films – both commercial disappointments – were made for its sister studio, TriStar Pictures.[13] Although not based on a literary 'classic', Warner Bros.' highly successful adaptation of Anne Rice's cult novel *Interview with the Vampire* (Neil Jordan, United States, 1994) can be seen as part of the cycle.[14] All three later films followed the lead of *Bram Stoker's Dracula* in targeting 'mainstream' and infrequent cinemagoers, especially women, beyond a 'core' horror audience perceived as predominantly male. This strategy can itself be seen as an attempt to replicate the success of *The Silence of the Lambs* (Jonathan Demme, United States, 1990), an Oscar-winning 'upmarket' horror/crime thriller hybrid featuring a 'strong' female protagonist.[15] *Bram Stoker's Dracula* – and *The Silence of the Lambs* – must also be contextualised in relation to the more general re-orientation of some action films towards female audiences over the 1980s and 1990s, via the incorporation of women protagonists and new emphases on emotional relationships.[16]

As 'quality' films, costume horrors were aimed at broader markets than the 'low horror' slashers and gore pictures which served the video sector in the late 1980s and early 1990s.[17] They also constituted a shift away from the successful comedy horror cycle of the previous decade, which included *Ghostbusters* (Ivan Reitman, United States, 1984, sequel in 1989) and *Gremlins* (Joe Dante, United States, 1984, sequel in 1990). The new cycle consisted of opportunistic combinations of pre-sold literary properties, familiar horror character types, expensive production values and major stars associated with non-horror genres such as Robert De Niro in *Mary Shelley's Frankenstein* and Julia Roberts in *Mary Reilly*. The Dracula and Frankenstein remakes also traded on a generic mix of romance and horror to pitch to a cross-gender market.[18] By contrast, *Interview with the Vampire* did not copy the romantic element but offered its own variant of 'feminised' horror by combining a high profile adaptation, period setting, a plot emphasising character development and quasi-familial relationships, and four male stars with proven appeal among female as well as male viewers (Tom Cruise, Brad Pitt, Christian Slater and Antonio Banderas). In addition to these 'historical' horrors, a number of familiar horror stories and characters were updated and relocated in contemporary settings, again with the intent of capturing broad, mixed-gender audiences. *Wolf* (Mike Nichols, United States, 1994) was a reworking of the werewolf myth as a romantic star vehicle for Jack Nicholson and

Michelle Pfeiffer, while the comedy horror *Vampire in Brooklyn* (Wes Craven, United States, 1995) starred Eddie Murphy. Despite Warners' success with *Interview with the Vampire*, the relative failure of *Wolf*, *Vampire in Brooklyn* and TriStar's two costume horrors presaged the end of the cycle.[19]

I have been tracing here moments in the continual redefinition of the horror genre – in this instance, via the decisions of film producers (I shall later turn to the role of commentators and audiences in this process). Rather than remaining fixed and static, the genre – and any other – should be seen as processual and subject to constant revision. Subsequent rewritings of horror from producers' perspectives have included the boom in teen horrors which followed the success of *Scream* (Wes Craven, United States, 1996), and the popularisation of documentary aesthetics initiated by the *Blair Witch Project* (Daniel Myrick and Eduardo Sanchez, United States, 1999). Genres thus encompass a degree of fluidity, but this is not infinite, and it does not make them simply interchangeable. The genre system still functions to demarcate different film types, even if the boundaries between such categories are mobile and variously defined or contested. Thus, the concept of a genre hybrid as a recognisable combination of distinct genres still has theoretical and practical validity, as will become clear in my study of *Bram Stoker's Dracula*. The point is that a genre needs to be recognised as such by some agents in the process of genrification. By writing about a 'costume horror cycle', I am of course acting as just such an agent myself. In my own way I am constituting a filmic category by including certain titles and excluding others. I have tried to indicate, however, not only the rationale behind my classification, but also how contingent such a definition remains, and some ways in which it might be broadened or redrafted. It is such acts of generic definition, and the conditions and implications of their production, reproduction and contestation, that I trace around *Bram Stoker's Dracula*. While it is important to acknowledge the productivity of film scholarship in the genrification process, I concentrate in this chapter upon generic taxonomies mobilised through the overlapping processes of film production and promotion, popular film journalism, and film consumption, including the diverse classifications made by viewers.

Production, marketing and reception contexts for *Bram Stoker's Dracula* were complicated by the sedimentation of previous incarnations of the vampire and Dracula myths. The film was preceded not just by Stoker's 1897 novel, but by hundreds of filmic, televisual, theatrical, literary and comic-book vampires. More than 600 films and 100 television programmes from around the world were listed in *The Illustrated Vampire Movie Guide*, itself published to coincide with the British release of *Bram Stoker's Dracula*.[20] This sprawling intertextual network presented both a bonus and a problem for the filmmakers. Such textual accretions guaranteed a high public awareness of the Dracula myth, but the endless repetitions and reworkings might have debased Stoker's story and eroded the impact of the central character. Audience expectations might have sunk beyond retrieval. Accordingly, the film had to be differentiated from the extensive constellation of Dracula and vampire texts. Jon Anderson, director of advertising and publicity at the United Kingdom distribution arm of Columbia TriStar Films, acknowledged this: 'Dracula was in many respects a "Pre-Sold" title, so our job was making it a special event that people would want to see'.[21] In this way, *Bram Stoker's Dracula* provides a particularly clear case of Hollywood's simultaneous standardisation and variation of its products.

The title presented *Bram Stoker's Dracula* as a faithful adaptation of the novel, and distinguished it from its predecessors. (Screenwriter and co-producer James Hart's script was originally subtitled 'The Untold Story'.) The film was also sold as unique via its allegedly unprecedented inclusion of the novel's gothic romance (a claim disputed by some commentators on the grounds of both fidelity and novelty).[22] Hart's script borrowed elements from the novel and innovated others, accentuating romance and so effectively creating a hybrid generic identity for the proposed film. As Altman has argued, the production of popular film is a process of innovation and imitation shaped in part by producers assaying previous hits and recombining their components in new exploitable forms that they hope will be successful.[23] In interviews Hart declared just such an intention, to reproduce the broad appeal of the book and so capture a hitherto untapped audience of women who enjoyed the novel's mix of thrills and romance but had avoided adaptations which foregrounded its horror content:

> The real Dracula has never been done. ... none of the previous film incarnations had done justice to Stoker's unnerving, sexually charged novel and its tragic hero. For *Dracula* to be done right on the screen, it needed a magnificent production on an epic scale, and a reading that reached to the heart of the character's seductiveness. Women more

than men have tended to read *Dracula* and other vampire stories, and
to understand the vampire's attraction.[24]

> The main thing that seems to me to be lost in most movie versions is
> the element of seduction, by which we become sympathetic to the idea
> of who and what Dracula is. To me, it's *like Gone With the Wind* with
> sex and violence.[25]

The claim to distinction made on behalf of the film here is rhetorical rather than reliable, however, and should not be taken at face
value. In his concern to differentiate *Bram Stoker's Dracula* from
previous adaptations, Hart exaggerates the romance elements in the
book, and effectively rewrites a number of earlier screen versions. In
fact, the film merely amplifies romantic and erotic elements already
present in pictures such as *Dracula* (Terence Fisher, United Kingdom, 1958), *Count Dracula* (Philip Saville, for BBC TV, 1973) and
Dracula (John Badham, United States, 1979).[26] Nevertheless, the
commercial opportunity presented by the female audience can be
seen as a crucial reason why Hart's script – initially due to be filmed
as a cable television movie[27] – was picked up and developed by Coppola's company American Zoetrope and by Columbia. From the
outset of the production, the strategy of widening the film's address
was envisaged in terms of a generic and gendered mixture. Lester
Borden, vice president of merchandising at Columbia's parent, Sony
Pictures, commented: 'It's a very exciting story to tell, and it's also
a male/female thing – a very romantic love story'.[28] Thus, to quote
Robert E. Kapsis, 'which genres finally get made depends on how
organizational gatekeepers at various stages of the film production
process assess the potential product in relation to their perception of
the audience's future tastes'.[29]

In the event, industry figures suggest that 50 per cent of the film's
cinema audience in Britain were female.[30] The assumption that all
these women were attracted to the film simply because of its high-
profile romantic elements must be avoided, however. As will become
clear, some of the female audience were habitual consumers of
horror, who did indeed enjoy *Bram Stoker's Dracula*, but not
because it was safely 'beyond' the horror category. Instead, they
found pleasures in its particular combination of scares with lush
mise-en-scène, engaging plot and characterisation, and the erotic
attractions that they had come to expect from vampire films. While
the 'female gothic'[31] tradition in the production and consumption of

horror literature has long been recognised within academic discourse, the 'invisibility' of female audiences for horror films only began to be reversed in the 1990s.[32] Moreover, both the 'classic' costume horror cycle of the early 1990s and the teen horror boom of the late 1990s involved industry professionals claiming to have 'rediscovered' female audiences for horror, following their neglect in earlier decades.[33]

Hart's script rewrites the novel by introducing a prologue in which Romanian knight Vlad the Impaler becomes a vampire following his wife's suicide. More than 400 years later, as Dracula, he finds that Mina, the fiancée of Jonathan Harker, bears a strong resemblance to his wife, and comes to London in the guise of Prince Vlad to find her. Employing Rick Altman's terminology, it is possible to trace in the film syntactic and semantic elements traditionally associated with both horror and romance.[34] The horror semantics include Dracula's castle, the lunatic asylum, and the more specific iconography of the vampire myth, such as coffins, bats, garlic, stakes, damsels in distress, and the stock location of Transylvania. The syntax of horror includes a familiar opposition between monster and humanity, complicated by parallels between the two terms, driven by sexual desire. The semantics and syntax of romance centre upon the pairing of Mina and Prince Vlad. The first category includes scenes depicting a candlelit dinner, dancing, kissing, music and lighting coded as 'romantic'. The syntax of romance in the film concerns a love which spans time and space, and which is confronted by social disapproval (whereby Dracula/Prince Vlad is opposed to Harker, the socially sanctioned partner). The two strands are entwined in the narrative structure of the film, which pursues the separation and reunion of Mina and Dracula (the latter achieved when she kills him and they are symbolically reunited), alongside the vampire's attacks and the quest of the vampire-hunters. Even this brief analysis effectively assumes more agreement on the recognition of 'romance' and 'horror' codings than is likely to exist among real, heterogeneous audiences, however. As Altman notes: 'disparate viewers may perceive quite disparate semantic and syntactic elements in the same film'.[35] It is nevertheless clear that the development of a romance between Dracula and Mina provided Columbia with a counterbalance to the story's well-known horror content which could be pushed aggressively in the advertising campaign. The poster tag line 'Love Never Dies' was intended to attract women viewers to a genre traditionally perceived as selling to male audiences.[36] The complex generic identity of the film was thus not just established by (nor is it simply readable from) its intratextual components. It was also constructed via extratextual advertising, publicity and merchandising, which signalled both Hart's innovations and more familiar horror elements, alongside further components such as star presences and Francis Ford Coppola as popular auteur. For example, the range of publicity stills put into circulation foregrounded codings of horror and romance, period costumes and settings, spectacular monster effects, and a number of star images.

Casting decisions extended the appeal of *Bram Stoker's Dracula* across age, gender and taste boundaries. A roster of stars supplemented the uncertain commercial potential of the adaptation. The presence of pin-ups Winona Ryder (as Mina) and Keanu Reeves (as Harker) was intended to hook into a mixed-gender youth market labelled the 'MTV audience'.[37] In the role of the vampire hunter Van Helsing, Anthony Hopkins combined a background in British theatre and arthouse cinema with a mass-market profile gained from *The Silence of the Lambs*. As Dracula, Gary Oldman was the source of some anxiety at Columbia, never having played the romantic lead in a major Hollywood production before. However, the familiar story and strong star line-up ensured that his name did not have to carry the film alone.[38] The presence of Coppola as star-director added to the list of attractions: 'The legend appeals to the broad market; the Coppola name appeals to the sophisticates'.[39] Thus, rather than standing in opposition to commercialism in popular cinema, the discourse of auteurism is readily incorporated within industry logics. The commodified author-name functions as a further means of marketing the film to certain audience fractions.[40]

In promotional discourses and press coverage, *Bram Stoker's Dracula* was often granted a romantic-erotic appeal for female audiences. For example, a feature in the *Daily Mirror* newspaper on the boom in vampire productions for television, film and video elaborated on Hart's claims in typical house style, proposing Count Dracula as the ultimate object of heterosexual female desire: 'Forget heart-throbs Mel Gibson, Richard Gere or Tom Cruise. Meet Count Dracula, Hollywood's latest and, soon-to-be greatest sex symbol. Handsome, charming, dangerous – and capable of giving unimaginable sexual pleasure. It's a combination that's proving irresistible to women.'[41] Heterosexual male desire was also catered for in the film package and marketing, and centred in particular on Winona Ryder's Mina, Sadie Frost's Lucy,[42] and on the three Brides of Dracula. Although less commonly debated than the erotic attractions offered female viewers, straight male sexual pleasure was highlighted in some press coverage.[43]

Released in the United States to tap into the 1992 Thanksgiving and Christmas market, *Bram Stoker's Dracula* opened in Europe the following January and February. In Britain, Columbia TriStar made multiple promises about the film across a range of satellite texts. The distributor arranged exposure over a spectrum of publications selling beyond the specialist horror market, including youth and women's magazines.[44] The strategy of dispersal, extending the film's social penetration, even capitalised on the casting of Reeves and Ryder to raise demand for merchandise and awareness of the '18'-rated title among those officially not old enough to see it. A poster of the stars and a competition to win branded products was placed in *Big!* magazine, whose target readership is girls aged nine to sixteen.[45] Columbia TriStar collaborated on a *South Bank Show* 'Dracula special' for ITV, and secured a slot on BBC television for *Bloodlines*, an account of the making of the film.[46] In cases such as this, the interface between distributors and broadcasters is mutually beneficial. The former secure exposure for their product, while the latter get access to cheap pre-packaged programming with a degree of 'guaranteed' audience appeal. *Bloodlines* was also released on video to buy the week that the film opened, entering the sell-through chart at number eight.[47] Thus, the video had a promotional function and also constituted an ancillary profit centre based on the *Bram Stoker's Dracula* property. As the trade paper *Screen International* commented: 'Columbia TriStar can start sucking video revenue from the title while it's still at the peak of its UK theatrical life.'[48]

The multiple address developed through extratextual materials was intended to maximise the dispersible text's reach, even if this necessitated making inconsistent or contradictory claims. But such materials also established demarcations between potential audiences, privileging some over others. Under Columbia's commercial imperatives the narrow horror market remained in some ways taken for granted, while mainstream audiences were targeted more enthusiastically. Beyond the specialist horror press, cast and crew members took steps to distance *Bram Stoker's Dracula* from the genre. In the press pack circulated to journalists, Ryder categorised the film as

2 Gary Oldman promotes *Bram Stoker's Dracula* on the cover of film magazine *Empire*

'very romantic and sensual and epic, a real love story ... It's not really a vampire movie'.[49] Questioned on *The South Bank Show*, Oldman compared the film to Jean Cocteau's fairy tale *La Belle et la Bête* (France, 1946): 'Francis always wanted to make a version of *Beauty and the Beast*, and he's sort of done it with this. ... scary monster film is the periphery of this really.' A concern to differentiate *Bram Stoker's Dracula* from the 'low horror' of youth culture was apparent in Hart's comment in the same programme: 'This is not *Freddy Krueger Goes to Transylvania*.'

The bid to win incremental markets risked upsetting horror enthusiasts, but for Columbia, this was a risk worth taking to reach a wider audience. The campaign did take some steps to persuade horror fans that the thrills they wanted had not been entirely displaced, however. Production information, personnel interviews and publicity stills (particularly of monster make-up and special effects) were made available to horror and fantasy publications, which gave the film extensive coverage even while often expressing doubts about its overall quality. The press pack noted that Coppola had directed the low-budget horror *Dementia 13* in 1963 and suggested that his new film was a return to a familiar genre, a reading taken up by some commentators.[50] Reassurance was also attempted through the bloody lettering of the ubiquitous title. The main poster mixed generic codings however, showing Oldman and Ryder in an embrace below a gargoyle, and combining the film's rubric with the romantic tag line.[51]

Merchandising

The diversity of market segments that *Bram Stoker's Dracula* was intended to capture was echoed in its spread of licensed merchandising. In the publishing sector, the British rights to the title logo and artwork were sold to Pan Books, which used them for a range of products aimed at different readerships: a novelisation of the script,[52] a 'moviebook' containing script, behind-the-scenes information and lavish illustrations,[53] and a paperback edition of *Dracula*. The film's profile was further enhanced through the opportunism of Penguin. Outbid by Pan for use of the film title, the company relaunched its own mass market paperback of *Dracula*, and brought out an edition of the novel in the 'upmarket' Penguin Classics imprint for the first time to coincide with the film's release.[54] The page-one blurb on Stoker and adaptations of his work concluded:

'Coppola's major film *Bram Stoker's Dracula*, arguably ... captures the spirit of the text most successfully.' Stoker's belated entry into the canon of English literature as defined by Penguin Classics was thus determined not so much by artistic merit as by market considerations. There is a certain circularity here: the film is pre-sold by the novel, which in turn is re-sold on the back of the film, which it plugs either overtly (Pan) or more discreetly (Penguin Classics).

Further merchandise in Britain included an 'official graphic novel',[55] a licensed board game, a video game and a music soundtrack. The last two items are examples of the much-touted synergy which consumer electronics giant Sony enjoyed after its $3.4 billion purchase of Columbia and TriStar Pictures in 1989.[56] In addition to licensing deals such as that with Pan, in-house tie-ups enabled the *Bram Stoker's Dracula* brand to be sold across various products under Sony ownership. While Columbia Pictures made the film, Sony Imagesoft brought out the video game, and Columbia Records released the soundtrack album. These two branded spin-offs were targeted at rather different markets. Unlike the film, which was aggressively pitched as having a cross-gender appeal, the video game was promoted to a tight core market of young males. An advert for the game carried on the sell-through video of *Bram Stoker's Dracula* played on intertextual references to target male adolescents: a male teenager, looking and talking like the Keanu Reeves' character in the cult comedies *Bill and Ted's Great Adventure* (Stephen Herek, United States, 1988) and *Bill and Ted's Bogus Journey* (Peter Hewitt, United States, 1991), plays the game while seated in a coffin. By contrast, the soundtrack album followed the film in aiming at a broader audience mix – a move facilitated by its generic hybridity. The combination of a classical score by modernist Polish composer Wojciech Kilar with Annie Lennox's end credits song and hit single 'Love song for a vampire', was designed to hook both adult and youth markets. The Lennox recording entered the British chart at number three in late February 1993 and spent seven weeks in the top ten, peaking at number two. The single was released on the RCA label to which Lennox was signed, and so made no money for Sony, but the promotional video – intercutting shots of the singer with clips from the film – pushed *Bram Stoker's Dracula* via heavy rotation on MTV and terrestrial pop shows during the theatrical release period.

Coppola's persona as a 'Hollywood Renaissance' auteur[57] may appear out of place alongside such a merchandise-heavy project. In effect, the author-name 'Coppola' only circulated in certain satellite texts addressing particular audience fractions: in the tabloid press intertextual frames of reference typically extended only to Hammer horror, *The Silence of the Lambs* and previous films starring Ryder or Reeves. While 'Coppola' clearly lacks the status of, say, 'Lucas' or 'Spielberg' in discourses of popular film journalism, this author-name was nevertheless still located within the commerce of auteurism in the early 1990s.[58] But if the commercial function of 'Coppola' as auteur persisted – with variable degrees of success – from the 1970s into the early 1990s, the economic context in which this persona was mobilised had certainly shifted. By 1992, Columbia TriStar executives were proposing an uneasy syncretism between an 'elite' authorial property on the one hand and a blockbuster product line on the other. They celebrated Coppola as an auteur whose individual commitment and attention to detail implicitly guaranteed the quality of the whole range of merchandise bearing the *Bram Stoker's Dracula* brand name:

> The Dracula campaign took director Francis Ford Coppola to places he'd never been before, including comic-book and S[cience] F[iction] conventions. Coppola's past work has never involved discussing the artwork of a graphic novel, the wardrobe of a collection of action figures or the inner workings of a high-tech video game. This time, however, the director assisted with all these marketing elements. ... 'Francis is very involved in every step', Clark says. 'The merchandising, publishing, what we're doing with the movie in terms of positioning it, everything.'[59]

Because the film's target audience and rating ('Restricted' in the US) limited the possibilities for licensed toys, the marketing campaign worked to encourage 'a Dracula style' as an alternative strategy of extension. In the US, designer dresses, coffin-shaped handbags and gargoyle earrings went on sale along with souvenir figurines, T-shirts and jackets, but many of these products were not available in overseas markets. Instead, Columbia TriStar invited journalists to a fashion show 'in the hope of triggering an international, Dracula-inspired, new-gothic trend'.[60] This move subsequently paid off with coverage in *Harpers and Queen*[61] and on BBC 1's *The Clothes Show*[62] and a boom in new-gothic styling, from Italian designers Dolce & Gabbana's 'funky pallbearer' style for men[63] to High Street spring fashions such as double-breasted jackets and coloured 'granny specs' based on those worn by Oldman as Prince Vlad.

Judging by both cultural profile and commercial performance, the assembly, marketing and merchandising of *Bram Stoker's Dracula* were largely successful in making the film an 'event' and encouraging a proliferation of possible avenues of access to it. Such strategies of dispersal also brought about some audience disappointments and clashes between disparate taste publics, however. These conflicts can be traced in both published accounts of the film and through audience research, and were often played out via the discursive construction of generic taxonomies.

Distinctions in press commentary

Press commentary mediated *Bram Stoker's Dracula* by inserting it into a number of different interpretive frames and writing its generic identity in various ways. Reviews discriminated between the film's heterogeneous components and the diverse implied audiences addressed by these elements. Such taste hierarchies were not always consistent with those established through Columbia's marketing campaign. However, some outlets did endorse the positioning of the film outside a narrow definition of horror. For instance, a multiplex programme guide described the film as an 'erotic thriller', locating it in a successful production cycle with cross-gender appeal.[64] A video review in *The Sun* newspaper commented: 'like *Jurassic Park*, it's the special effects that really stand out. But in the end it's a love story. Puritans may not approve of what Coppola has done to it – the added lust and humour. But you won't be able to resist it.'[65] The coalition of different age and gender groups addressed by *The Sun* partially mirrors the wide audience targeted by *Bram Stoker's Dracula*. This may explain the absence in this review of distinctions based on class, age, or gender, which were evident in titles with narrower readerships. The reviewer does make an important differentiation, however – between 'puritans' and *Sun* readers, who, it is implied, value fun and (sexual) entertainment above moribund ideas of generic or cultural purity.[66] *The Sun*'s review is the first of several I shall examine which discursively construct like-minded audiences for the film, and which often distinguish the preferences of these imagined audiences from less 'valid' tastes. Other published commentaries made very different distinctions, often enacted through the attribution of particular genre identities to the film. While the

details vary, the rhetorical strategy of differentiation and the selective ratification of taste fractions is a common one.

One vector of the film's multiple address was towards a 'cultured'
audience. Borrowings from literature and painting, and the use of
costumes designed by Japanese artist Eiko Ishioka, endowed it with
an aura of 'good taste'.[67] High art references to Klimt and Cocteau
in particular were flagged in the press pack and 'moviebook'.[68] These
gestures towards elite culture were largely ignored by the youth
press and popular tabloids. The cues were picked up and elaborated
upon in the so-called 'quality' press, however. For example, the
Independent on Sunday's review noted 'tableaux vivant that nod to
Tissot'.[69] Coppola's status as an auteur – certified in 'middle market'
and 'upmarket' publications – further elevated the cultural standing
of the film.[70]

On occasions, commentators asserted distinctions between
'knowing' audiences who could recognise the film's high-art cita-
tions and the 'base' tastes of less elevated viewers. In a *Sunday Telegraph* review freighted with a number of assumptions and
judgements, Anne Billson wrote: '[The film] runs aground on the
lovey-dovey scenes, which are not just inept but boring. By turning
the bogeyman into a Mills & Boon heart-throb, screenwriter James
V. Hart has drained the story of most of its plasma.'[71] The film's
romantic elements are rejected here through their association with a
culturally denigrated 'female' genre, that of 'low-brow' romantic fiction. Billson erected a second axis of distinction in rejecting another
'common' taste formation, that of an implicitly Americanised youth
culture: 'Those of you with deliciously shivery memories of Christopher Lee or Bela Lugosi will not be disposed to look favourably
upon *Bram Stoker's Dracula* … Coppola's film is a Dracula for the
Nineties, aimed not at classicists but at a fang-de-siecle generation
weaned on MTV.' The inclusion of Lee, a star of the often-derided
Hammer horror cycle, under the heading of 'classic horror' testifies
to the flexible borders of such critical categories across time. When
Billson considered positive effects of the film's 'feminisation', she
mobilised an 'upmarket' image of the female spectator: 'This has all
the makings of a classic Accessory Film: one ought never to under-
estimate the cumulative aesthetic effect of all those nice scratchy
fountain pens, pebble-lensed spectacles and pearly earrings. Eiko
Ishioka's truly fabulous costumes mix Symbolist art with Gray's
Anatomy and London Zoo, and have already sent me scurrying to

the shops to buy fluttering lengths of chiffon.'[72] In this (admittedly playful) review, three target audiences are stratified and only one is legitimated – that made up of adult, middle-class, art-loving, female spectator-consumers. Whereas Columbia's strategy was to appeal to both teenagers and adults, to 'elite' and 'common' tastes,[73] Billson makes a clear distinction between the terms of each couplet. This is an instance of the 'refusal' of the preferences of the Other which, according to Bourdieu, places tastes in mutual opposition.[74] Those who share Billson's taste draw on cultural capital provided by education and class background, and are thus differentiated from the 'masses'.

Just as some reviews in the 'adult' press denigrated youth tastes, so sections of the youth press derided the 'mainstream' culture of the over-30s. For instance, the music weekly *New Musical Express* refuted the film's cultural aspirations and labelled it 'the most expensive teen exploitation pic ever'.[75] A less subtle polarisation of adult and youth cultures was proposed by *Smash Hits*, a pop music magazine bought predominantly by young females in their early teens. A review comparing *Bram Stoker's Dracula* (by now available to rent on video) with the about-to-open costume horror *Mary Shelley's Frankenstein* discriminated between the two largely on the grounds of the age and appearance of their respective stars. In particular, the Americans Reeves and Ryder were contrasted with Frankenstein's older and less glamorous English stars, Kenneth Branagh and Helena Bonham Carter. Publicity stills from the films carried the following captions:

Saucy, yummy Winona Ryder snogs the yummy, saucy Keanunu [sic] ...... and old beard-face Kenneth Branagh kisses old bird Helena Bonham Carter.

He's big, he's sexy, he's rugged ... [Reeves]... can we help you, Gramps? [Branagh]

Keanununu [sic] snogs loads of birds ... [Reeves with the brides of Dracula] ... Gramps and Mumsy ponce about. [Branagh and Bonham Carter in ballroom dancing scene][76]

The age difference between Branagh and Reeves, and between Bonham Carter and Ryder, is five years. From the perspective of *Smash Hits* this is a significant gap. Relative youth is a contributory factor in the 'cool' which Ryder and Reeves are presented as possessing. *Bram Stoker's Dracula* is read as offering 'hip' young American stars (with, crucially, no mention made of Oldman or Hopkins), and thus can be integrated into the youth culture in which *Smash Hits* readers are seen to participate. With its relatively old actors, *Mary Shelley's Frankenstein*, on the other hand, is represented as part of an unexciting adult 'mainstream'.

In the specialist horror press, commentators often took on the role of gatekeepers of the genre, judging the film by its fidelity or otherwise to the norms of horror. Those deeming *Bram Stoker's Dracula* successful allowed it entry to the generic corpus as productively different, a worthwhile innovation sometimes labelled 'epic' horror.[77] Other writers rejected the film because it was too different, citing the incursion of romance. Oppositions between an informed horror audience and ordinary cinemagoers ignorant of the genre structured reviews in the British horror magazines *The Dark Side* and *Samhain*. In contrast to Hart's approving comparison, the reference to *Gone With the Wind* here stands as a measure of the film's failings:

> *Bram Stoker's Dracula* is a high-profile, low-risk venture, with no real attempt to explore the intellectual depth the material can provide … Instead of Murnau's "symphony of Horror" we have Coppola's pop promo of Horror, or even, a rather unwieldily modified *Gone With The Wind* plus fangs.[78]

> The picture's hype has preceded it to an exceptional degree and ensured it an audience who wouldn't normally venture out to something as 'coarse' as a horror film – precisely the sort of punter this picture needs! … it's a horror movie that never once exudes or creates fear, menace or terror. It's a love story without a remotely believable scenario … – Mills and Boon Gothic at best.[79]

Like *The Sunday Telegraph*, these reviews characterised the film through its association with juvenile and 'lowbrow female' tastes. All three commentaries rejected perceived commercial priorities in proposing alternative taste hierarchies. By contrast, *Cinefantastique* – a magazine devoted to screen horror, fantasy and science fiction[80] – held out the prospect of an accommodation between a horror/fantasy subculture and the 'mainstream': 'Okay, so it's a little hard to get worked-up about yet another film version of Bram Stoker's *Dracula*. … Nevertheless, I'm excited by the prospect of *Bram Stoker's Dracula* and I think our lavish preview of director Francis Ford Coppola's forthcoming horror epic will get even die-hard skeptics in the mood.'[81] A gatekeeper's concern for the standards and reputation of the horror genre was shared by writers at *Cinefantastique*, *The Dark Side*, and *Samhain*, despite their different views of the film.[82] Thus, an investment in, and evaluation of texts according to, a notion of 'authentic' horror did not determine the reaction of critics in the specialist press. Rather, it shaped the ways they framed the film and expressed their diverse judgements of it.

To unpack further the differentiations made in the horror press, I shall draw on Sarah Thornton's theory of 'subcultural capital'.[83] This modification of Bourdieu's model of cultural capital is designed to take account of the accumulation of 'additional' cultural resources beyond those derived from education and family background. Displayed in record collections, fashionable haircuts – or knowledge about films – subcultural capital 'confers status on its owner in the eyes of the relevant beholder'.[84] Its differential distribution underpins taste distinctions such as 'cool' youth's disparagement of 'mainstream' culture. In opposing sanctioned versions of the Dracula myth with Columbia's offering, horror reviewers display subcultural capital (implicitly held by their readers too) and establish dichotomies between an authentic horror culture and 'mainstream' Hollywood, which sells inferior products to easily pleased audiences. These distinctions also attest to the paradoxical status of horror fans' relations with the 'mainstream'. On the one hand, horror is to be vigorously defended against criticism from outside – and a big-budget production provides an institutional acknowledgement of the legitimacy of horror. On the other hand, ideas of ignorance, misunderstanding and disapproval on the part of 'society in general' are central to the appeal of certain taste publics.[85] Thus the 'mainstream' is a discursive construct against which the horror consumer can define him/herself as a member of a popular cultural 'elite'. The horror fan subculture in which publications such as *Samhain* and *The Dark Side* circulate is commercial, but often represents itself as less so than the 'blind commercialism' of 'mass-market' Hollywood. Horror fans are at the very least differentiated as more discerning consumers than the cinemagoing crowd, whose preferences render them 'taste-less'. In all the reviews considered so far, 'average' and 'inauthentic' audiences are characterised as 'inferior' not just through their tastes, however, but also via marks of age, gender and/or class. In the process, *Bram Stoker's Dracula* is implicitly infantilised, feminised

and/or banalised in contrast to tastes ratified by cultural or subcultural capital.[86]

Press responses to *Bram Stoker's Dracula* reveal negotiations made
by commentators participating in a wide range of taste publics. Their
responses to the film, whether approving or disapproving, display significant and value-laden suppositions about the social and (sub)cul-
tural positions that they and their assumed readerships occupy. These
locations are most clearly established in relation to, and through symbolic rejection of, the 'mainstream'. Exactly how this despised mass is
perceived, in terms of class, age, gender, and/or taste, varies according
to the self-definition current among each taste formation. As Bourdieu
puts it, 'social subjects, classified by their classifications, distinguish
themselves by the distinctions they make'.[87]

There is no inevitable match between the generic audience segmentation employed by Columbia and those constructed in the press
(nor is there necessarily any between the views of commentators and
those of their readers). The studio sought to capture (older)
teenagers of both genders, women and infrequent cinemagoers, in
addition to a specialist horror audience defined as predominantly
male. This strategy was endorsed by some reviewers, but others proposed their own hierarchies by making distinctions grounded in
generic competences and preferences which were often made to
carry signifiers of gender, class, age or (sub)cultural capital. The critical reception of *Bram Stoker's Dracula* thus foregrounds the articulation of taste conflicts with these social and cultural identities. The
film succeeded commercially not by resolving these ongoing conflicts and assembling a unified or homogeneous mass audience, but
by selling to an aggregation of different taste formations. This objec-
tive is not endangered by taste disputes, so long as enough audience
segments find that a part of the film package speaks to them.

Audience responses

How did viewers respond to the multiple address of the dispersible
text? How did they classify the film generically? In what terms was its
perceived success or failure expressed? What distinctions did individuals make between its different audiences? In this section I draw on
questionnaires handed out to cinemagoers attending my local multiplex shortly after the film's first screening on terrestrial television to
track, among other things, audiences' engagements with, and uses of,

generic categorisations.[88] The questionnaire covered film tastes in general and responses to *Bram Stoker's Dracula* in particular, and included both open-ended and more specific questions. Of 250 questionnaires given out, a total of 49 were returned. The vast majority of this self-selected sample was white, with ages ranging from 16 to 48. Twenty women and eleven men had seen the film in some format. (See appendices 5–7 for the full questionnaire plus breakdown of respondents.)

I asked respondents to state their preferences for, and dislikes of, film types and genres. Gender is the sociological factor that is usually assumed by industry personnel and commentators to correlate most closely with genre preferences,[89] and on occasion it was employed here as a mark of difference in taste. The correspondence between gender identity and genre preference was not always as neat as stock assumptions would imply, however. While some favoured films did conform to stereotyped 'female' and 'male' tastes, others confounded these and sometimes cut across 'incompatible' genre categories. For instance, one woman listed as her favourites 'Disney, true stories, murder, action'. Some respondents did not adhere to received genre typologies at all, but organised films under more idiosyncratic headings such as (for likes) 'clever' 'well directed' and 'intelligent cool films' or (dislikes) 'stereotyped' or 'most British films after 1970'. This kind of taxonomy appears to coexist with an awareness of more familiar classifications, while effectively overwriting them. I have been tempted to employ a 'public'/'private' dichotomy here, but it is somewhat problematic. What I might have termed 'private' typologies are less likely to be picked up by the media or otherwise endorsed in the public domain, and so lack the institutional consolidation which marks and constitutes a film genre. But, like 'public' genres, they too contribute to viewers' self-perceptions, and can be 'converted' into a limited social currency through peer-group interaction.[90] Moreover, all (institutionally sanctioned) genres are 'privatised' to the extent that individuals are able to recognise and deploy them. Indeed, genres rely on such shared recognitions to function successfully – even while viewers variously refashion, reconfigure and valorise or denigrate them in the process. It is clear that established film genres may also be entirely rewritten into idiosyncratic groupings such as those listed above. Some such groupings even get to be endorsed more publicly. Although 'clever' 'well directed' and 'intelligent cool films' are not as yet installed as fully fledged genres, similar categories are often proposed in critics' top tens or in scheduling decisions for televised film strands such as BBC 2's *Moviedrome*. By employing these terms, informants may be drawing upon such public discourses, and presenting themselves as 'experts' with knowledge, taste, and the ability to evaluate films across a range of genres. Viewers and commentators will of course disagree about the films to be included and excluded from any such corpus, but, as this chapter demonstrates, similar border skirmishes occur around more familiar, established genres.

Audiences approached *Bram Stoker's Dracula* anticipating pleasures that were shaped both by prior viewing experiences and awareness of diverse attractions flagged through advertising, publicity and ancillary products. There was no simple consensus about the film's generic status. Instead, it was ascribed various identities, as 'sensual, sad, romantic', a 'gothic-horror-love story', 'a thriller', and a 'normal Dracula movie with a bit more sex'. Horror fans[91] of both genders judged the film against favoured examples of the genre. Some rejected *Bram Stoker's Dracula* as a 'mainstream' mishandling of horror, so prioritising generic fidelity over mass appeal and implying alternatives to Columbia's operative taste hierarchy. The primary complaint was a failure to frighten. Such accounts lamented a dilution of horror's promise of a certain affect, even while sometimes noting the presence of additional values in the production:

> My first reaction to it was that it was visually stunning, with first rate sets/costumes etc. Also, I found the sound brilliant – better than in any other film I'd seen. At times, I found it slow, but Gary Oldman's performance made up for that. Winona was fairly convincing, but Keanu Reeves was simply dire.
>
> I didn't really have any expectations, but it did fulfil my entertainment values, but I had longed for some more gore and scares.
>
> (*16: anon. male. School student, age 16. Part two; Q.31.)

> I thought it was very good – visually stunning, with some brilliant set-pieces, tremendous camerawork and a great scene-stealing performance by Anthony Hopkins. The problem I had with it is that Gary Oldman's Dracula wasn't especially frightening … When the film *did* concentrate on the 'horror' aspects, I thought it was very effective … On the whole, I was impressed, although I still think the 1958 Hammer *Dracula* is by far the best adaptation of the novel ever.
>
> (*1: anon. male, *Samhain* sample, letter only.)

In characterising the film's ideal audiences as lacking in generic knowledge and subcultural capital, the following informants implicitly distinguished themselves from these less 'educated' taste publics, much as press commentators with various preferences had done:

> Why I watched the film – the story is a classic, scary … [The film was] Crap. I simply was not scared enough. Watching it for the second time – hated it even more.

> I thought it would be much much scarier – the music was the best thing – that was scary.

> [who do you think *Bram Stoker's Dracula* appeals to most?]
> Those uneducated in film.
>   (*17: anon. female. Charity worker, age 22. Part two; Q.31; Q.35.)

> [who do you think *Bram Stoker's Dracula* appeals to most?]

> People who mistakenly believe that Hammer = hammy. Fans of style over content.
>   (*3: anon. male. Media worker, age 26. *Samhain* sample. Q.35.)

Some respondents had strategically lowered their expectations in anticipation of concessions to 'other' tastes:

> Didn't want to see it because I was sure they'd butcher it. Saw $^1/_2$ of it on TV recently.

> [who do you think *Bram Stoker's Dracula* appeals to most?]

> 13 year olds, girls who wear itty bitty backpacks, fools.
>   (* 19: anon. male. Student, age 23. Part two; Q.35.)

Not all horror fans were so disappointed, however:

> I liked the sound of the film and generally enjoy dracula/vampire type films. I also think Gary Oldman is a great actor and went to see the film partly because he had the lead role.

> I thought the Gothic atmosphere was portrayed excellently. The make-up effects on Gary Oldman were good, and his portrayal of dracula was quite moving.

> The 'long lost love' angle … was more interesting than the usual blood and gore type of vampire film.
>   (* 10: anon. female. Biomedical scientist, age 33. Part two.)

This account evinces a dislike of gratuitous gore, an enjoyment of involving and 'moving' characterisation, and a sympathy for the dilemma of the vampire, all of which echo some of Brigid Cherry's findings about female horror fans.[92] Cherry's research points to women's pleasurable investments in the relationships between vampires, and to a wider affinity for the monsters and 'outsiders' portrayed in the horror genre. While no simple and clear-cut gendered division emerged in my project, such pleasures were less likely to be mentioned by men in the sample.

Some informants' statements effectively corroborated Hart's claims about the sexual appeal of the film for female viewers. It is notable that these women also enjoyed being scared:

> I'm an avid fan of horror – books and films alike, so there was no way I was going to miss *Dracula*. But I suppose one other reason why I watched it was because of all the hype – that it was unmissable, blah, blah … The bit where the girl came out of the house wearing that red dress was the most memorable bit. I'm a girl, but I though it was very sexy nevertheless. … I do remember getting the impression that the film was rather sexual in a subtle way. I think I got a bit aroused by it!
>
> [what elements did you particularly like?]
>
> Fantasy. Erotic. Good looking actors.
> > (*11: Evonne. Female student, age 21. Part two; Q.35.]

> I watched it because I quite like horror films and I thought it would be quite erotic and beautifully filmed. I was interested in the type of imagery used. I like being scared.
> > (*9: anon. female. Student, age 21. Part two; Q.35.)

Cherry's suggestion that vampire films may function as a 'form of erotica for some women',[93] providing the opportunity for sexual fantasy along with pleasurable tension and suspense, is borne out here. Among respondents, more women than men found the film erotic.[94] In a rare admission of sexual pleasure, a male *Samhain* reader wrote:

> I guess it just came down to a combination of a few things … Desperately wanting a bloody great Dracula movie, and the chance to watch gorgeous people in gorgeous costumes just being gorgeous. … I appreciate the way Hart and Coppola attempted to give the novel more resonance by adding the 'eternal love' aspect … by trying to appeal to two separate audiences: the horror fan, who wants to be scared, and those who find the vampire idea sexy as hell, there were two disparate avenues it could have explored. Unfortunately, Coppola tried both, and fell between them. As a viewer who wanted both aspects in my film, I was a bit happier than most … I loved it.
> > (*3: anon. male. Media worker, age 26. Part two.)

This informant notes the double appeal that Hart located in the Dracula myth. What is also striking here is the coexistence of a conception of the filmmakers' commercial imperatives (the appeal to two markets) alongside a high degree of personal investment in the film. Such a dual perspective on the valued artefact has been located in other studies of fans' engagements with mass media products.[95] Elsewhere in the sample, viewers less happy with the film typically attributed its failure to 'Hollywood-isation' – a phrase used to imply crass commercialism, Americanisation, simplification and/or overstatement of the original material. For example:

> [what elements of the film did you dislike?]
>
> the accents, the background scenes, the Hollywoodized sexuality.
>> (*29: Allison. Female student, age 20. Q.34.)

Whatever their final opinion, many horror fans evaluated *Bram Stoker's Dracula* according to their 'rules' of the genre and favourite instances of this film type. Such judgements were similar, but less public, than those made in specialist publications. In this way, generic regimes may be policed privately by audience members as well as publicly by reviewers.

Despite attempts to sell the film to audiences wary of horror, it was expressly defined as such by some people – particularly women – for whom the term was clearly pejorative. The following account draws upon a popular 'folk theory' of media influence to express concern about the adverse effects of horror films:

> I went to see it not out of choice but because a friend wanted to see it. I watched very little of it.
> Disliked it. Not my kind of film. I get nightmares very easily. I think horror films (cinema or TV) deaden one's sensibilities and make one less sensitive to, and hence less caring about, the real horror in the real world.
>> (*21: anon. female. Tax consultant, age 35. Part two; Q.12.)

By contrast, enthusiastic viewers often perceived the film to be addressed to audiences shaped in their own self-images:

> [who do you think *Bram Stoker's Dracula* appeals to most?]
>
> Young, imaginative people.
>> (*11: Evonne. Female student, age 21. Q.35)
>
> Goths! horror and vampire fans
>> (*8: anon. female. Unemployed/voluntary worker, age 24. Q.35.)[96]

Audiences are able to read markers of genre in advertising and publicity as one set of a series of 'publicly distributed orientations'[97] offering patterned ways of preparing for and responding to a film. They may participate in the contractual transactions which film genres propose (to which they bring payment and knowledge, and from which they expect a pleasurable combination of the familiar and the novel). Or they may read generic markers not as incitements to consume but as reasons to avoid a film. In all cases, potential viewers are mediating industrial procedures of production, advertising and publicity, mobilising assumptions about the nature of a film and its target audience by drawing on extratextual materials and their experience of films similarly classified. Exactly how (non-)viewers perceive a genre – its value, boundaries, pleasures and audience – will vary according to their different histories as viewers, their competences, repertoires and dispositions. As Gemma Moss puts it, the exact places that users construct for a genre are shaped by their socially specific 'histories of engagement'.[98] In the process, they are also asserting something about themselves. In watching a film or declining invitations to do so, individuals use markers of cultural preference to negotiate their own sense of self. Identity is constructed and (re)asserted both through positive self-images (as 'imaginative', knowledgeable or tasteful, for instance) and by distinguishing oneself from those with 'invalid' tastes – for example, 'girls', 'boys', 'fools', or horror consumers with deadened sensibilities.

Watching and remembering films

Like some of the responses to *Basic Instinct* assessed in the previous chapter, a process of viewer negotiation, a filtering out of 'good' and 'bad' elements, can be located in several respondents' accounts of *Bram Stoker's Dracula*. For example, respondent *2 (anon. male, self-employed, age 34, *Samhain* sample) particularly enjoyed Oldman's performance, foregrounding this as a highlight of the film. He also picked out Reeves' performance, but as a notably unfavourable element, or lowlight. In another example, the 'good' and 'bad' components were expressed in generic terms:

> [I]n playing up the romantic element of the story, I felt the film diluted the horror.
>
> (*1: anon. male. *Samhain* sample, letter.)

Salient elements can be either single moments or continuing strands, but they both stand out from, and come to stand for, the whole film experience. This pattern of sifting though a film's disparate components to focus on highlights and lowlights appeared repeatedly in respondents' statements in all three case studies. The extraction of filmic modules in advertising and media publicity appears to have had some influence on viewing strategies, priming audiences to look out for certain attractions. What is under consideration here is not simply a question of how people react while watching the film, however. It is also how the experience is talked over with friends and colleagues before and after viewing. The following remarks (made in response to a question about who informants had talked to about *Bram Stoker's Dracula*) suggest that such discussions often employ inventories of outstanding items, marked as sources of pleasure, fright, desire, disappointment or ridicule:

> After I saw it, I spoke with my friends (one male, one female) about it, mainly saying how Keanu was dreadfully miscast. ... They wanted to know about the oral sex scene!
>
> (*16: anon. male, age 16.)

> Colleagues at work. The effects/make-up. Gary Oldman – his accent and sexiness as the young Dracula. Keanu Reeves' awful accent!
>
> (*10: anon. female. Scientist, age 33.)

> Yes, because it's a wonderful film with special effects with beautiful males (Reeves, Oldman). So I spoke about it with schoolfriends.
>
> (*15: Jessica. French au pair, age 20.)

> Keanu Reeves' rubbish accent and the fake blood at the start of the film.
>
> (*17: anon. female. Charity worker, age 22.)

> Mostly I praised the design and atmosphere and complained that there was no villain or really scary bits.
>
> (*3: Anon. male. Media worker, age 26.)

Viewing experiences were reconstructed retrospectively, not only in post-film discussions, but also in the narratives written in response to my questionnaire – sometimes two or three years after the event. The model of salient elements may describe one important way in which viewers formulate their responses to a film in peer group discussions, as well as in written submissions to a researcher such as myself – that is, by remembering these elements and the reactions they produce and then representing them to others. Processes of memory formation and articulation, in particular the act of writing down and so reifying one's response to a film, appear to encourage the arrangement of the film experience into highlights and lowlights. Memory cannot encompass or exhaust the entire event of viewing. It holds on to certain moments or elements, which ultimately represent the whole. In other words, such memories work synecdochically. Not surprisingly, visual memories are particularly common in accounts of film watching, but sound – music, dialogue, accents – also figures.[99]

The layout of the questionnaire also has a part to play here. In particular, the question which asked 'what elements of the film did you particularly like or dislike?' could be seen to invite such itemisations. But many respondents used this form of writing about the film in the open-ended section (part two) which preceded more specific questions. This section asked viewers simply to 'write about why you watched *Bram Stoker's Dracula* [and] your reactions to it'. It seems that the very act of writing about a film, without any further specific prompting, often leads to the citation of highlights and lowlights. These considerations should not obscure the point I am making about processes of viewing, whereby certain outstanding elements – sources of pleasure and displeasure, triggers of emotional and physical affect such as desire, terror, laughter, admiration, sympathy, anxiety, discomfort, surprise or irritation – are registered during the film. This pattern of response suggests that films are not necessarily always experienced as the integrated narrative structures still assumed and effectively constituted as objects of scrutiny within much orthodox film studies. In certain instances at least, they may be consumed as essentially disintegrated and fragmented collections of disparate highlights and lowlights (with attendant pleasures and displeasures) standing out from a less memorable background.[100]

Conclusions

To have a chance of success, the dispersible film text must offer multiple invitations-to-view to a number of taste publics, even while commercial imperatives may privilege some market segments over others. Further distinctions between audience fractions may be constructed in media reviews and commentary. This kind of coverage is not simply an unproblematic conduit between industry and audience: commentators mobilise their own taste hierarchies and differentiations in the light of professional conventions, personal inclinations and target readerships, and thus mediate strategies of the film industry. Audiences operate within contexts shaped not only by macro- and micro-social factors, but also by the institutional procedures of marketing and publicity – in part by drawing on, modifying or explicitly rejecting associated taste classifications. Thus, in viewers' accounts, the film's generic status may emerge as a point of intersection for their negotiations of differentials in taste, competence and identity. The circuit of production and consumption is completed by filmmakers' decisions about future projects, which are informed by perceptions of popular demand based on previous films' success or failure in finding an audience.

Accounts of genre in film studies need to examine in more detail audiences' differentially distributed knowledges of, and participations in, the generic regimes of Hollywood and other popular cinemas. As a first step, I hope to have demonstrated how this turn to the audience can produce new understandings of the interplay between industrial and critical logics and audience activities of discrimination and self-definition. Viewers may enjoy belonging to taste publics (commonly invoked in reviews and advertising campaigns) based on shared patterns of consumption, such as a preference for horror films or for appearances by Keanu Reeves or Winona Ryder. These communities are more often imagined or implied rather than convened in a literally shared space.[101] But they can nevertheless offer consumers a powerful sense of identity. So can the symbolic rejection of such taste formations. Both positions were evinced in the affiliations and distinctions found in informants' accounts. In deploying generic markers, audiences are not simply accepting commercially and critically recognised categories in a passive fashion, but are taking them up and making them work for their own purposes. In the process, they shape the meaning, value, and frontiers of established genres according to their tastes and motives. Respondents' decisions about whether or not to classify *Bram Stoker's Dracula* as 'horror' suggest some variance over the definitions and contents of traditional genre categories. It seems that individuals can maintain ensembles of preferences which are not necessarily coterminous with industrial and critical typologies, while simultaneously knowing that they are addressed as members of institutionally constituted and demarcated constituencies through production, marketing, and reviewing strategies. Such personal 'taste maps' may incorporate institutionalised categories such as horror, as well as groupings such as 'intelligent cool films' which cut across more established generic headings. It is not time to jettison the familiar taxonomies proposed by film genres. But it is necessary to recognise that they are subject to constant rewriting – by audiences in addition to producers and reviewers – and that they exist alongside, and their members are always being (re)arranged into, discursive categories which are yet to attain institutional consolidation.

Notes

1 The term is Richard Maltby's. See Richard Maltby and Ian Craven, *Hollywood Cinema: An Introduction* (Oxford, Blackwell, 1995), pp. 30–5. The extent and particularities of textual aggregation will of course vary from film to film.

2 Duncan Clark, Columbia TriStar's senior vice president of international marketing, quoted in Ana Maria Bahiana, 'Tooth and nail', *Screen International*, 13 November 1992, 12.

3 *Bram Stoker's Dracula* grossed $82 million in the United States and Canada, ranking 13th in the rolling box office chart. 'US top grossers to date: Jan 3 1992 – Jan 3 1993', *Screen International*, 8 January 1993, 37. It was more successful in overseas markets, where it grossed $110m. Source: imdb.com

4 See Steve Neale, *Genre and Hollywood* (London, Routledge, 2000), especially pp. 231–42.

5 See Steve Neale, *Genre* (London, British Film Institute, 1980), pp. 22–3; Maltby and Craven, *Hollywood Cinema*, chapter 3, especially pp. 109, 112; Maltby, '"Sticks, hicks and flaps": Classical Hollywood's generic conception of its audiences', in Melvyn Stokes and Richard Maltby (eds), *Identifying Hollywood's Audiences: Cultural Identity and the Movies* (London, British Film Institute, 1999) pp. 23–41.

6 Neale, *Genre*, p. 54.

7 See also Rick Altman, *Film/Genre* (London, British Film Institute, 1999), p. 16.

8 Alan Williams, 'Is a radical genre criticism possible?' *Quarterly Review of Film Studies*, 9:2 (1984), 124.

9 Three exceptions appear in a recent volume of the *Journal of Popular British Cinema*. See Claire Monk, 'Heritage films and the British cinema audience in the 1990s'; Joanne Lacey, 'Seeing through happiness: Hollywood musicals and the construction of the American

dream in Liverpool'; and Sue Harper and Vincent Porter, 'Cinema audience tastes in 1950s Britain', all in *Journal of Popular British Cinema*, 2 (1999).

10 James Naremore, 'American film noir: the history of an idea', *Film Quarterly*, 49:2 (1995/6), 12–28. Naremore is himself borrowing from Foucault's notion of the 'author function', which proposes that discourses of authorship construct the object they claim to find by unifying a diverse set of texts under a common heading. See Michel Foucault, 'What is an author?' in V. Harari (ed.), *Textual Strategies* (Ithaca, Cornell University Press, 1979), pp. 147–53.

11 On this last point, see also Andrew Tudor: 'To take a genre such as a "Western", analyse it and list its principal characteristics, is to beg the question that we must first isolate the body of films which are "Westerns". But they can only be isolated on the basis of the "principal characteristics" which can only be discovered *from the films themselves* after they have been isolated. That is, we are caught in a circle.' Tudor, *Theories of Film* (London, Secker and Warburg, 1973) cited in Peter Hutchings, 'Genre theory and criticism', in Joanne Hollows and Mark Jancovich (eds), *Approaches to Popular Film* (Manchester, Manchester University Press, 1995), pp. 66–7. Italics in original. Tudor proposes a solution to this dilemma by suggesting that a genre is 'what we collectively believe it to be'. This in turn begs a number of questions about who participates in shaping such a consensus, questions addressed by Naremore, and by Rick Altman in his *Film/Genre*.

12 Altman, *Film/Genre*, especially pp. 30–82. On genres in process, see also Neale, *Genre and Hollywood*, especially pp. 207–57.

13 *Mary Shelley's Frankenstein* grossed $22 million in the US. *Mary Reilly* (based on Valerie Martin's 1990 novel of the same name) grossed a mere $6 million in the US. Figures from imdb.com

14 Although published in 1975, *Interview with the Vampire* is set partly in the eighteenth century. The film grossed $105 million in the US. Source: imdb.com

15 See Mark Jancovich, 'Genre and the audience: genre classifications and cultural distinctions in the mediation of *The Silence of the Lambs*', in Melvyn Stokes and Richard Maltby (eds), *Hollywood Spectatorship: Changing Perceptions of Cinema Audiences* (London, British Film Institute, forthcoming, 2001). The film grossed $130 million in the US. Source: imdb.com

16 This trend is most apparent in the work of director superstar James Cameron, from *Aliens* (1986) to *Titanic* (1997). See Peter Kramer, '"Women first": *Titanic* (1997), action-adventure films and Hollywood's female audience', *Historical Journal of Film, Radio and Television*, 18:4 (1998), 599–618, and 'A Powerful cinemagoing force?

Hollywood and female audiences since the 1960s', in Stokes and Maltby (eds), *Identifying Hollywood's Audiences*, pp. 93–108.

17 The mini-boom in 'classic' horror was noted in both trade and fan publications of the time. See Allan Hunter, 'Undying attraction', *Screen International*, 14 October 1993, 16–17; Lizzie Francke, 'They're back!' *Premiere*, November 1994, 65–7.

18 This formula was imitated by some producers – for example in Roger Corman's straight-to-video production *Dracula Rising* (Fred Gallo, United States, 1993).

19 *Wolf* grossed $65 million in the US, on a budget of $70m. *Vampire in Brooklyn* grossed $20 million in the US. Source: imdb.com

20 Stephen Jones, *The Illustrated Vampire Movie Guide* (London, Titan Books, 1993).

21 Jon Anderson, letter to the author, 19 July 1993.

22 On the common fixation with fidelity to a literary source in critical discourses around screen adaptations, see Brian McFarlane, *Novel to Film: an Introduction to the Theory of Adaptation* (Oxford, Clarendon Press, 1996), pp. 17–18.

23 Altman, *Film/Genre*, pp. 41–7. Of course, this process does not guarantee success, as evinced by commercial flops such as *Mary Shelley's Frankenstein* and *Mary Reilly*.

24 James V. Hart, 'The script that wouldn't die', in Francis Ford Coppola and James V. Hart, *Bram Stoker's Dracula: The Film and the Legend* (New York, Newmarket Press/London, Pan Books, 1992), pp. 6–7.

25 Suzi Feay, 'Staking reputations', *Time Out*, 28 October 1992, 18–19.

26 Ira Konigsberg makes a similar observation in 'How many Draculas does it take to change a lightbulb?' in Andrew Horton and Stuart McDouglas (eds), *Play it Again Sam: Retakes on Remakes* (Berkeley, University of California Press, 1998), pp. 250–75. Konigsberg notes that in the novel: 'Dracula ... always has the stench of the grave and the pallor of the dead. In the films he is too much a seductive lover to have these qualities'. *Ibid.*, p. 264.

27 Columbia Pictures, *Bram Stoker's Dracula: Production Notes*, 1992, p. 4

28 Bahiana, 'Tooth and nail', 12.

29 Robert E. Kapsis, *Hitchcock: The Making of a Reputation* (Chicago, University of Chicago Press, 1992), p. 6.

30 Cinema Advertising Association 1997.

31 Ellen Moers, *Literary Women* (London, The Women's Press, 1978), cited in Brigid Cherry, 'Refusing to refuse to look: female viewers of the horror film', in Stokes and Maltby (eds), *Identifying Hollywood's Audiences*, pp. 187–203.

32 See, for example, Cherry, 'Refusing to refuse to look'. She suggests

that the perception of a male cinemagoing audience for horror has persisted in part because many women watch horror 'in private' on video or television. In her own audience study, Cherry found that female horror fans rated vampire films as the most pleasurable type of horror, and were least likely to enjoy the slasher subgenre. *Ibid.*, pp. 192–3.

33 '[H]orror film audiences used to be heavily male. If they could drag their girlfriends along, you were lucky.' Miramax president Mark Gill in Andrew Hines, '*Scream 2* showcases demographic power', *Variety*, 16 December 1997, cited in Cherry, 'Refusing to refuse to look', p. 188. As Rhona J. Berenstein has pointed out, women constituted a significant fraction of the audience for horror in the 1930s. Berenstein, *Attack of the Leading Ladies: Gender and Performance in Classic Horror Cinema* (New York, Columbia University Press, 1995).

34 The 'semantics' of a genre are its 'building blocks': familiar settings, props, costumes (often known as 'iconography') and character types. 'Syntax' refers to the meaning-bearing structures (such as oppositions and parallels) in which semantic elements are arranged. See Rick Altman, 'A semantic/syntactic approach to film genre', *Cinema Journal*, 23:3 (1984), reprinted in Altman, *Film/Genre*.

35 Altman, *Film/Genre*, p. 207. For a further consideration of Altman's model, see Neale, *Genre and Hollywood*, pp. 215–17.

36 Anderson, letter to the author.

37 Bahiana, 'Tooth and nail', 12.

38 For a relatively rare feature on Oldman as the main star of the film, see Pauline McLeod, 'Born to be Dracula', *Daily Mirror*, London Xtra, 28 January 1993, 8–9.

39 Anderson, letter to the author.

40 See Timothy Corrigan, 'Auteurs and the new Hollywood' in Jon Lewis (ed.), *The New American Cinema* (Durham, Duke University Press, 1998), pp. 38–63. On the viability of auteurs with idiosyncratic, that is to say recognisable and marketable, visual styles in the industrial context of 'post-classical' Hollywood's package system of production, see Henry Jenkins, 'Historical poetics', in Hollows and Jancovich (eds), *Approaches to Popular Film*, pp. 114–15.

41 Lorraine Butler, 'Out for the Count', *Daily Mirror*, 20 November 1992, 22–3. On women enjoying the depiction of sex in *Bram Stoker's Dracula*, see also Francke, 'Back to Life'.

42 See Jeff Dawson, 'Journey to glory', *Empire*, 45 (March 1993), 64–5.

43 A review in *The Sun* commented: '[Reeves is] left to spend the movie wrestling with a bevy of Dracula's brides who put it about for the Count. And we're talking 400 years of great mammaries here!' Peter Cox, 'Gary's a suck-cess', *The Sun*, 29 January 1993, 17. Italics in original.

44 Anderson, letter to the author. 'You ask us', *Bella*, 3 February 1993, 22; Chris Hulme, 'Winona's painful coming of age', *Woman*, 1 February 1993, 54–5; Edwin J. Bernard, 'Winona takes all', *Sky Magazine*, January 1993, 6–10; Harold von Kursk, 'Winona takes all', *Time Out*, 13–20 January 1993, 16–18; Chris Heath, 'My bloody Valentine', *Empire*, 45 (March 1993), 56–66; 'Win! A wardrobe's worth of clothes!' *Empire*, 45 (March 1993), 96–7; Michael Pye, 'Sure fang', *Esquire*, February 1993, 36–41; Tom Shone, 'Film', *ES* (*Evening Standard*), January 1993, 72–3; Adriaane Pielou, 'Winona's first love bite', *You Magazine* (*Mail on Sunday*), 24 January 1993, 76–7.

45 'Winona Ryder and Keanu Reeves', *Big!* poster, *Big!*, 10–23 February 1993; 'Win! Dracula bits', *Big!*, 10–23 February 1993, 38.

46 Anderson. *The South Bank Show: Dracula*; *Bloodlines*, BBC1, 30 January 1993.

47 'UK film sell-through top 20', *Screen International*, 12 February 1993, 31.

48 'The blood and guts of film-making', *Screen International*, 12 February 1993, 31.

49 Columbia Pictures, *Bram Stoker's Dracula: Production Notes*, p. 5.

50 Columbia Pictures *Bram Stoker's Dracula: Production Notes*, p, 2; Coppola and Hart, *Bram Stoker's Dracula: The Film and the Legend*, p. 4; Steve Biodrowski,,Coppola's horror roots', *Cinefantastique*, 23:4 (December 1992), 44–6, and 'Fang warfare', *The Dark Side*, 29 (February 1993), 5–8.

51 Three posters were released. The initial 'teaser' carried horror connotations, featuring the single word 'BEWARE'. The second poster introduced a gargoyle along with the copyline 'Love Never Dies'.

52 Fred Saberhagen and James V. Hart, *Bram Stoker's Dracula* (London, Pan, 1992).

53 Coppola and Hart, *Bram Stoker's Dracula: The Film and the Legend*.

54 Tim Bates, letter to the author, 5 January 1994.

55 Roy Thomas, Mike Mignola and John Nyberg, *Bram Stoker's Dracula* (London, Pan, 1993).

56 Sony had previously acquired CBS Records for $2 billion in 1987. On problems experienced by Sony in Hollywood, see Barbara Rudolph, 'So many dreams so many losses', *Time*, 28 November 1994, 60–1.

57 See Robert Philip Kolker, *A Cinema of Loneliness: Penn, Kubrick, Coppola, Scorsese, Altman* (New York and Oxford, Oxford University Press, 1980). Significantly, Kolker responded to the perceived failure of Hollywood's 'modernist project' by replacing Coppola with Spielberg for the second edition in 1988.

58 See Corrigan, 'Auteurs and the new Hollywood', in Lewis, *The New American Cinema*. Over the last decade, the market value of 'Coppola' as a 'celebrity auteur' has declined quite rapidly. Despite some suc-

cesses as a producer, Coppola has been working more or less as a director-for-hire on projects such as *Jack* (United States, 1996) and *The Rainmaker* (United States, 1997) – an adaptation marketed under the author-name of novelist John Grisham.

59 Bahiana, 'Tooth and Nail', 12, quoting Duncan Clark, Columbia TriStar's senior vice-president of international marketing. Compare an article in a Californian magazine in which Coppola expresses anxiety about the power of film industry 'bureaucrats' to shackle his auteurist intentions for the film, while presenting himself as in complete personal control of the products from his Napa Valley vineyard. Jim Wood, 'A taste of the holidays', *San Francisco Examiner Image*, 22 November 1992, cited in Jim Collins, *Architectures of Excess: Cultural Life in the Information Age* (New York and London, Routledge, 1995), p. 204.
60 Bahiana, 'Tooth and nail'.
61 Iain R. Webb, 'Study in scarlet' (featuring Monica Bellucci, one of the film's brides of Dracula) *Harpers and Queen*, September 1992, 154–165, 222.
62 14 February 1993.
63 Nick Sullivan, 'Vamping it up,' *Esquire*, April 1993, 32.
64 Showcase Cinemas, Leeds, Programme Information (1993): 'Dracula'.
65 Rosie Horide, 'Eternal lust of Drac-u-like', *The Sun*, TV Super Guide, 31 July 1993, 7.
66 For a critique of the film's representation of sexuality from a gay male perspective, see Richard Dyer, 'Dracula and Desire', *Sight and Sound*, 3:1 (NS) (January, 1993), 8–12.
67 On the influence on Ishioka's costumes of oriental, symbolist, surrealist and decadent art, see *Production Notes*, pp. 9–10; Hilary Alexander, 'Out for the Count', the *Sunday Telegraph*, 24 January 1993, ix; Francis Ford Coppola, Eiko Ishioka and David Seidner (ed., Susan Dworkin), *Coppola and Eiko on Bram Stoker's Dracula* (San Francisco, Collins, 1992); Peter Popham, 'Dressed to thrill', the *Independent Magazine*, 3 April 1993, 34–8. The film won an Oscar for best costume design.
68 See Coppola and Hart, *Bram Stoker's Dracula: The Film and the Legend*, pp. 39, 70. The book also contains an afterword by American academic Leonard Wolf (editor of the *Annotated Dracula*), and a list of suggestions for 'further reading and viewing'. The press pack quotes Wolf, refers to Freudian and Jungian concepts, and suggests further reading on Dracula. *Production notes*, pp. 8, 59.
69 Anthony Quinn, 'Absolutely ravishing', *Independent on Sunday*, 31 January 1993, 19.
70 *Ibid*. Jonathan Romney, 'At the court of Coppola', *The Guardian*, 21 January 1993, G2, 2–3.

71 Anne Billson, 'Vlad the Mills & Boon hero', the *Sunday Telegraph*, 31 January 1993, Arts section, xv.

72 For less enthusiastic perspectives on the film's use of costume, see Tom Hutchinson, 'A Dracula drained of his own life blood', *Mail on Sunday*, 31 January 1993, 37; Adam Mars-Jones, 'The beautiful and the damned', *The Independent*, 29 January 1993, 16.

73 Cinema Advertising Association figures suggests that 54 per cent of the film's British cinema audience were from classes ABC1, and 46 per cent were from classes C2DE. 44 per cent of the audience were under 24, and 22 per cent were over 35 (May 1997).

74 Pierre Bourdieu, *Distinction: a Social Critique of the Judgement of Taste*, trans. Richard Nice (London, Routledge & Kegan Paul, 1984), especially pp. 31–4.

75 Nick Hasted, 'The Kids are all bite', *New Musical Express*, 30 January 1993, 20–1.

76 'Frankenstein versus Dracula', *Smash Hits*, 26 October 1994, 55. The magazine erroneously listed both films as classified '15', when Coppola's film was in fact rated '18'.

77 Frederick S. Clarke, untitled editorial comment, *Cinefantastique*, 23:4 (December 1992), 3.

78 Ian Calcutt, 'Bram Stoker's Dracula', *Samhain*, 37 (March–April 1993), 38.

79 Stefan Jaworzyn, 'Bram Stoker's Dracula', *The Dark Side*, 29 (February 193), 9

80 Published in the United States, the magazine is sold in British film merchandise stores and by mail order.

81 Clarke, untitled.

82 *Samhain*, *Cinefantastique* and *The Dark Side* are all almost exclusively male-authored, and tend to perpetuate conceptions of horror subculture as a largely masculine arena.

83 Sarah Thornton, *Club Cultures: Music, Media and Subcultural Capital* (Cambridge, Polity, 1995). John Fiske makes a similar argument in outlining his concept of 'popular cultural capital'. Fiske, 'The cultural economy of fandom', in Lisa Lewis (ed.), *The Adoring Audience* (London, Routledge, 1992), pp. 30–49.

84 Thornton, *Club Cultures*, p. 11.

85 Gina Marchetti 'Subcultural studies and the film audience: rethinking the film viewing context', *Current Research in Film: Audiences, Economics, and Law*, 2 (1986), 64.

86 The legitimacy of the film was also contested over the terrain of the gothic. See Duncan Barford, 'On Coppola's Dracula', *The Goth*, June 1993, 19–20. The article concluded: 'It's enough to make any self-respecting, traditionalist vampire heartily sick. And it's a million miles

away from the sumptuously Gothic depiction of lust and disease in Bram Stoker's original.'

87 Bourdieu, *Distinction*, p. 6.

88 ITV, Saturday, 24 October 1996, 10pm. In 1995 I asked the editor of *Samhain* to publish a request for readers to write to me. The reaction was disappointing: just three letters and one subsequent question- naire. Because of this poor response, I tried a new approach, which had the benefit of enabling me to access a wider spectrum of cinema- goers.

89 This has not always been the case. For instance, Richard Maltby points out that the assumed correlation between gender and genre prefer- ences was complicated in trade discourses of the 1930s by considera- tions of audience location (urban or rural). He suggests that this was due to the boom in talkies which appealed to 'metropolitan' tastes. See Maltby, '"Sticks, hicks and flaps": classical Hollywood's generic con- ception of its audiences', in Stokes and Maltby (eds), *Identifying Hol- lywood's Audiences*.

90 Audience research offers one way of converting private discourses of taste and genre by bringing them into limited public view. On 'con- version', see Roger Silverstone, *Television and Everyday Life* (London, Routledge, 1994), pp. 130–1.

91 By this term, I mean respondents who identified themselves as such, or who listed horror among their favourite genres.

92 Cherry suggests that women fans may not reject gore or violence *per se*, but that they are more often concerned with the way these elements are used in a film. Cherry, 'Refusing to refuse to look', p. 196.

93 *Ibid.*, p. 196.

94 Some male responses may of course have been coloured by self-cen- sorship or a desire to maintain privacy in the face of my inquiry, but this is nevertheless a fair indication of a lack of male (hetero)sexual pleasure in the film. The presence of countless features on 'scream queens' in largely male-oriented horror publications such as *Fangoria* suggest that the erotic is a major attraction for many straight male horror fans.

95 See for example, Daniel Cavicchi, *Tramps Like Us: Music and Mean- ing Among Springsteen Fans* (New York, Oxford University Press, 1998), pp. 83–5. Thanks to Matt Hills for pointing me to this book.

96 'Goths' in youth culture parlance are fans of doom-laden 'indie' (as opposed to 'heavy' or 'adult-oriented') rock music, given to wearing black. They are often keen consumers of gothic and horror novels and films. In September 1997, several goth bands played at the Whitby Weekender, a Dracula festival in the town where part of Stoker's novel is set.

97 The phrase is from Martin Barker and Kate Brooks, *Knowing Audiences: Judge Dredd, its Friends, Fans and Foes* (Luton, University of Luton Press, 1998) p. 142.

98 Gemma Moss, 'Girls tell the teen romance: four reading histories', in David Buckingham (ed.), *Reading Audiences: Young People and the Media* (Manchester, Manchester University Press, 1993), pp. 119, 133.

99 Jackie Stacey has called frozen visual moments 'iconic memories'. On these and other 'generic features' of viewers' memory texts, see Jackie Stacey, 'Hollywood memories', *Screen*, 35:4 (1994), 318–19.

100 This may be particularly true of action movies. Drawing on audience research, Martin Barker and Kate Brooks describe plot as a 'carrier wave' taking viewers 'from action to action, from effect to effect.' Martin Barker and Kate Brooks, 'Bleak futures by proxy', in Stokes and Maltby (eds), *Identifying Hollywood's Audiences*, p. 170.

101 See Altman, *Film/Genre*, pp. 156–65.

Chapter 5

Natural Born Killers: a film for hooligans?

Compared to the highly successful *Basic Instinct* and *Bram Stoker's Dracula*, *Natural Born Killers* (Oliver Stone, Warner Bros./Ixtlan/New Regency, United States, 1994) was merely a moderate hit at the United Kingdom box office, grossing £4.7 million in 1995.[1] While it enjoyed widespread, if often hostile, media exposure, the film's stars were not top-rank, and its assembly and marketing did not exploit the logic of textual and audience aggregation on the same scale as the other two titles. Instead, *Natural Born Killers* was pitched to a relatively narrow audience of young adult males. It was positioned in the marketplace as something of an 'outlaw' film and was in many ways received as such, by commentators and individual viewers. Withheld from video release in Britain throughout the 1990s, but screened regularly in repertory cinemas and at late shows, *Natural Born Killers* can be characterised as combining elements of both a cult film and a mainstream hit. Both content and form offer support for readings of it as an 'outlaw' work. The film tells the story of two young 'white trash' killers in love and on the run. They commit many murders and instigate a prison riot before settling down and raising a family.[2] The film quotes repeatedly from television shows, advertising and other films, and includes an omnipresent rock soundtrack, black humour and several drug references. Its form is a collision of visual styles and rapid editing (achieved through new digital techniques) often compared in reviews to the quick-cutting collage style of pop music videos popularised by MTV. *Natural Born Killers* combines various black and white and colour film stocks, video footage, and animation. The plot of murderous youth rebellion can thus be seen to be reinforced by a form that rejects certain 'classical' codes of narrative continuity and formal unity, and appears to assume a media-aware youth audience. The film's maverick status was enhanced by the reputation of its director, Oliver Stone, who has a public image as a rebel, a successful but controversial Hollywood auteur. Even so, like many nominally 'independent' films, *Natural Born Killers* was financially supported and distributed by a major studio, in this case Warner Bros., the film division of Time Warner (now AOL-Time Warner), one of the largest and most powerful multimedia corporations in the world. Stone's 'outlaw' film thus benefited from the industrial muscle and expertise of a conglomerate whose advertising and publicity strategy entailed promoting *Natural Born Killers* as challenging and unconventional entertainment.

In Britain, the film was supported by specialised commercial mechanisms and strategies calculated to sell it to its target audiences. These marketing efforts were inadvertently aided by a panic in the British media over the film's 'violent' content. Shortly before its British release, *Natural Born Killers* became the latest in a long line of popular entertainments accused of encouraging anti-social and dangerous 'copycat' behaviour. The controversy resulted in the postponement of its certification by the British Board of Film Classification (BBFC). This decision effectively confirmed the film's reputation as 'beyond the pale'. *Natural Born Killers* had arrived in Britain loaded with discourses of anxiety, specifically claims that it inspired acts of violence in viewers. The mechanism through which reports marked *Natural Born Killers* as a 'dangerous' film was thus centred on its professed effects on (susceptible, unstable and potentially dangerous) audiences. While offering up such alarmist notions of the film and the audiences expected to enjoy it, the media outrage had the accidental effect of abetting its commercial prospects.

The general shape, if not the details, of my investigation into the circulation of *Natural Born Killers* in Britain will be familiar from previous chapters. First, I consider the film's industrial setting, including how it was marketed as a film with a distinctive appeal, and the influence upon this strategy of the BBFC delay. Then I examine in detail how the press responded to *Natural Born Killers*, how the film's potential viewers were represented, and how an approving audience (largely assumed to be young and male) was figured as a problem. I thus pursue various constructions of the film's audience put forward via marketing tactics and journalistic discourses – as 'hip' and in the know, or as moronic, sick, impressionable, and dangerous. In the process I trace a series of discursive

connections between formations of class and gender, and understandings of violence on screen and in society at large. In the final
sections of the chapter I draw on audience research to explore actual
viewers' responses to the film and the promotional and disapproving discourses surrounding it. I assess viewers' perceptions of themselves and 'other' audiences, and ask to what extent these coincided
with or diverged from constructions of audience identity proposed
by the distributor and/or the press.

The classification delay and the marketing of *Natural Born Killers*

Natural Born Killers is described in the official press pack as 'a satire
on our culture of violence and the media's ratings-driven exploitation of that culture', and 'a hallucinatory journey that shocks and
disorients as it reveals and informs'.[3] The original script was written
by aspiring film-maker Quentin Tarantino and sold to fledgling producers Jane Hamsher and Don Murphy in 1990. Three years later,
following Tarantino's debut directorial success *Reservoir Dogs*
(United States, 1991), the *Natural Born Killers* script was filmed by
Oliver Stone as a project involving his own production company,
Ixtlan, and Warner Bros. Before the American opening in August
1994, Tarantino had his script credit changed to 'story by' after
reportedly objecting to Stone's reworking of his script. Tarantino's
version had centred on a television reporter following killers Mickey
and Mallory, while Stone chose to focus on the murdering pair
themselves.[4]

Before discussing the marketing of *Natural Born Killers* in Britain,
it is necessary to examine the delay in the film's classification by the
BBFC, since this decision had a significant impact on Warner Bros.'
advertising strategy. Rather like *Basic Instinct*, *Natural Born Killers*
became surrounded by discourses of outrage in the period leading
up to its British release. However, the careers of the two controver-
sies were notably different. Protestors lobbying against *Basic
Instinct*'s representations of lesbianism and bisexuality had to work
hard to gain space (let alone support) for their views in the mainstream press. By contrast, many of the anxieties about *Natural Born
Killers* were instituted by press commentators and reviewers in the
first place. They mobilised concerns about direct audience effects
(largely absent from journalistic discussions of *Basic Instinct*) which

SCENES TO SHOCK: Natural Born Killers starring Woody Harrelson and Juliette Lewis could be outlawed from our screens

By RICHARD WALLACE

Ban these natural born killers

AN ANGRY "ban it now" outcry erupted last night over the gruesome Hollywood film Natural Born Killers.

Its launch in Britain next month was shelved after censors had failed to agree whether they should outlaw the movie.

The "body count" is nearly 100 and it is being blamed for copycat murders in America and France.

Censors here are expected to meet again in December. But last night MPs demanded an immediate ban on the movie likened to the British-made shocker of the 70s, A Clockwork Orange. Michael Alison, a Church Commissioner and Tory MP for Selby, North Yorks, said: "There is only one rule on this issue. If there is any hint that people could be exposed to danger, the film should not be shown.

"We should be concerned about potential victims of crime, and not worry about viewers who might miss cheap thrills."

Justify

Labour's Frank Cook said: "I find it difficult to imagine any artistic argument which could justify the inclusion of so many fatalities."

Liberal Democrat David Alton said that a cerficate for films which glorify violence would act as "a downward pressure on the industry".

In the film, stars Woody Harrelson — the Cheers barman — and Juliette Lewis go on a three-week orgy of violence.

Police, hitch-hikers, petrol attendants and waitresses are all massacred in scenes resembling an MTV-style rock video.

But in America and in France, the £38million movie is said to have inspired real-life murder.

In the USA, Eric Elliot, 16, and Lewis Gilbert, 22, are accused of murdering Ohio pensioner Ruth Loader, 79, for her car.

It was found 650 miles away in Missouri, where the pair allegedly shot a husband and wife. Three days later, the couple's car was found in Oklahoma City near the body of Roxie Ruddel, whose pick-up truck had gone.

Earlier this month a 14-year-old boy in Dallas was accused of decapitating a girl after seeing the movie. "I want to be famous and kill someone like the natural born killers," he is reported to have told a friend.

In Paris three weeks ago, 19-year-old Florence Rey and her boyfriend Audry Maupin, 22, killed three policemen and a taxi driver. Natural Born Killers memorabilia was found at their apartment.

The film and the controversy has echoes of A Clockwork Orange, released in 1971 but later withdrawn by American director Stanley Kubrick.

The story of murderer and rapist Alex (Malcolm McDowell) and his gang was blamed for a wave of violence across Britain.

Natural Born Killers directed by Oscar-winner Oliver Stone and due for release on November 18 — came before the British Board of Film Classification in July. One source told of "very heated debates." A cooling-off period was needed before it was looked at again.

Censors director James Ferman said yesterday "At the moment it has not got a classification and the board will not make a comment on a film that has not been classified."

Distributors Warner Bros are "very disappointed" by the delays.

COPYCAT: Suspect Elliott

COPYCAT: Suspect Gilbert

COPYCAT: Suspect Rey

VICTIM: Ruth Loader

Blood on the screen

THE 70s was the era of the violent movie – as a string of screen shockers caused outrage.

Marlon Brando on a bike had started it all in 1953 with THE WILD ONE. Censor condemned its "unbridled hooliganism" and it was effectively banned in Britain until the late 60s.

In 1966 WILD ANGELS, another biker movie, was banned for years before substantial cuts earned it a certificate. Then came the vicious 70s.

1970: TRASH. Andy Warhol's film was outlawed by the censor as grossly offensive.

1971: A CLOCKWORK ORANGE. Withdrawn by director Stanley Kubrick after copycat crimes.

1971: STRAW DOGS. No video certificate.

1973: THE EXORCIST. Released without cuts but many protests and banned on video.

1974: TEXAS CHAINSAW MASSACRE. Banned from video, along with two sequels.

1974: DEATH WISH. Fears that vigilante hero might be imitated came true when New Yorker Bernard Goetz shot a subway mugger.

1979: SCUM. Appeared as a movie after play was banned by the BBC. Film shown on Channel 4 in 1983. In 1982 there was BRIMSTONE & TREACLE, the screen version of the Dennis Potter TV play banned by the BBC. Play shown in 1987.

In 1992 came BAD LIEUTENANT. Irish censor deemed it unsuitable for viewing until after the year 2000.

Last year RESERVOIR DOGS hit trouble. Still to be granted a video certificate.

3 Some of the 'copycat' allegations levelled against *Natural Born Killers*

centred upon incidents of murder and violence allegedly encouraged by the film. In the months before the scheduled opening in November 1994, the press ran stories of 'copycat' killings in the United States and France reportedly inspired by *Natural Born Killers*.[5] Various outraged commentaries added to the media hysteria.[6] In October the BBFC responded to the clamour by postponing its award of a certificate.[7] This decision was defended as necessary in order to investigate media allegations against the film. Rather than the 'vertical' movement of pressures upwards from members of the public to the regulatory body, a 'horizontal' model of communication can be seen to operate in this instance: the BBFC responded directly to, and effectively entered into a dialogue with, the British press. The mediating role of elected representatives or lobby groups such as the National Viewers' and Listeners' Association was largely absent.

Nearly two months later, the film was finally issued with an '18' certificate, with no cuts required.[8] A press statement released by the BBFC declared:

> After a very full investigation of alleged links between real-life murders in the United States and France and the film *Natural Born Killers*, the BBFC is satisfied that there has been no instance in which this film could be held to have been responsible for homicidal behaviour. … The idea that ordinary people had been turned into killers by being exposed to a particular film was not one with which the FBI or local police forces in America had any sympathy. … Having satisfied itself that the film *Natural Born Killers* has not had the pernicious effect it was reported as having, the Board has now classified the work '18' without cuts.[9]

The BBFC postponement of classification must be situated in the context of the political and media climate that prevailed during lobbying over the Criminal Justice and Public Order Bill, which became British law in November 1994. The new Act required the BBFC, when considering videos for classification, to take into account the possibility of harm to potential viewers (by implication, children and the mentally unstable in particular), and, as a consequence of viewers' resulting behaviour, the possibility of harm to society in general. The BBFC took care to point out in its statement that it habitually undertook such considerations with regard to films as well as videos:

> The suggestion that such links [between *Natural Born Killers* and real murders] existed was one the Board had to take seriously, since the

possibility of harm to potential viewers or, through their behaviour, to society is not only the new statutory test which Parliament has laid down for video; it is also one which the Board has traditionally applied to every film or video submitted for classification.

As will become apparent, there is a clear overlap between the logic and assumptions structuring the BBFC's initial approach to *Natural Born Killers*, and some of the discourses of anxiety mobilised in the press to demand the banning of the film outright. In each case, 'susceptible' viewers are perceived as both vulnerable to certain representations (here, of violence) and, via their consequent imitative actions, present a threat to members of society at large.[10] Unlike the Board's statements, the press typically detailed this 'problem' audience for 'problem' films, – simultaneously vulnerable and dangerous – in terms of gender (male), socio-economic background (working class), and age (adolescent), even when heterosexual couples were accused of copycat crimes. Both Warner Bros.' marketing tactics and the moral panic over the film in the press ignored potential and, later, actual female audiences to concentrate in their own ways on male viewers.

Following the classification of *Natural Born Killers*, Warner Bros. set a new release date of 24 February 1995. This gave the company eight weeks after the Christmas break to run its advertising campaign. According to Ian George, then director of advertising and publicity at Warner Bros. Distributors Ltd. in London:

> [T]here was a feeling that we were just never going to get the females, certainly ridiculous trying to advertise specifically to females. I mean you would get females going, but they would be the sorts of people who would want to go to that [kind of film]. So [the target audience] was definitely male, it was definitely younger males, by that we classify 18 to 24 – I mean actually it was 16 to 24, but it's an '18' certificate film, so officially they're not supposed to go.[11]

This target market comprised two main groups, which were differentiated from each other according to cultural preference and class. The first of these was conceived of among industry professionals as a largely working-class audience, enthusiastic about violent films in general. The second was made up of more 'discerning' cinemagoers, essentially from the middle classes. These were labelled as fans of the 'new violence' popularised by Tarantino's stylish cult hit *Reservoir Dogs* and his highly successful follow-up *Pulp Fiction*, which was released in Britain in autumn 1994, shortly before the planned opening of *Natural Born Killers*.[12] Despite publicised differences between Stone and Tarantino over *Natural Born Killers*, it was hoped that Tarantino's input would still attract a significant fraction of this taste grouping. Warner Bros. viewed its film as selling to a 'hip' audience similar to that for *Pulp Fiction*, although narrower and less gender-mixed: 'It won't be as big as *Pulp Fiction*, because ultimately *Pulp Fiction* has got a broader appeal.'[13] The company paid to run the *Natural Born Killers* trailer prior to screenings of *Pulp Fiction* in late October and early November 1994 to target 'new violence' fans. Ultimately, the gender profiles of the audience for each film were different, but not by a great deal. The figures for *Natural Born Killers* were 71 per cent male, 29 per cent female, compared to 65 per cent male and 35 per cent female for *Pulp Fiction*.[14]

Warner Bros. staff felt that a more extensive advertising campaign was required to hook the 'downmarket' audience grouping. Ian George explained the constitution of the two distinct core markets thus:

> [T]here was a feeling that there was your *Guardian*-type, *Independent*-type reader, who are all into genre film, into Tarantino as a director and into the whole ethos of this different type of movie coming out. And there's also a target market which is described in the States as shit-kickers. And these are your meat-heads, your people who go out on a Saturday night, go to the pub, get assholed, go with the lads, after the pub, go into the pictures and watch that really violent movie. Now as far as we were concerned, we were going to direct the major bulk of our advertising towards the shit-kickers, because we felt that the more upmarket target would go and see the film anyway, because that's the sort of people they are. So whilst we did do a bit of advertising in the more sort of quality type press, generally it was all amongst the down-market people.[15]

George's stereotyping of 'downmarket' viewers as unthinking males, caricatured as 'meat-heads', bears some correlation with the classed formulations of *Natural Born Killers*' audience mobilised by disapproving media commentators, discussed in detail below. However, unlike hostile reviewers, George also stressed the safety and 'normality' of the audience for *Natural Born Killers*: 'We did talk about it, if there is a copycat killing, how would we all feel, and that sort of thing. But ultimately, a film doesn't turn anybody into a killer. You've got to be pretty mad to go down that route anyway, there's gotta be something wrong with you. You don't go in there a guy with two point four kids and come out Mickey and Mallory sort of thing, you know?'

A third fraction in the film's target market, cutting across and supplementing 'meat-heads' and 'new violence' audiences, was made up of rock music fans: 'We also recognised that there was a key audience amongst the student population, amongst [listeners to] alternative radio stations, or alternative rock programmes and independent music programmes.'[16] The soundtrack to *Natural Born Killers* provided a significant opening into this market. It featured more than 100 songs and musical extracts from a variety of artists and musical genres. The soundtrack album was compiled and produced by Trent Reznor of American alternative rock group Nine Inch Nails, and released through Time Warner's recording group Atlantic via its subsidiaries Interscope and Nothing. Piggybacking on existing market trends in popular music, from alternative rock to hip-hop, it comprised 27 tracks 'from and inspired by' the film.[17] Made available to buy five months before *Natural Born Killers* finally opened, the album effectively promoted the film in certain market sectors, as well as circulating in its own right. Advertised as 'the soundtrack of the decade',[18] the album gained extensive exposure in the music press and had sold 84,000 copies in the UK by November 1995.[19] In addition to the revenue which the album brought in via Atlantic, the soundtrack gave the film an entry into rock music subculture which Warner Bros. exploited aggressively. The company borrowed an advertising technique from the recording industry in fly posting the film. Posters had the Warner Bros. logo removed, and provoked complaints from some local authorities, but the distributor considered these 'guerrilla tactics'[20] successful in reinforcing the unofficial, 'underground' and subculturally 'hip' image of *Natural Born Killers*. Warner Bros. worked closely with EastWest Records, securing displays in independent record stores and big name chains. The distributor collaborated with a company called Beatwax to put together show reels, including the *Natural Born Killers* trailer, to play in university film societies and student bars. Warner Bros. also contracted Revolution Promotions to visit selected universities, displaying posters, standees and T-shirts, and arranging competitions and coverage in student publications.[21]

Meanwhile, the media outrage over the film – fuelled by allegations of copycat violence and further inflamed by the BBFC's postponement and final award of a certificate – inadvertently gave a huge boost to Warners' advertising and publicity campaign. While not specifically engineered by the company, and sometimes motivated by a desire to see the film banned outright in Britain, the moral panic over *Natural Born Killers* and its alleged link to 'real life' murders was nevertheless of great commercial significance. Not only did press reports raise the film's profile generally, but such disapproval effectively authenticated for some viewers the attraction of the film as daring, exciting and dangerous.

A similar point about the commercially beneficial 'advertisement' effects of media hysteria can be made about the marketing and reception of *Basic Instinct*. In the case of *Natural Born Killers*, however, Warner Bros. had time to deliberately capitalise upon the moral panic and to adjust its advertising strategy accordingly, once the certificate had finally been awarded. In interview, George noted that media reports of the BBFC postponement had produced a widespread impression that the film was banned outright, rather than merely awaiting classification. While this belief had to be corrected by Warners' advertising campaign in early 1995, the press furore ultimately proved highly advantageous for the distributor: 'the media controversy and the media hysteria was unbelievable – "the film that's banned", "*Natural Born Killers*, killer film banned" – you couldn't have bought that sort of publicity. Now as far as we were concerned, we were disappointed because we wanted a release November 18, [but] ... it did nothing but good for us.'[22] Tracking reports, undertaken on behalf of Warner Bros. to trace market expectations of *Natural Born Killers*, put audience awareness of the film at 77 per cent two weeks before the February opening, against a norm of 30 per cent.[23] By the week of release, general audience awareness stood at 83 per cent against a norm of 50 per cent, with an impressive 94 per cent awareness among the target audience of males under 25. Interest among young women was also above average. The report stated: 'Opening prospects look good to very good. ... "Definite" interest is an above average 32 per cent overall (norm is 20 per cent). It is concentrated among younger males, where a far above average six in ten (60 per cent) express "definite" interest in seeing the film. ... First choice among opening and released films is 19 per cent overall. Among males and younger females, it leads all other films in the marketplace by a wide margin.'[24] Research for Warner Bros. also showed that the film was most commonly characterised by respondents as 'violent'. Asked what they specifically remembered hearing about *Natural Born Killers*, 32 per cent of those aware of the film mentioned violence.[25] The same document reported that 'all the hype' was the 'positive' factor most widely mentioned by those aware of the film (18 per cent of the sample).[26]

In this context, Warner Bros.' new advertising task was not to boost awareness of the existence of the film – this had effectively been achieved by media coverage – but to clear up lingering confusion about whether or not it was banned and to stress its imminent release. 'We said, right the job we've got to do is just say, "the film is here, it's ready to see",' noted George. The company reduced its television advertising spend drastically, cutting the length of its commercials by two-thirds and targeting them very closely on its core audience. Two adverts were assembled, one featuring Woody Harrelson as Mickey, aimed at men, the other, featuring Juliette Lewis as Mallory and backed by the film's 'love theme' (a cover of Lou Reed's 'Sweet Jane' by Cowboy Junkies) aimed at women. The Mickey version was the most widely used. The most important advertising spots were booked in programmes with guaranteed large male audiences showing in the third week of February: the heavyweight boxing bout between Frank Bruno and Rodolfo Martin; the League Cup football semi-final between Liverpool and Crystal Palace; *The Yardies*, a programme about crime syndicates in Jamaica and Britain; and the James Bond film *The Living Daylights*. A commercial was also booked for the more gender-mixed audience watching the British music industry awards. George explained:

> Normally we would go with 30-second commercials trying to explain the story. In this case we didn't have to explain the story. Everybody knew it was a film about killers, it was a film from Oliver Stone, it was about serial killers featuring Woody Harrelson and Juliette Lewis, and it was bad and it was violent and it was nasty and all that sort of stuff. So all we had to say was 'the most controversial film you've seen [sic] this year is now available'. Ten seconds. Very specific targeting of the TV spots we bought. And we also didn't buy as many ratings as we would normally buy. We would normally buy something like 200, 250 ratings. In this case we just bought about a hundred, literally just cherry-picking the TV spots that we wanted.[27]

The press advertising campaign was aimed largely 'downmarket'. Warner Bros. booked adverts in *The Sun*, *Daily Mirror*, *Daily Star*, *Today*, *Daily Express*, *Daily Record*, *News of the World*, *Sunday*

Mirror and *Sunday People*. The company used *The Big Issue*, *Evening Standard*, *Time Out*, *The Guardian* and *The Independent* to target more 'upscale' audiences. The advert featured a head-shot of Harrelson as Mickey and was tagged with the line, 'The controversy starts when you see the film'. The company also paid for a series of London Underground six-sheet posters with the same tagline. Inserted in quotation marks, the line was a 'cheat' drawn up by company staff rather than a genuine press comment, and was necessitated by the lack of positive reviews.[28] George commented:

> We sat here and said let's use a quote and we didn't really have any quotes, the critics didn't really like it. So we said what the bloody hell can we do? So we just came up with five [sic]: 'Fuel the controversy. See the film.' 'Most films claim to be. This one is. Controversial.' And there was another two, but we felt those other ones were sort of like Warner Bros. trying to whip up the controversy, which we didn't want to be seen to be doing. So it was a statement of fact, but we put it in a quote which was 'controversy starts when you see the film'.[29]

Heavy publicity schedules were arranged for director Oliver Stone (who was featured in 'mainstream' television and press)[30] and producer Jane Hamsher (featured largely in niche publications). Stars Harrelson and Lewis, who had been on the original European press tour in November, were not brought back to Britain.

After initially causing dismay at Warner Bros. amid fears of the film being refused a certificate outright, the BBFC delay resulted in substantial cost savings for the distributor, and also boosted revenue. The estimated rental (distributor's share of box office gross) for the scheduled November release was £800,000, with advertising and publicity spend set at around £600,000. In the run-up to the film's February opening, Warner Bros. kept its rental estimate at £800,000 but the advertising and publicity budget was cut to £450,000. However, after *Natural Born Killers'* relatively strong opening, the rental was revised upwards to £1.3 million, giving the company a £500,000 improvement on initial income predictions, to add to a saving of £150,000 on advertising costs.[31] *Natural Born Killers* opened on 203 screens nationally. This exhibition pattern was not as wide as the saturation releases enjoyed by *Basic Instinct* and *Bram Stoker's Dracula*, or by Warner Bros.' big spring release, *Disclosure* (Barry Levinson, United States, 1994). Nevertheless, distribution staff reasoned that potential viewers for *Natural Born Killers* had been successfully reached by the marketing campaign and so would be prepared to make a slightly longer trip to the cinema if neces- sary.[32] The moral panic in the media, and the resulting delay in the classification of the film effectively facilitated the company's differ- entiation of *Natural Born Killers* as an outrageous and attractive product. George commented:

> We've done better in this country than any other country in Europe, but they all released in November. What it was, as a marketing tack, was that there were so many things out of our control – censorship issue, media hysteria, trying to fix a date – so many things outside our control, but what you have to do with that ... is, the bits you can con- trol, [you] try and do the best with.

What constructions of, and attitudes towards, audiences for *Natural Born Killers* were mobilised in press coverage of the film, both before and after the BBFC finally classified it? What were the inter- nal logics of discourses of anxiety, and how did these compare to Warner Bros.' perceptions of its target markets? It is to these ques- tions that I now turn.

Natural Born Killers' reception in the press

A number of distinct templates for thinking and writing about *Nat- ural Born Killers* and its audiences can be located in the media cov- erage of the film. In the mainstream press, reviews were often characterised by a pervasive hostility to the idea of any 'healthy' viewer deriving pleasure from the film, along with a common dis- course of assault on the audience, in which the film was described in terms such as 'mind-numbing' and 'overkill'.[33] Thus the reviewer in the Sunday tabloid *The People* wrote of Stone's 'efforts to shock us into submission'.[34] A review in the *Daily Mirror* commented simi- larly: 'Stone is the main exponent of the sledgehammer school of film-making, hitting us again and again with his idea that the media is responsible for society's ills'.[35] (This particular review was posi- tioned beneath two illustrated interviews with the film's stars[36] and was preceded by a full-page colour picture of Mickey and Mallory, headlined, 'Shocker they tried to ban is here'. The film was thus granted a large amount of visual impact in the pages of the *Daily Mirror*, with its 'event' status and star presences highlighted, even while the newspaper's critic lambasted it. This example illustrates the importance of locating any press review in its context on the page, and of paying proper attention to visuals and layout as well as to text.) Martin Barker has noted the guilty pleasure registered by less hostile reviewers of the film and points to 'the effective absence of any space to be an enjoying audience without condemning oneself as in some way bad'.[37] While Barker's observations hold for much of the mainstream (written) coverage accorded the film, they do not always apply to niche publications, which were more likely to be unashamedly positive about *Natural Born Killers*. Nevertheless, beyond these niche markets the film was widely excoriated for portraying murder as glamorous and fun. It was labelled a 'feature-length advertisement for mass killing' in the *Daily Mail*, and 'a tacit glorification of the two young casual killers' in *The Guardian*.[38]

While Stone repeatedly contended that *Natural Born Killers* was a serious investigation of the links between the popular media and social violence, the film was often accused of exemplifying just such a connection, via its effects on 'susceptible' audiences. These 'problematic' viewers were routinely marked in terms of class, gender and age. Mainstream press attacks on the film often noted its appeal to teenagers and young adults. As in the case of *Bram Stoker's Dracula*, denigrations of the film and an approving youth audience sometimes took the form of disparaging comparisons with MTV. This was perhaps not just because both *Natural Born Killers* and MTV use a music soundtrack and rapid editing styles, but because MTV commonly stands for popular youth culture in disapproving 'adult' discourses. Thus *Natural Born Killers* was described in *The Guardian*'s negative review as a 'two-hour slice of MTV'.[39] Another way of decrying the vacuity of the film was via a discourse hostile to styles in youth clothing. An article in *The Sunday Times* accused the film of glorifying murder via fashion, a link encapsulated in the pun that *Natural Born Killers* had inspired 'a fashion for violence'. The 'grunge' or 'punk' look of the film's costumes was placed on a spectrum of imitative behaviour being, or likely to be, undertaken by its young audience, which led all the way to possible murder: 'However vigorously Stone rejects the accusation that his film will incite more violence, he must still be thankful that most of the film's fans have only emulated Mickey and Mallory in the fashion stakes. For the time being at least.'[40]

An enjoying and influenced audience was thus a crucial part of the 'problem' presented by *Natural Born Killers*. An example of this thinking appears in the following *Sunday Times* report on copycat allegations and the BBFC classification delay, which quotes American film critic and anti-screen violence campaigner Michael Medved:

> In the most recent case a 14-year-old boy in Dallas, Texas, was accused of decapitating a girl, 13, after seeing the film; he told friends he wanted to kill someone and be 'famous, like the natural born killers'.

> Public concern increased this month after a young couple killed four people during a shooting spree in Paris. Police speculated it might have been an attempt to emulate the violence in *Natural Born Killers*, released in France a few weeks earlier.

> Michel Medved, chief film critic of the *New York Post*, believes *Natural Born Killers* is 'more dangerous than the average movie'. He said: 'Stone may claim it is a satire, but for any hormone-raddled 14-year-old the film's strongest message, that killing people is sexy, is very dangerous.'[41]

The logic of the argument here is similar to that considered but ultimately rejected in the BBFC statement discussed above. The film constitutes a problem via the subsequent violent, anti-social behaviour of its viewers. Vulnerable and yet dangerous, they may go on to victimise others. The 'hormone-raddled 14-year-old' adolescent stands as the figure of this unhealthy and dangerous audience. Familiar medical tropes of contagion and sickness, both mental and moral, are deployed here.[42] The gender of the problem viewer remains unclear in this article, although elsewhere it is evident that he is male. For example, this is how the *Daily Telegraph* anticipated the arrival of *Natural Born Killers* in Britain:

> Medved vividly describes the audience for violent films: 'drooling, hormone-addled, violence-prone, sub-literate males'. This is pretty much on target. They are the new generation of mostly white suburban teenagers, often with poor schooling, some money from 'McJobs' and time on their hands. Their latest hot fashion item is a big, baggy t-shirt bearing the slogan 'Natural Born Killer'. ... The blood from Hollywood's jackpot of violence seeps into soil already thick with the roots of dangerous social ills. At the very least, it must enrich that soil. And in that lies the argument for refusing a certificate to *Natural Born Killers*, a film which is part of the media culture it itself portrays as accelerating the cycle of real-life violence.[43]

The long-established folk devil of the hooligan raises his head here, condensing 'with great power a cluster of anxieties ... around masculinity and youth, read through the lens of class'.[44] In addition to being young, male, and 'unfit', the problem audience is represented as working class, 'sub-literate' and employed in menial jobs. (This figure bears some striking similarities with the representation of Mickey within the film as 'white trash' initially employed as a butcher's delivery boy.) There is a strong sense that this audience cannot grasp Stone's avowed satirical intentions, which, by implication, more 'mature' and educated viewers could assess and evaluate. Instead, the adolescent male will enjoy what he sees as the film's prime attraction, its violence: 'Oliver Stone claims it's satire, but American teenagers love it for the gore'.[45] News reports alleging 'copycat' killings tended to reinforce this stereotype. Five out of six reported murderers were male, and all six were in their teens or early twenties – an age range almost identical to that of the film's target audience.

Press notions of an unthinking working-class male audience for violent films have something in common with Ian George's target market of 'shit-kickers' and 'meat-heads', but crucially they pathologise them, rather than regarding them as legitimate viewers. Moreover, another significant market identified by the distributor, that provided by middle-class fans of Tarantino and 'new violence', was largely absent from hostile press accounts of the film. Clearly, it would not fit the class logic of these discourses of anxiety. In the cases where such an audience was mentioned, commentators typically suggested that it would be disappointed because Stone's film lacked Tarantino's subtlety and wit.[46] In this formulation, critics argued that Stone had underestimated an audience which deserved better. For example, a review in *The Times* commented: 'The flimsy, derivative storyline becomes almost obliterated; while Stone hammers his satirical points so relentlessly that he seems to share [reporter character] Gayle's withering view of his audience – "the nitwits out there in Zombieland"'.[47] The problem audiences discussed above were typically marked as other in terms of age (younger) and class (lower) than the commentators and implied readerships of mainstream newspapers. By contrast, articles in diverse publications accusing Stone of patronising an implicitly intelligent audience tended to make no such distancing efforts, but rather to include the writer and reader in the assumed audience for the film. A review in the best-selling Sunday tabloid the *News of the World* commented: 'It's loud, violent, glossy and superficial. It expects nothing more from its audience than they sit back and let it wash over them, offering the feeblest and most overstated point of view – too much TV is bad for you. ... Stone even has the words TOO MUCH TV projected onto Harrelson's chest. Duh. Subtle it really isn't. Insulting it is.'[48]

Some articles that made positive claims for *Natural Born Killers*, including several based on interviews with Stone, offered alternative notions of its effect upon the audience. They assumed a hitherto unthinking, passive audience which, instead of being entertained by dangerously enjoyable violence and gore, was to be shocked awake by the film's confrontational stance and its refusal to allow the conventional pleasures of spectatorial identification. Interviewed in *Sight and Sound* magazine, Stone claimed to challenge audiences' complicity in violent entertainment:

> Mickey and Mallory are in charge of the world, they're having fun killing and you're having 'fun' watching it. It makes you confront yourself. ... The usual characters are not there – who is the good guy, what is the catharsis of the film? It robs the audience of that and makes them question their watching, which is subversive.[49]

An ambivalent assessment was offered by the reviewer for *Today*, who combined two of the models of audience response discussed so far. From this perspective, the assault on the viewer launched by the film is ultimately worthwhile, because it makes him or her think: 'The result is an assault on the senses that will make you wince, maybe on occasion force you to avert your eyes, but which dictates that you think about the supply and demand factor in the mass media kaleidoscope of life's darker colours.'[50]

Natural Born Killers' problematisation of audience pleasure was also noted by the popular film magazine *Empire*, which nevertheless located consoling attractions in its innovative form, its observations on contemporary America, and the incongruous casting of Woody Harrelson (previously best known for his part in the widely syndicated American sitcom *Cheers*) as a mass murderer:

> It's very difficult to describe NBK as 'good entertainment' in any classical, Merchant-Ivory sense of the phrase. ...While by no means a work with universal appeal, NBK is nevertheless a must-see for anyone with even a cursory interest in the exploitation of violence, the state of 90s society, or stunningly innovative filmmaking. You also get to see the formerly wide-eyed and innocent Woody from Cheers going

bananas with a shotgun, which has to be worth the ticket price on its own.[51]

With its acknowledgement of legitimate and 'healthy' viewer invest-ments in *Natural Born Killers*, both 'serious' and fun-oriented, this is perhaps the nearest a British press review came to Warner's for-mulation of a self-consciously hip 'new violence' audience for the film.

Some other youth-oriented publications located in the film further opportunities for audience pleasures which had been largely over-looked or pathologised in the mainstream press.[52] This was true, for example, of British heavy metal weekly *Kerrang!* – a title serving the third target market identified by Warner Bros.' Ian George, that of rock fans. *Natural Born Killers* was granted extensive exposure in *Kerrang!* in the week of its release, comprising a front cover, a one-page poster and three full feature pages, plus a competition to win a T-shirt and soundtrack CD, and further references in three articles on film music.[53] Interviews with producer Jane Hamsher and Trent Reznor, producer of the *Natural Born Killers* soundtrack, testified to the con-vergence of audience tastes for certain films (particularly horror) and heavy rock music. The magazine presented a relatively rare positive portrayal of an approving viewer and mocked anxieties in the main-stream media about the film and its anti-social audience effects:

> So is it a good film? Yeah, definitely. In its own, hyper-modern, sign-of-the-times kind of way, 'NBK' is an OTT classic. It's got ultraviolence, even if it's often surprisingly restrained in depiction; it makes you chuckle, flinch and generally relish the sheer chaotic wickedness of it all. It also makes you go out and kill strangers. That last one was, of course, a joke.[54]

In summary, press constructions of an approving audience for *Nat-ural Born Killers* bore some similarities with conceptions mobilised by the distributor. Both sectors characterised the film's core viewers as young and predominantly male. However, press accounts varied widely in their attitude towards this imagined audience. In main-stream publications such as newspapers, the film and its audience were commonly pathologised, with little or no space allowed for 'healthy' viewer pleasures. The denigration of the film was often achieved through the expression of concerns about its supposed 'problem' audience. This was marked as 'other' and distinguished from such publications' assumed readerships by being young, moronic and impressionable. The film was labelled an advert for murder, its violent prescriptions about to be slavishly followed by susceptible teenagers and young adults. Such accounts typically constructed and scapegoated a male, undereducated and working-class spectator. His predicted anti-social behaviour on seeing the film stood as justification for banning it in Britain. The gender and class of this archetypal 'problem' viewer had something in common with the paradigm circulating at Warner Bros. of a working class male 'meat-head' who enjoyed violent films. However, a crucial difference is that distribution staff conceived of this target spectator as safe, and his pleasure in screen violence as valid, in contrast to the dangers perceived by disapproving commentators. The distributor's other significant target markets, namely rock fans and the audience for 'new violence' films (seen as largely middle class), were typically ignored in the mainstream press. Beyond the adult mainstream, some youth and subcultural publications endorsed spectatorial enjoyment of *Natural Born Killers* as healthy and, moreover, as 'hip'. For magazines such as *Kerrang!* (and, to a lesser extent, *Empire*) the violent content, humour and music of the film were seen as legitimate attractions, while crucially remaining outside the mainstream. Disapproving perspectives were ridiculed and rejected, and the film's nonconformity and 'anti-social' stance were celebrated rather than lamented.

Audience responses

In the last part of this chapter I make use of audience research to investigate how actual cinemagoers perceived themselves and 'other' viewers, asking to what extent they shared, or deviated from, constructions of the audience for *Natural Born Killers* made by the distributor and commentators in the press. In the process I examine respondents' views on screen violence and its possible impact upon audiences. I also investigate the significance of secondary texts in providing information about the film, asking how potential viewers made use of this material. A total of 300 questionnaires were given out to cinemagoers at a multi-screen town centre cinema, in two separate batches over a period of four weeks. The first questionnaire, timed to coincide with the run-up to *Natural Born Killers*' release, was largely concerned with what respondents knew about, and expected from, the film. The second targeted viewers at screenings of the film in its first two weeks of release. As in the two preceding audience studies, this survey produced a self-selected sample, rather than a statistically representative one. Ultimately, 104 questionnaires were returned, with the response spread fairly evenly across both batches. Gender breakdown was also even, with 50 questionnaires returned by women, and 54 by men. The overwhelming majority of respondents described themselves, via the option provided, as 'white European'. (In addition, three respondents wrote their own categories as 'white British', and one as 'African/European'.) Around half of all respondents fitted the film's target audience profile of 18 to 24. The spread of informants' occupations indicated that both middle-class and working-class cinemagoers were represented in the survey. (See appendix 10 for details.)

The first batch of questionnaires was given out to cinemagoers in the two weeks prior to the opening of *Natural Born Killers*. Questions were devised to assess whether respondents intended to see the film, and their conceptions of *Natural Born Killers* and its likely audience.[55] I wanted to investigate perceptions held by those who had no intention of watching the film, as well as among those planning to see it. One hundred questionnaires were handed out, of which 45 were returned. Of those responding, 36 had heard of the film in one way or another. Of these, 11 stated their intention to see the film, while 12 had no desire to see it, and 11 remained undecided. A further two respondents had already watched *Natural Born Killers* on pirate video. If informants had heard of the film at all, they were highly likely to be aware of its controversial reputation. Of 36 respondents, 27 mentioned one or more of the following: a delay in the film's release (often remembered as a 'ban'); 'hype' or 'fuss' over the film; 'controversy'; and allegations of 'copycat' killings. Press and television coverage were regularly cited as sources of information, as were marketing forms such as cinema trailers and press advertising (each of which was recalled far more commonly than television spots for the film), and conversations with friends, relations and work colleagues. Among those not intending to see *Natural Born Killers*, the film was commonly understood and characterised as 'violent'. (The same was true of undecided respondents. As noted above, research for Warner Bros. came to a similar conclusion.) This was the prime reason given for avoiding the film at the cinema. Nevertheless, these respondents often expected the film to be a commercial success precisely because of its violent con-

tent, which was perceived as appealing to other viewers. Unenthusi-
astic informants often appeared to share common media assumptions about, and suspicions of, an approving audience, which they
typically characterised as relatively young and immature, and often
as male. However, the very media controversy over *Natural Born
Killers* which raised these doubts was also seen by disapproving
respondents to be abetting the film's commercial prospects:

[Have you heard of *Natural Born Killers*? If so, please say what you
know about it.]

The director. violent? being blamed in the States for copycat killings.

[Where did you get this information from?]

News, friends.

[Do you intend to see *Natural Born Killers*? Please give reasons for
your answer.]

No. Don't like violence.

[Do you think *Natural Born Killers* will be a commercial success?
Please give reasons for your answer.]

Yes. Papers condemning a film always inspires interest.

[Who do you think *Natural Born Killers* will appeal to? Please tick an
answer] Young men.
                (*1:35: anon. male. Financial software consultant, age 27.)

[Have you heard of *Natural Born Killers*? If so, please say what you
know about it.]

violent – little else known.

[Where did you get this information from?]

Media and press action on whether it should be released in U.K.

[Do you intend to see *Natural Born Killers*? Please give reasons for
your answer.]

No. Not my type of film.

[Do you think *Natural Born Killers* will be a commercial success?
Please give reasons for your answer.]

Yes. Notoriety and publicity gained. The 'shock' factor and the social
standing of having seen it amongst young adults.

[Who do you think *Natural Born Killers* will appeal to? Please tick an answer]

Young men and women.

(*1:44: anon. female. Information manager, age 32.)

In some cases, the audience for *Natural Born Killers* was perceived as unstable and potentially dangerous, again much as media discourses had suggested. For instance:

[Have you heard of *Natural Born Killers*? If so, please say what you know about it.]

Directed by Stone. Interviewed on Radio 4 *Start the Week*. ... Sounded violent, unhappy, ignoring victims of crime concentrated on glorifying criminal actions – disgusting.

[Do you intend to see *Natural Born Killers*? Please give reasons for your answer.]

No. Film makers should produce a product which entertains, educates and enlivens one's being. I see that being horrified and disgusted is a human reaction and can cause a lot of debate but it does not add to my human condition – after all stepping into a dog turd gets the same reaction Q.E.D.

[Do you think *Natural Born Killers* will be a commercial success? Please give reasons for your answer.]

Don't know. There are a lot of degenerate 'loonys' out there who would be stimulated by this sort of film.

[Who do you think *Natural Born Killers* will appeal to? Please tick an answer]

Young men.

(*1:11: Peter, male Paramedic, age 44.)

Thus, informants who had decided not to watch *Natural Born Killers* typically characterised the film as violent, and its audience as young, male or mixed in gender terms. For some, there was a risk that an element of this audience could be 'stimulated' by the film in dangerous ways. *Natural Born Killers* was also often seen to be the commercial beneficiary of widespread media coverage, which respondents themselves had made use of in forming their conceptions of the film. These conclusions also hold true for several undecided cinemagoers. Two further points emerge here. Firstly, the dangerously susceptible 'other' audience is always located elsewhere; the concerned informant typically places him/herself beyond media influence. Secondly, some of the anxieties expressed here are significantly similar to those mobilised in the British press. It is important, however, not to conclude from this that the press sets an agenda which is automatically followed by its readers. Such an assertion simply substitutes one mode of direct media effects (that of the press) for another (that of moving images). Instead, the researcher needs to take account of what Graham Murdock calls the dynamics of 'translation'.[56] Concerns such as those raised here – and in other cinemagoers' accounts discussed below – may certainly be shaped by moral panics in the press, but the exact ways in which such discourses are taken up and made use by individuals will be variable and context-specific.

Respondents intending to see *Natural Born Killers* were less concerned about the potentially damaging effects of the film's depiction of violence. Indeed, if violence was mentioned, it was usually cited as a prime attraction:

[Have you heard of *Natural Born Killers*? If so, please say what you know about it.]

It's about serial killers as US folk heroes. ultra violent. It was initially banned. Lots of the most interesting scenes have probably been censored.

[Where did you get this information from?]

Mags, *Newsnight*, *Late Show*, newspapers, friend who saw it in Paris.

[Do you intend to see *Natural Born Killers*? Please give reasons for your answer.]

Yes. sounds like the kind of film I like.

(*1:42: anon. male. Student, age 23.)

The following positive account of *Natural Born Killers* – already seen by the informant on pirate video prior to its theatrical release – offers a characterisation of an approving audience which contrasts with those propounded in media outrage over the film. Here, *Natural Born Killers* is seen to appeal to young men and 'any intelligent people' rather than the unhealthy, moronic or susceptible cited in press scares:

[Have you heard of *Natural Born Killers*? If so, please say what you know about it.]

I know it's the story of Micky [sic] and Mallory a young couple who go on a killing spree that starts a la *Badlands* with the girls parents. They are jailed but escape on live television. I know the so called 'uncut' version coming out is in fact the heavily censored American version. Quentin Tarantino has disowned it.

[Where did you get this information from?]

Firstly from 'Ban the filth' stories in the papers and on T.V. Secondly I received a pirate video for my birthday and watched it on Xmas Day instead of *Robin Hood*.

[Have you spoken to anybody about *Natural Born Killers*?]

I believe the film should be released uncut. My mother disagreed after reading all the ignorant journalism.

[Do you intend to see *Natural Born Killers*? Please give reasons for your answer.]

Yes. I enjoyed it so much on video I wanted to see it on the 'Big Screen'.

[Who do you think *Natural Born Killers* will appeal to? Please tick an answer]

Young men, 'any intelligent people'.

(*1:1: David. Unemployed male, age 23.)

Camille Bacon-Smith and Tyrone Yarborough have argued that press stories and reviews 'train' viewers in how to approach a film.[57] In the case above, however, the dynamic at work is not so straightforward and unidirectional. Instead of being cued to mobilise a certain set of expectations, the informant actively derives information from press coverage explicitly demanding that the film not be screened ('ban the filth'). He thus displays a dual response to the moral panic in the media. Negative coverage of the film is both utilised and dismissed as 'ignorant journalism'. A positive orientation towards *Natural Born Killers* enables details of the film to be gleaned from hostile reports even while the respondent rejects the interpretive frame in which such data is embedded.

Among some respondents, advertising and media 'hype' could be seen to play a part in establishing intent to view and raising expectations of the film. (This evidence supports and elaborates upon the findings of Warner Bros.' audience tracking report.) For example:

[Do you intend to see *Natural Born Killers*? Please give reasons for your answer.]

Yes, DEFINITELY. Woody's image has completely changed and the hype of the film is contagious. I also think the title is one that is very gripping – hopefully an indication of the film.

[Do you think *Natural Born Killers* will be a commercial success? Please give reasons for your answer.]

Don't know. I have seen films before that have been hyped up and I have been disappointed with the film itself. ... I hope it will live up to what I am expecting – I always do!

[Who do you think *Natural Born Killers* will appeal to? Please tick an answer]

Young men and women.

(*1:33: anon. female. Student, age 23.)

Prospective viewers typically failed to share anxieties expressed in the media about the film's likely effect upon its audiences, and some explicitly rejected these fears. Nevertheless, media coverage appeared to be an important source of low-level information about the film, even when accompanying negative judgements were ignored or refuted. Whatever their opinions of the film, the majority of respondents saw its commercial prospects benefiting from extensive coverage in the media, as well as from the marketing campaign.

I shall now draw on the second batch of questionnaires to investigate further responses to the film and, in particular, notions of 'dangerous' or 'safe' audiences. Questionnaires were handed out to cinemagoers following screenings of *Natural Born Killers* during the first two weeks of its release. Of 200 questionnaires given out, 59 were returned.[58] Respondents were initially asked to state why they had gone to see *Natural Born Killers*, and their reactions to it. This section was followed by more targeted questions (see appendix 9). One effect of the marketing campaign for, and media coverage of, *Natural Born Killers* was to encourage people to see the film to make up their own minds, and to decide whether the attention and criticism it had received were warranted. As in the two previous case studies, *Basic Instinct* and *Bram Stoker's Dracula*, this motivation was mentioned repeatedly by informants. The opinion of friends who recommended the film was also cited regularly.

Among positive respondents, *Natural Born Killers* was often characterised as a 'cool' film. Factors cited as contributing to this status included the participation of Stone, Tarantino, and Harrelson, along with the film's notoriety, violence, visual style, music soundtrack and black humour (the last was an attraction only very rarely mentioned in the marketing campaign or reviews). In addition, the love story element of the film, which was underplayed in advertising and all but ignored in media coverage, featured as a significant and unexpected attraction in one woman's account. This raises the question: how many more female viewers would *Natural Born Killers* have attracted had it been aggressively marketed to women as a (violent) romance, in much the same way that *Bram Stoker's Dracula* was positioned as a gothic romance?

Approving viewers often inserted *Natural Born Killers* into interpretive frames based on entertainment values, rather than on anxieties raised in the press and by broadcasters. The majority appeared largely unconcerned by the hostile media climate surrounding the film. Several expressed an interest in seeing *Natural Born Killers* more than once, or had already done so. Five examples will serve to illustrate such positive accounts. Judging by the films to which *Natural Born Killers* is compared here, this selection includes people understood in industry terms as 'new violence' fans and so-called 'meat-heads'. But this division is blurred by the first account, which draws on repertoires assigned to both groups. It appears, then, that from audience perspectives these two groups might not always have been as distinct as institutional constructions suggested:

[Reasons for seeing the film:]

Because I like who starred in it and the writer/director, looked like a good story in reviews I've seen and I like a bit of violence in a well made film.

[Reactions:] Very very good, loved it, better than I'd hoped it would be, Mickey and Mallarie [sic] were so 'cool'! The story was so strong and the directing was so good, the stars were cast well, I didn't move once the whole film, it had my total attention from beginning to end, it's the sort of quality film I'd like to see more of. [Part One]

[Are there any elements of the film that you particularly liked or disliked?]

When Mallarie kicked shit out of those blokes at the very start, every thing was calm till that bloke called her 'pussy'. When the reporter picked up a gun and started shooting the guards in the prison.

[Do you think *Natural Born Killers* will be a commercial success?]

Yes. I'm a pretty good judge of films plus I'll tell everybody I know to watch it. Plus a lot of people still just watch films for violence, ie, Seagal, Van Damme type films.

[Is there anything else you would like to say about *Natural Born Killers*?]

It's nice to see the bad guys win for once.

(*2:54: Steven. Unemployed male, age 22.)

I like Tarantino and Ol[iver] Stone. I was mesmerised during film. Liked it a lot. Would like to watch it again. [Part One]

[Are there any elements of the film that you particularly liked or disliked?]

Liked script, acting, PHOTOGRAPHY (V. MUCH) and MUSIC.

[Is there anything else you would like to say about *Natural Born Killers*?]

Cool film – very mesmerising.

(*2:37: anon. male. Student, age 22.)

I saw *Natural Born Killers* initially on a pirate video at a friends house before its release in the cinema. I probably would not have chosen to go to the cinema to see it. Having seen and enjoyed it I went to see it at the cinema with a friend. I enjoyed the film very much, particularly the cinematic effects and the black comedy. [Part One]

[Did *Natural Born Killers* remind you of any other films?]

It provoked the same reaction as *Thelma and Louise* ie. exhilaration, liberation.

(*2:29: anon. female. Homeless worker, age 27.)

[Was the film what you expected or not?]

No, it wasn't as violent as I thought, it was violent but not what I expected. Didn't expect it to be particularly romantic but it was.

[Are there any elements of the film that you particularly liked or disliked?]

Liked the romance in the storyline because it wasn't the sickly, soppy normal romance in films, liked the flashbacks and imagery.

(*2:30: Heidi. Female sixth-form student, age 18.)

[Reasons for seeing the film:]

Told it was good. Looked good/tv clips etc (*Moviewatch*).

[Reactions:] Best film I've ever seen. Brilliant.

[Would you say *Natural Born Killers* has a message?]

kill kill kill

[Is there anything else you would like to say about *Natural Born Killers*?]

Brilliant The Bollocks Fuck the censors
                                   (*2:26: anon. male. Soldier, age 27.)[59]

The last account here consists of a particular presentation of self, centred on a specific kind of overtly aggressive (heterosexual) masculinity – an identity both validated and regimented through employment in the military.[60] It also asserts particular pleasures in nonconformity, produced firstly by investing in *Natural Born Killers* as an enjoyable celebration of an unregulated fighting ability (deployed by Mickey and Mallory), and secondly in the social act of viewing the film – a confrontational gesture which flouts the official disapproval of 'the censors'.

Natural Born Killers thus appeared 'cool', exciting and/or liberating to some viewers. With its challenging visual form, powerful music soundtrack, and plot centred on violent social transgression and law-breaking by two relatively young protagonists, the film can be seen to have something in common with what J.P. Telotte has termed the 'midnight movie'. This is a type of cult film appealing to an audience of teenagers and young adults who view themselves and their cultural tastes as distinct from the 'adult' mainstream. According to Telotte, a cult film is partly the product of identifiable textual structures and properties such as themes of alienation from society and rebellion against social constraints, references to sex and drugs,[61] and a rock music soundtrack. It is also 'produced' through the activities of subcultural communities and audiences.[62] Exhibition practices may also play their part here: 'The transgression of exhibition applies especially to the phenomenon of "midnight movies" for such screenings by definition go against the logic of traditional "prime time" exhibition.'[63] Thus, although the cult film is to a large extent 'made' by its audience, certain textual characteristics and extratextual factors which signal transgression may predispose viewers towards cult devotion. *Natural Born Killers* appeared to fit these criteria for several positive respondents. The appeal of social transgression was even acknowledged by some who were ultimately disappointed with the film:

> [Reasons for seeing the film:] I like Quentin Tarantino films – Because of the media hype surrounding the problems allowing NBK's to be shown. ie – the trouble/problems the film encountered trying to be allowed to be shown encouraged my perception of the film as shocking/violent/against societal values therefore of added attraction.
>
> [Reactions:] I was shocked, disgusted, frightened and a little bit horrified.
>
> (*2: 53: LP. Female care worker, age 18.)

The appeal of *Natural Born Killers* as a cult film which polarised opinion and was disliked by those not 'in the know', was expressed by a member of the audience at a sold-out one-off screening of the film at the Prince Charles, London – an independent cinema devoted to repertory and cultish screenings.[64] This viewer owned the soundtrack album and film poster, and had seen *Natural Born Killers* 'six or seven' times previously on pirate video:

> It's a rush of blood, love and philosophy. … Either you love it or hate it, there's nothing in between.
>
> (*3:7: Lissy. Female nanny, age 19.)

Despite the BBFC's investigation and ultimate certification of *Natural Born Killers*, the film's career since 1995 has been shaped by continuing fears over copycat violence. At the time of writing in 2001, Warner Home Video has yet to release *Natural Born Killers* on video in the UK. The company postponed video release indefinitely in 1996 in the wake of events at Dunblane, Scotland, where 16 children and one adult were killed by a gunman who then shot himself.[65] The BBFC had granted the video an '18' classification, uncut. Even allowing for the (unquantified) availability of *Natural Born Killers* on pirate video, it seems that the lack of an official video release enhanced the film's life in repertory cinemas and at late-night screenings. (For example, *Natural Born Killers* played at the Warner West End cinema in Leicester Square, London, daily from its initial release in February 1995 until June of that year. It was then screened at late shows and one-offs in the capital a total of 62 times between mid-June 1995 and May 1997.[66] It appears that this patchy but continuing theatrical run was sustained (at least partly) by cult interest, with fans making repeat viewings of the film.)[67] Despite Warners' decision to withhold the video, *Natural Born Killers* was screened in November 1997 by the new terrestrial television operator Channel Five, in a move greeted with dismay by the National Viewers' and Listeners' Association.[68] In the United States, the controversy over the film was revived by celebrity author John Grisham's well-publicised suggestion that Stone and Warner Bros. be sued over an alleged copycat murder in Mississippi.[69]

'Safe' and 'dangerous' audiences

Several respondents who did not enjoy, or were disturbed by, *Natural Born Killers* employed schematic models of unhealthy, vulnerable and/or potentially dangerous approving audiences. One reason for this may be that if one is upset or unimpressed by a film, the denigration of 'other', more enthusiastic reactions both stems from and supports a 'positive' self-identity associated with the original response. Another reason may concern viewers' exposure to satellite texts around the film. As I have shown, similar models of 'problem' audiences were evident in several media accounts of *Natural Born Killers*. There is thus a notable convergence of the discourses, constructions and interpretive frames mobilised in disapproving journalistic narratives and those of some informants. It is not my aim to prove here any causal relationship leading from the one to the other. However, it seems possible that discursive frameworks and schemata derived from, and/or reinforced by, popular media texts, such as stereotypes and oppositions, became integrated into cinemagoers' broader opinions.[70] This is not to argue that disapproving viewer reactions to *Natural Born Killers* were determined in a straightforward, unmediated and unidirectional fashion by media coverage. Research suggests that readers are typically most responsive to press reports which reconfirm their existing attitudes, orientations and world views.[71] Moreover, integration and other means of information processing involve active and negotiating individuals rather than passive ones, and are complex, indirect and individually variable rather than direct or uniformly enacted.[72] Such processes may take place not only through exposure to the press, television or radio, but also through the dissemination and mediation of media discourses via everyday talk.[73] The following cases show respondents framing their responses in rhetorical patterns similar to those mobilised in the media reception of *Natural Born Killers*. These accounts express concern about the film via models of audiences marked variously as unhealthy, possibly dangerous, or as impressionable teenagers.

A disappointed Stone fan, who rated the film 'very' violent, 'a bit' offensive and 'not at all' enjoyable, wrote:

> [Are there any elements of the film that you particularly liked or disliked?]:
>
> The editing is amazing. The film is worthless.
>
> [Who do you think *Natural Born Killers* will appeal to?]
>
> If this film actually appeals to anybody those people have serious problems.
>
> [Should it have been banned, as some papers suggested?]
>
> It should have been banned, full stop.
>
> [Is there anything else you would like to say about *Natural Born Killers*?]
>
> 'Don't see it' should be sprayed across all the posters.
>
> (*2:38: Jude. Male decorator, age 30.)

Initially attracted to *Natural Born Killers* by its association with Tarantino and its controversial, anti-establishment reputation, the next respondent found the film shocking and frightening, and thought it should have been banned. Her concerns about the impact of the film were expressed via speculation about its possible effect on children, standing here as the prototype of a vulnerable and inappropriate audience:

> I was shocked, disgusted, frightened and a little bit horrified. My first thought was – Christ what if children watched this film? I actually found the film (in terms of stress) very heavy and difficult; also as it pulls on all negative feelings/emotions, with very little dramatic relief. [Part One]
>
> (*2:53: LP. Female care worker, age 18.)

The respondent also cited an American 'copycat' killing in expressing concern about violence perpetrated by spectators of *Natural Born Killers*.

[Do you think *Natural Born Killers* can be blamed for violence in society?]

Not on its own, but it could be seen to contribute ie. copy of Mickey and Mallory in USA already.[74]

The absence of a reassuring, prophylactic distance between fictional images and 'real life' is very clear in the next account. The respondent is concerned not with the effects of the film upon others, but with its impact on her own anxieties:

I went to see *Natural Born Killers* because I heard from a couple of people that it was good. ... I also hadn't been to the cinema for a while and as my friends were going already to see it I thought I might as well.

My initial reaction was total shock and I felt generally stunned. This was mainly because of the fact that those situations where people were being brutally murdered could happen to anyone at any time – it just takes some maniac to go out and kill and your whole life could be ripped apart. With a horror film you can put it out of your mind as unreal and would never happen to you. But the fact that this could happen to you (be victim of maniacs) made it really frightening.

I also found the portrayal of their total disrespect for life very disturbing and frightening – the thought that some people may really think that way was really distressing. This film really brought home some of the fears I have after watching the national news – but it made a much bigger impression on me.

(*2:52: Jolene. Female student, age 19.)

This viewer's sense of the proximity and relevance of the violence enacted on screen is what produces her feeling of being at risk. In her account, the random murders represented in *Natural Born Killers* cross the border dividing 'unreal' violence (as in a horror film) from everyday experience, and are compared instead to the 'real' violence mediated through television news.[75] However, it is the film images which have more immediacy, and hence pose a more potent threat, inculcating in the respondent a sense that the violence could happen to her.

In the next case, the informant does not go so far as to call for *Natural Born Killers* to be banned. However, in discussing motives for repeat viewings of the film, she adopts a binary logic, distinguishing between defensible and indefensible audience activities. Initial curiosity and thoughtful critical analysis are seen as legitimate, unhealthy pleasure and enjoyment are not:

> [Do you think *Natural Born Killers* will be a commercial success?]
>
> Don't know. People may watch it out of curiosity initially but I think if people go back and watch the film two or three times for reasons of enjoyment rather than analytically there's something wrong.
>
> [Who do you think *Natural Born Killers* will appeal to?]
>
> It depends on the individual's mental balance it may appeal to people who like the violence, but also because it is thought provoking.
>
> (*2:48: Jacqueline. Female housewife and student, age 25.)

Having testified to the influence of the film on their own attitudes, some respondents then rhetorically shifted this influence on to viewers marked as 'other', typically represented as more vulnerable and/or dangerous than themselves. The construction of, and differentiation between, distinct audiences occurred even among some respondents who enjoyed the film. In the next case, an informant expresses anxiety about the film's possible effects on others who may be vulnerable or susceptible, while she herself remains safely beyond influence:

> I thought it was a good film, I liked the camera tricks of distorting the faces etc. It was different, basically about a very wild and violent couple which [illegible] the worlds not so perfect anymore anyway. I thought the film was good but could disturb some people or influence some. [Part One]
>
> [Does film violence matter?]
>
> Yes, to some people who can be influenced by things like this, but to some people I don't think it does anything, it doesn't to me.
>
> (*2:23: anon. female. Beauty therapist, age 21.)

Other viewers noticed changes in themselves during or after watching *Natural Born Killers*. A Woody Harrelson fan wrote:

> A very disturbing film, but one that I would definitely go and see again although I wouldn't recommend it to the faint hearted. I did find that being a very placid person, it did make me feel quite aggressive when I left the cinema. [Part One]
>
> (*2:46: Christine. Female secretary/computer operator, age 25.)

The next informant reported that her value system temporarily shifted while watching the film. In addition, she differentiated between different modes of screen violence, by drawing a distinction

between the style and impact of killings in *Natural Born Killers* and
those portrayed in conventional action films:

> Overall, I enjoyed the film a lot. A tremendous effort must have gone
> into making it. The actors/actresses were particularly well cast.
> Towards the end of the film I started to believe that murder isn't really
> a bad thing at all. [Part One]

> [Do you think *Natural Born Killers* can be blamed for violence in soci-
> ety?]

> I think this film could help push people 'over the edge' more than a
> straightforward 'action' film, as you are constantly being bombarded
> by images of killing.
>
> (*2:25: anon. female. Civil servant, age 30.)

While she herself is not pushed 'over the edge' by *Natural Born
Killers*, the respondent has already attested to the powerful, if less
drastic, effect the film has had on her. This is an essentially positive
account of the film which nevertheless shares some ground with discourses of anxiety and audience effects used to pathologise the film
and its audience in the popular media. Here, as in many press attacks
on the film, *Natural Born Killers* is characterised by an egregious
level of violence which constitutes an assault or bombardment on
the audience, and by the potentially destabilising effects it has on the
moral and social values of viewers.

By contrast, other respondents overtly rejected media scares. Discourses about a dangerous film creating dangerous audiences were
countered by audience members identifying themselves, and hence
the film they enjoyed, as safe and non-threatening. These accounts
offered explicit rebuttals of the logic which argued that the film was
problematic because of its effects on viewers' behaviour. For example:

> I went to see the film to see if it was as bad as the media said and for a
> night out. At first I thought 'what a load of rubbish', but as I got into
> it I thought it was good and wondered what all the fuss was about it
> being so violent. It was not as bad or violent as the picture the papers
> painted about it. When I left the cinema I did not want to kill anyone
> after all it's only a film. [Part One]
>
> (*2:35: Sid. Male motor mechanic, age 24.)

Viewers' self-images as sane, rational and safe individuals were often
articulated through the assurance that they could differentiate

between representation, or fantasy, and reality. Thus watching violent acts on screen would not lead them to emulate or admire violent behaviour in 'real life'. An impervious border between screen fiction and 'reality' is central to this reasoning, as is evident in the following account. The respondent asserts that her enjoyment of mass murderers Mickey and Mallory as 'heroes' is founded on their fictional status, and would not apply to comparable non-fictional events. Indeed – and in contrast to Jolene's account discussed above – 'exciting' films such as *Natural Born Killers* are attractive to her partly because of their (safe) distance from 'reality', from which they provide an escape:

> I went to see the above film because: I like to watch exciting films which I personally don't relate to reality (my escapism). Because I wanted to see if I thought it to be as bad as the press said. I like Woody Harrelson as an actor. I did enjoy the film. It took me on a journey through love and death which I found exciting. I found it different because it portrays the murderers as heroes. It made me see them as heroes but in the film not in reality. If this story occurred in reality my views would be different. Have to see it as it is. A film (not real). [Part One]

> (*2:27: Catherine. Female post office worker, age 23.)

An assertion of competence in recognising and engaging with conventions of screen fiction, and a concomitant defence of screen violence as a valid form of entertainment is also apparent in the next account. Here watching images of 'mindless killing' provides a 'total release from the daily grind':

> Having little to do and being 200 miles from home a colleague and I decided to 'go to the movies'. We were torn between *N.B.Killers* and *Stargate*, I was keen to see *NBK* because I felt like watching some mindless killing as a total release from the daily grind. I am well able to differentiate between reality and fantasy.

> My reactions = gory, exciting, shocking and thought provoking. I could believe it could happen but only in the USA, quite simply your average American malcontent is quite likely to think they could copy the film but we in Britain I feel have more sense. [Part One]

> (*2:21: David. Male security officer, age 35.)

As in previous accounts, the non-threatening nature of *Natural Born Killers* is reliant upon its separation from 'real life'. According to the respondent this gap could be bridged through copycat behaviour, but only in America. The geographical and psychological distance between 'other' American and British audiences is crucial to his perception of the film as safe.

Conclusions

Through the case study of *Natural Born Killers* I have further developed my inquiry into some of the interrelating mechanisms shaping popular film culture in Britain: marketing practices, popular critical and journalistic coverage, and the responses and attitudes of viewers. Warner Bros.' advertising and publicity strategies worked to identify and pursue target audiences, constructing identities for the film and its consumers in the process. Viewers could appear 'hip', 'in the know' and/or socially transgressive by watching *Natural Born Killers*. The popular media contextualised the film in other ways, inserting it into certain interpretive frames, and its viewers into discursive models such as that of a classed and gendered 'problem audience'. As with *Bram Stoker's Dracula*, viewer accounts of *Natural Born Killers* sometimes articulated social and cultural distinctions. In varying rather than identical ways, the statements of respondents attesting to enjoyment of the film could be seen to contribute to their own self-perceptions as beyond the cultural 'mainstream'. The fictional events that the film portrayed on screen – law-breaking, prison riots, murder, and black or 'sick' humour – enabled it to be read as transgressive. Most of these attractions were highlighted in the marketing campaign and (often inadvertently) through media exposure. The invitation in the poster tagline to 'fuel the controversy' could be seen as an attempt to exploit the appeal of transgression. In addition, the film's 'outlaw' status was effectively certified by the BBFC delay in classification, often recalled by respondents as a 'ban'. The film could appear to some as a subcultural artefact which had been misunderstood and interfered with by 'mainstream' institutions such as 'ignorant journalism' and the BBFC. Hence, watching and enjoying *Natural Born Killers* could become a symbolic act of social transgression in itself: a defiance of authority, a message to 'fuck the censors', a rejection of media disapproval, perhaps even a positive embrace of the 'anti-social' identity mobilised in the press scare.

I have been interested here in tracking the ways in which audiences conceive of themselves and 'others', and how they relate to discourses of anxiety and concern, rather than in evaluating or attempting to (dis)prove such discourses myself. Among some respondents, the film was regarded as appealing to a 'problem' audience, characterised as unstable, susceptible to influence, and possibly anti-social and violent. This was true of some viewers who had enjoyed the film, as well as of several who had not. Approving informants sometimes drew a distinction between a vulnerable, dangerous or inappropriate audience and themselves as reasonable and safe audience members. Such conceptions of the 'problem audience' for *Natural Born Killers* often showed similarities with press attacks on the film. It was seen as assaulting the audience and posing the threat of destabilising viewers – crucially differentiated from respondents themselves as 'other', already unstable or 'on the edge'. Respondents who identified this 'other' audience appeared to have self-images as safe and sane viewers. The same is true of those who voiced no concerns about the film. They typically characterised *Natural Born Killers* as valid, enjoyable and safe entertainment. These respondents' justifications of the film and their own positive responses to it were usually based on the assertion of their ability to differentiate between violence 'in reality' and in screen fiction, and so refuted media-derived models of screen violence and audience effects.

Notes

1   'UK Top 20 Dec 1, 1994 – Nov 26, 1995', *Screen International*, 15 December 1995, 15.

2   Stone shot an alternative ending in which Mickey is killed by a prisoner who has escaped jail with him. In this version, the film ends with the prisoner taking aim at Mallory. Information from www.melonfarmers.co.uk. See also Jane Hamsher, *Killer Instinct: How Two Young Producers Took on Hollywood and Made the Most Controversial Film of the Decade* (London, Orion Media, 1997).

3   Warner Bros., *Natural Born Killers: Production Information*, 1994, p. 1.

4   See Baz Bamigboye, 'Too much blood for trendy Mr Violence', *Daily Mail*, 3 June 1994, 43; William Shaw, 'Uh-oh! You're in trouble!' *Select*, April 1995, 74–9; Hamsher, *Killer Instinct*. After some delay, Tarantino's version of the screenplay was published in the UK in autumn 1995.

5   'Murder link to violent screen role', *The Times*, 2 November 1994, 14; '"Natural Born Killers" link to murders', *Daily Telegraph*, 7 September

1994, 13; Richard Wallace, 'Ban these natural born killers', *Daily Mirror*, 28 October 1994, 9; Paul Webster, 'Natural Born Killer', 'Deadly date with destiny', *The Guardian*, 27 October 1994, G2, 1–3.

6   Geordie Greig, 'When film violence finally turned American stomachs', *Sundy Times*, 30 October 1994, section 2, 8; 'A poisonous film' (editorial comment), *Daily Mail*, 28 October 1994, 8.

7   See Grace Bradbury, 'Murder-spree movie is put on pause by the censor', *Daily Mail*, 28 October 1994, 11; Dan Conaghan, 'Film blamed for murders is held up by censors', *Daily Telegraph*, 28 October, 1994, 4; Mike Ellison, 'Censors hold up *Natural Born Killers*', *The Guardian*, 28 October 1994, 24; Caroline Lees, 'Kiss and kill film runs foul of censors', *Sunday Times*, 23 October 1994, section 1, 1.

8   The Motion Picture Association of America had originally rated the film as 'NC-17'. After Stone submitted re-edited versions five times, cutting around 3 minutes, the film was given an 'R' rating. It was this version which was viewed and passed by the BBFC. See Brad Stevens, 'Choice cuts', *The Dark Side*, 64 (January 1997), 53–5; Hamsher, *Killer Instinct*, pp. 194–6.

9   British Board of Film Classification, 'Press statement: *Natural Born Killers*', 19 December 1994.

10   The web of journalistic and institutional concerns over *Natural Born Killers* was further complicated by a French murder inquiry in 1996. An investigator on the case speculated that a video of the film may have inspired a teenage couple to kill. As David Kerekes and David Slater note, 'here we have a case of police officers being influenced by press reports of what other police officers have theorised'. Kerekes and Slater, *See No Evil: Banned Films and Video Controversy* (Manchester, Critical Vision, 2000), p. 338. Thanks to Matt Hills for pointing me to this book.

11   Ian George, director of advertising and publicity, Warner Bros. Distributors Ltd., personal interview, 21 March 1995. According to the Cinema Advertising Association, 55 per cent of *Natural Born Killers*' audience were aged 24 and under. Figures provided by the CAA, May 1997.

12   An indication of the popularity of Tarantino among a certain audience grouping is his performance in readers' polls in best-selling film magazine *Empire*. In 1994 *Reservoir Dogs* was voted best film and best debut, and in 1995 *Pulp Fiction* was voted best film, and Tarantino best director. 'Results!' *Empire*, 58 (April 1994), 54–5; 'And the winner is …', *Empire*, 70 (April 1995), 10–11. *Empire*'s 'typical reader' is 24 years old, with gender split of 70–75 per cent male, 25–30 per cent female. Philip Thomas, editor and managing editor of *Empire*, telephone interview, 5 May 1995.

13   George, personal interview.

14 *Natural Born Killers* was seen by 1.8 million cinemagoers, *Pulp Fiction* by 4.3 million. Figures (which include repeat visits) provided by the CAA.

15 The bifurcated audience proposed by George finds an intriguing parallel in far more judgmental comments attributed to James Ferman, then secretary of the BBFC. Ferman distinguished between healthy and unhealthy audiences on the basis of class, as realled by Carl Daft, of video distribution company Exploited: 'At the National Film Theatre at the back end of the *Texas Chain Saw Massacre* ... Ferman says that ... it was fine playing for middle class intellectual audiences at the NFT ... but imagine the effect it might have on the average car worker in Birmingham.' Kerekes and Slater, *See No Evil*, p. 374. Thanks to Matt Hills for bringing this to my attention. *Natural Born Killers* appears to have been seen by rather more middle-class than working-class viewers. The CAA puts 57 per cent of its audience in the ABC1 bracket and 43 per cent in the C2DE bracket.

16 George, personal interview.

17 The synergistically motivated inclusion in the film of tracks featuring Interscope artists Dr Dre and Snoop Doggy Dogg angered producer Jane Hamsher. She also wrote scathingly of Reznor's commercially oriented track selection for the album: 'There was so much range to the music we'd chosen for the film – everything from the Ramsey Lewis Trio to Steven Jesse Bernstein to Anton Webern – and none of the extensive variety was displayed in the tracks he'd picked.' Hamsher, *Killer Instinct*, p. 184.

18 *Natural Born Killers* soundtrack album, promotional flyer.

19 Letter to the author from R. Engler, Warner Music, 3 November 1995.

20 George, personal interview.

21 *Ibid.*

22 *Ibid.*

23 This figure comprises unaided awareness (cinemagoers are asked unprompted what new films they have heard about or seen advertising or) and aided awareness (cinemagoers are read a list of titles and asked which they have heard of). A total awareness level of 60 per cent or more is generally reckoned to be needed to successfully launch a film on wide release. See Olen J. Earnest, '*Star Wars*: a case study of motion picture marketing', *Current Research in Film: Audiences, Economics, and Law*, 1 (1985) 13–14.

24 National Research Group, Inc., Los Angeles, 'UK tracking notes for the week of 20 Feb 95', p. 1. *Natural Born Killers* was in competition with the following films on release at the same time: *Star Trek: Generations, Heavenly Creatures, Andre, Black Beauty, Rudyard Kipling's The Jungle Book, Quiz Show*, and *The River Wild*.

25 National Research Group, Inc., Los Angeles, 'UK Tracking Program:
    Week of 20 February 1995, *Natural Born Killers*, Table One'. Of the
    total sample, only 6 per cent listed violence as a 'positive' factor, with
    another 7 per cent listing 'action'. 23 per cent rated violence as a 'neg-
    ative' factor. Of those unaware of *Natural Born Killers* and asked 'what
    do you think the film will be about?' 31 per cent mentioned violence.
    Ibid.

26 National Research Group, Inc., Los Angeles, 'UK tracking program:
    week of 20 February 1995, *Natural Born Killers*, Table Two'. A further
    7 per cent mentioned 'controversy'.

27 Ratings gauge estimated audience exposure to a television advert.
    Thus, 100 ratings would 'guarantee' that 100 per cent of a product's
    target audience would see an advert; 200 ratings would 'guarantee'
    that 100 per cent of the target audience would see the advert twice.
    Thanks to Helen Branwood on this point.

28 George, personal interview. Some press adverts carried a quotation
    taken from the British music magazine *Vox*.

29 *Ibid.*

30 See Lynn Barber, 'Oliver Stone: natural born director', *Telegraph Mag-
    azine*, 25 February 1995, 34–8; Andrew Clarke, 'Blood from a Stone',
    East Anglian Daily Times, 25 February 1995, EA, 2–3; Gavin Martin,
    'Carnage fan club', *New Musical Express*, 4 March 1995, 30–1, 33;
    Moving Pictures, BBC 2, 12 February 1995; David Robinson, 'A film-
    maker for our time?' *The Times*, 22 February 1995, 37; Gavin Smith,
    'Oliver Stone: Why do I have to provoke?' *Sight and Sound*, 4:12 (NS)
    (December 1994), 8–12. Stone had made earlier media appearances in
    November 1994. See for example, *Film 94*, BBC 1, 7 November, 1994.
    As Janet Wasko notes, star visits to overseas markets are an effective
    and relatively cheap means of promotion. Wasko, *Hollywood in the
    Information Age: Beyond the Silver Screen* (Cambridge, Polity Press,
    1994), p. 232.

31 The final UK gross suggests a rental figure of nearer £2m.

32 George, personal interview.

33 See also Martin Barker, 'Violence', *Sight and Sound*, 5:6 (NS) (June
    1995), 10–13. Barker cites the *Daily Express* ('overkill', 'bludgeon')
    and *The People* ('Mind-numbing'). See Rachel Simpson, 'The Killers
    can leave you Stone cold', *Daily Express*, 24 February 1995, 52–3;
    William Hall, 'Quentin's natural yawn overkill', *The People*, 26 Febru-
    ary 1995, 45. The notion of assault on the audience is also found in
    Andrew Clarke, 'Assault on audience', *East Anglian Daily Times*, 24
    February 1995, 12; Jonathan Romney, 'High bludgeon', *The Guardian*,
    23 February 1995, G2, 11.

34 Hall, 'Quentin's natural yawn overkill' .

35 Simon Rose, 'Aimless kids dead on target', *Daily Mirror*, 23 February 1995, Screen Mirror, 5.

36 Sarah Gristwood, 'My killer Dad should watch this in prison', *Daily Mirror*, 23 February 1995, Screen Mirror, 5; Gill Pringle, 'Crime pays for wild child Juliette', *Daily Mirror*, 23 February 1995, Screen Mirror, 5.

37 Barker, 'Violence'.

38 Christopher Tookey, 'Oliver's twisted bloodfest', *Daily Mail*, 24 February 1995, 44; Derek Malcolm, 'Faster Oliver kill! kill!' *The Guardian*, 23 February 1995, G2, 10. See also: Clarke, 'Assault on audience'; Julie Burchill, 'Blood out of Stone', *The Sunday Times*, 26 February 1995, 10: 6–7.

39 Malcolm, 'Faster Oliver kill! kill!'. See also Philip French, 'The hype remains the same', *The Observer*, 26 February 1995, Review, 7.

40 Lucy Broadbent, 'Dressed to kill', the *Sunday Times*, 18 September 1994, section 9, 4–5.

41 Lees, 'Kiss and kill film runs foul of censors'.

42 On medical language in discourses of concern over media effects, see Graham Murdock, 'Reservoirs of dogma: an archaeology of popular anxieties', in Martin Barker and Julian Petley (eds), *Ill Effects: The Media/Violence Debate* (London and New York, Routledge, 1997), pp. 67–86, especially pp. 76–8.

43 Charles Laurence, 'Our worst nightmare', the *Daily Telegraph*, 28 October 1994, 27. For a contrastingly disapproving citation of Medved, see Dan Glaister, 'London Film Festival: Is NBK OTT?' *The Guardian*, 14 November 1994, G2, 9.

44 Bill Schwarz, 'Night battles: hooligan and citizen', in Mica Nava and Alan O'Shea (eds), *Modern Times: Reflections on a Century of English Modernity* (London, Routedge, 1996) p. 119, quoted in Murdock, 'Reservoirs of dogma', p. 73. On the class dimension to moral panics over media influence, see also Julian Petley, 'Us and them', in Barker and Petley, *Ill Effects*, pp. 87–101.

45 See also Geordie Greig, 'When film violence finally turned American stomachs'.

46 On contrasts in the styles of Stone and Tarantino, see Geoff Andrew, 'Natural Born Killers', *Time Out*, 22 February – 1 March 1995, 65; Burchill, 'Blood out of Stone'; Malcolm, 'Faster Oliver kill! kill!'. See also Ian Calcutt, 'Natural Born Killers', *Samhain*, 49 (March–April 1995), 38–9; Shaw, 'Uh-oh! You're in trouble!'; Terry Staunton, 'Which homicide are you on?' *New Musical Express*, 25 February 1995, 26; Chris Watts, 'Metal Means Murder', *Kerrang!* 534 (25 February 1995), 50–2.

47 Geoff Brown, 'Stone cold killers not up to snuff', *The Times*, 23 February 1995, 33. See also Nick James, 'Natural Born Killers', *Sight and*

Sound, 5:3 (NS) (March 1995), 44–5.

48 Jonathan Ross, 'Born-again killers', *News of the World*, 26 February 1995, 42–3. See also: Romney, 'High bludgeon'; Staunton, 'Which homicide are you on?'

49 Smith, 'Oliver Stone: Why do I have to provoke?'. See also: Steve Sutherland, 'Which homicide are you on?' *New Musical Express*, 25 February 1995, 26; Richard Corliss, 'Stone Crazy', *The Times*, 12 September 1994, 58–9; Clarke, 'Blood from a Stone', and the review in *Samhain* magazine: 'viewers who consistently rely on "identifying" with a suitable character will have big problems here!' Calcutt, 'Natural Born Killers'.

50 Bill Hagerty, 'Stone makes a killing out of hype', *Today*, 24 February 1995, 36–7. See also Larry Gross, 'Exploding Hollywood', *Sight and Sound*, 5:3 (NS) (March 1995), 8–9.

51 Clark Collis, 'Natural Born Killers', *Empire*, 66 (December 1994), 28.

52 Youth style magazine *The Face* carried an admiring interview with star Woody Harrelson. Rob Tannenbaum, 'Blood relations', *The Face*, 75 (December 1994), 60–6.

53 Jason Arnopp, 'Killing is my business!', *Kerrang!* 534 (25 February 1995), 28–30; Jason Arnopp, 'Full metal racket!', *Kerrang!* 534 (25 February 1995), 38–40; 'Killer queens!' 30; 'Lights! Camera! Metal!' 38–9; 'Metal stars in the movies!' 36–7.

54 Jason Arnopp, 'Kill for thrills!' *Kerrang!* 534 (25 February 1995) 29.

55 Other issues, such as cinemagoing habits in general, were also covered by the questionnaire but are not pursued here. The questionnaire is reproduced at appendix 9.

56 Murdock, 'Reservoirs of dogma', p. 82.

57 Camille Bacon-Smith with Tyrone Yarbrough, '*Batman*: the ethnography', in Roberta E. Pearson and William Uricchio (eds), *The Many Lives of the Batman: Critical Approaches to a Superhero and his Media* (New York and London, Routledge//British Film Institute Publishing, 1991), pp. 98–9.

58 The reasons for this rate of return being lower than that for the first wave are unclear. However, some viewers refused questionnaires on the grounds that the film was such a disappointment they were not interested in anything connected with it.

59 My audience research took place in a garrison town.

60 The respondent listed his hobbies as 'sex, murder, football' and regular reading material as *Playboy* and *Penthouse*.

61 Surprisingly, while *Natural Born Killers*' visual form was labelled 'hallucinatory' in the press pack, the film was not compared to a hallucinogenic drug experience or 'trip' by any of the reviews or respondent accounts that I saw.

62 J.P. Telotte, 'Beyond all reason: the nature of the cult', in Telotte (ed.), *The Cult Film Experience: Beyond All Reason* (Austin, University of Texas Press, 1991).

63 Barry Keith Grant, 'Second thoughts on double features: revisiting the cult film', in Xavier Mendik and Graeme Harper (eds), *Unruly Pleasures: The Cult Film and its Critics* (Guildford, Fab Press, 2000) p. 19.

64 The following account comes from one of ten questionnaires returned by members of this audience. Research was carried out in August 1997.

65 See Dan Glaister, 'Release of "Killers" video halted', *The Guardian*, 17 May 1996, 13; Philip Johnston, 'When the censors failed to match the public mood', *Daily Telegraph*, 6 November 1996; 'Natural Born Killers video is held back', *Daily Telegraph*, 14 March 1996.

66 *Time Out*, May 1995 – May 1997. This figure includes 37 shows at the Warner West End in the summer of 1995, and 14 screenings at the Prince Charles over the whole period.

67 Although the size of the sample is very small, several respondents from the Prince Charles audience had seen the film at least once before. Evidence of cult investments in the film on the Internet includes a *Natural Born Killers* fan club website and an American fan newsletter, called the 'Batongaville Times' after the prison from which Mickey and Mallory escape. Seven issues of the newsletter were published online between October 1994 and April 1995.

68 See Sean Poulter, 'Outrage at Killers' TV screening', *Daily Mail*, 29 October 1997; 'Channel 5 bosses shot down over "mindless" movie', *Daily Mail*, 26 February 1998, 46.

69 John Grisham, 'Natural Bred Killers', *The Oxford American*, 1996, reprinted in Karl French (ed.), *Screen Violence* (London, Bloomsbury, 1996). Stone's response, 'Don't sue the messenger', was published in *LA Weekly*, and is also reprinted in *Screen Violence*.

70 There is of course an extensive and varied literature on 'media effects', although the best-known of this work focuses more on television than on the press. For a useful overview, see Jack M. McLeod, Gerald M. Kosicki and Zhongdang Pan, 'On understanding and misunderstanding media effects', in James Curran and Michael Gurevitch (eds), *Mass Media and Society* (London, Edward Arnold, 1991), pp. 235–66.

71 See Teun A. van Dijk, *News as Discourse* (Hillsdale, Erlbaum, 1988), pp. 180–1.

72 See McLeod *et al.*, 'On understanding and misunderstanding media effects', pp. 252–3. See also Stuart Hall, 'Encoding//decoding', in Stuart Hall, Dorothy Hobson, Andrew Lowe, and Paul Willis (eds), *Culture, Media Language: Working Papers in Cultural Studies, 1972–79* (London, Hutchinson, 1980), pp. 128–38, and my discussion of this paper in chapter 2.

73   There is a certain circularity here: media texts themselves draw on dis-
     courses current in everyday speech. See Roger Fowler, *Language in the
     News: Discourse and Ideology in the Press* (London, Routledge, 1991),
     pp. 41–2.
74   While the respondent could be seen to be partially cued by the question
     to express concern, not all informants took up this opportunity. More-
     over, the means through which her concern was expressed was not pre-
     determined by the question.
75   As Martin Barker has noted, 'screen violence' is a problematic concept
     that must be defined according to its specific textual location, for exam-
     ple, in news or documentary footage, or any of a number of fictional
     genres, from cartoons to horror. Thus, 'there simply isn't a "thing"
     called "violence in the media" that either could or couldn't "cause"
     social violence.' Barker, 'Violence', 10.

Chapter 6

Conclusion

The multi-dimensional approach pursued in this book has been designed to address a series of questions about the significance of popular film in everyday life, and about the power relations in which films and their audiences become enmeshed. To this end, I have worked across some received inter- and intradisciplinary divisions, tracing interfaces between industrial practices, textual organisation, viewing strategies proposed through marketing and film journalism, and the contextually located actions of viewers. I have drawn on work undertaken within both cultural studies and film studies, borrowing investigative tools from the critical traditions of qualitative audience research, reception studies and the political economics of Hollywood. More specifically, this inquiry has coalesced around a number of issues raised via my three case studies. My scrutiny of the *Basic Instinct* phenomenon examined protests against the film's representation of sexual minorities, and the professional ideology of entertainment mobilised to defend the film against these accusations. It also revealed how audiences used the film as a resource from which various fantasies, pleasures and knowledges could be derived, and as a means to assert sexual and gendered identities in a range of social settings. The chapter on *Bram Stoker's Dracula* assessed and revised orthodox theorisations of film genres through an examination of taste coalitions and conflicts formed around the film. The commercial and social fate of both these films was shaped by a double dynamic of dispersal and stratification, through which textual assembly and marketing strategies both canvassed and effectively hierarchised multiple audience fractions. Commercial logics can be seen to intersect with (in the case of *Basic Instinct*) wider social discourses on, and the normative organisation of, relations of sexuality and gender, and (in the case

of *Bram Stoker's Dracula*) the differentiation and selective legitimation of audiences according to notions of taste and identity. Picking
up on another strand from these two chapters, my analysis of the
promotion and reception of *Natural Born Killers* explored viewers'
images of themselves and 'others', by examining working distinctions between 'safe' and 'dangerous' audiences. In this instance, my
triangulation between text, contexts and audiences concentrated on
discourses of concern about 'copycat' violence. *Natural Born Killers*
was thus engulfed in a very different kind of controversy to that
which framed *Basic Instinct*. While mainstream publications worked
in the main to defend the latter as 'just entertainment', the former
was widely indicted by the British press in a campaign which, in per-
suading the BBFC to postpone classification of the film, effectively
authenticated its transgressive attractions for some viewers.

In their differing ways, all three case studies have traced continuities across, and differences between and within, institutional and
'ground-level' perspectives on films and their audiences. What, then,
is the status of the text within such an integrative methodological
framework? I have tried to hold on to a sense of the significance of
textual formations and structures for the production of meanings,
pleasures and uses, while avoiding the pitfalls of textual determinism. Let me revisit this dilemma by returning briefly to *Basic
Instinct*. As an example of what I have termed a dispersible text, the
film was organised intratextually and promoted extratextually to
offer a multiple address to diverse audience segments, so achieving
a broad social and cultural reach. Such a dynamic of extension is not
infinite, however. The 'invitations-to-view' presented by a film and
associated satellite texts do not proliferate endlessly. Of course, a
host of social factors – including viewers' knowledges and dispositions, and contexts of reception – shape audience encounters with
film texts. In addition, as I have attempted to demonstrate though
my use of John Corner's triple-decker model of meaning production, any film text operates with a low degree of ambiguity at the
'primary' level, that of denotation, even if higher-level meanings are
more open to dispute. This is true of *Basic Instinct*, notwithstanding
its deliberately engineered open ending, which invites viewers to
complete the narrative themselves. Furthermore, the multiple
promises made on behalf of a film in marketing discourses and
reviews may be contradictory at times, insofar as one may under-
mine another for a particular viewer confronted with such diverse

offers. I have argued that this is true, on occasions, of the actual, realised engagements audiences made with *Basic Instinct*. The consequence in these instances is an effective hierarchisation of audience appeals and viewing strategies. In the case of *Basic Instinct*, the film was pitched primarily to straight men and straight women. In addition, some lesbian and bisexual women enjoyed the film, interpreting it as a celebration and/or legitimation of their sexual identities. These viewing strategies were not prohibited by the structure and marketing of the film, but its most familiar and widely circulating invitations were made to heterosexuals. These were also arranged in structures of dominance, shaped by generic conventions, commercial imperatives and normative discourses and practices, which converged to endorse most enthusiastically a male 'appraising gaze' at the female body. Thus, I have suggested, straight male pleasures in the sexualised display of women, which are already sanctioned in much of Anglo-American society and culture, were the primary promise made on behalf of *Basic Instinct*. This invitation (and others, including the thrills of the detective plot) ran alongside the celebration of Catherine Tramell as a figure of 'post-feminist' assertion. Crucially in this instance, the two particular appeals cannot be regarded as unrelated. There is an element of mutual incompatibility about these viewing strategies at the level of many individuals' approaches to the film.

According to this logic, there are some clear limits on the avenues to *Basic Instinct* that may be taken up by a viewer at any one time. Some interpretive frames and pleasures can be termed 'dominant' and some 'marginal', in terms of both their textual cues and their degrees of social endorsement. These two groundings for viewing strategies do not necessarily coincide, of course, but in the case of *Basic Instinct* there is a large degree of overlap. Thus I have argued that the film was sometimes made use of as a space for the celebration of female fantasises of empowerment and sexual agency, but that these pleasures were often subordinated to, and compromised by, 'straight male' pleasures, both within sections of the mainstream press and in certain 'local' viewing scenarios. By contrast, I found very little evidence of the inverse – that is, of the impairment of male (hetero)sexual pleasures by an awareness of female perspectives – beyond some admissions of 'guilty' enjoyment. This leads me to suggest that the film and its promotion proposed and validated certain straight male viewing pleasures with more vigour and success than it did female pleasures of agency and autonomy. I would argue that any further textual invitations to women along these lines might have threatened *Basic Instinct*'s ability to travel socially and commercially among heterosexual male audiences who were looking for certain sexual pleasures and uses. This is not, of course, to assert that *Basic Instinct* was simply and for all viewers 'a straight male film', but to argue instead that there were interacting factors – both textual and social – that limited its polysemy and structured its appeals.

The model upon which I have been elaborating here should not be taken to imply that mainstream films such as *Basic Instinct* always and inevitably endorse and reproduce the *status quo*. As I argued in chapter 3, less urgently solicited viewing strategies deployed by members of marginal social groups will also feed into talk about, and uses and (higher-level) meanings derived from, a film at any particular historical moment. But they will not do so regardless of the text's own structures and surrounding discourses. A balance must be struck in critical analysis between scrutiny of the complexities of actual viewers' diverse and socially situated engagements with popular film; an associated recognition of the historical contingency of uses, pleasures and meanings produced in these encounters; and an awareness of how viewing strategies and supporting discourses are variously sought, (in)validated and hierarchised both within and beyond film texts. In attempting to strike such a balance, I hope to have moved beyond some existing paradigms of textual determinism, while pursuing an investigation of certain operations of social and cultural power. This is a move that I hope will have some significance beyond the specific findings of the three case studies developed within these pages.

Appendices

Appendix 1

Basic Instinct audience research, published request (edited on occasions)

Have you seen the film *Basic Instinct*? If so, I'd like to hear from you. Why did you watch it? Where and when? What were your reactions to the film? If you haven't seen it, why is that?

I am doing research at the University of East Anglia into cinema audiences. Please write to me about your views of the film, and for a small questionnaire.

I look forward to hearing from you.
Thomas Austin
English and American Studies
University of East Anglia
Norwich NR4 7TJ

Appendix 2

Questionnaire used for *Basic Instinct* case study

(A slightly different format was sent to respondents who had not seen the film.)

Questionnaire on *Basic Instinct*

Please note that the questionnaire is in three parts. Part One is left blank for you to write about your own feelings about the film. Part Two contains some specific questions. Part Three covers basic details about you.

It is important for my research that you answer Part One first, as it is useful to see what you think about the film independent of my own avenues of inquiry.

Your reply will remain confidential, unless you agree otherwise in Part Three.

Part One
PLEASE COMPLETE THIS SECTION BEFORE READING PART TWO.

Please use this page to write about (i) why you saw *Basic Instinct*, and (ii) your responses to it. Feel free to use an additional page if required.

Part Two
This section covers general information about where and when you saw the film, as well as areas I am particularly interested in – including the role played by publicity and promotion around the film, issues raised by the film itself and some responses to it in the media. Please forgive the repetition of the initial questions, and don't worry if you repeat some of your response to Part One.

1: Where did you watch *Basic Instinct*?
2: When did you watch it?
3: Did you watch it alone? If not, who did you watch it with?

4: If you watched it in a group or couple, who in the group/couple decided to watch it?

5: If you watched it in a group or couple, did you have different reasons for seeing it? If so, please give details.

6: If you watched it alone, was this because someone refused to see it with you? If so, please give details.

7: Please say what you knew about the film before you saw it.

8: Where did you get this information about the film from? Please give full details.

9: Did the film fulfill or contradict your expectations? Please give details.

10: Did you talk with anyone else, either before or after seeing it? Please say who, and give details of what you talked about.

11: If you saw the film in a group or couple, did you agree in your verdict on the film? Please give details of any differences of opinion.

12: Were you aware of protests against the film by:
   a. lesbians
   b. gay men
   c. women's groups
   d. censorship campaigners
   e. others (please specify)

13: Were these protests in:
   a. the US
   b. the UK
   c. both

14: How did you become aware of the protests? Was this before or after you watched the film, or both?

15: What was your reaction to the protests? Did it change after watching the film? Please give details.

16: Which star do you feel got most publicity in the promotion of the film?
   a. Michael Douglas
   b. Sharon Stone
   c. both

17: Who do you think was the main character in the film?
   a. Detective Nick Curran (Michael Douglas)
   b. Catherine Tramell (Sharon Stone)
   c. both
   d. other (please specify)

18: What did you think of the film's portrayal of the following (please give details)
   a. Catherine Tramell
   b. Beth (the police psychologist)
   c. Roxy (Catherine's girlfriend)
   d. Hazel Dobkins (Catherine's older friend)

     e. lesbians and bisexuals in general
     f. women in general
     g. Nick Curran
     h. men in general
     i. sex
     j. violence

19: Which character appealed most to you, and why?

20: Please state what you thought of:
     a. The ending
     b. The opening scene

21: Who do you think was the ice pick killer?

22: Would you say *Basic Instinct* has a message? Please give details.

23: Are there any elements of the film that you particularly liked or disliked? Please give details.

24: Are films getting more violent?
     a. Yes
     b. No

25. Does this matter?
     a. Yes
     b. No
     Please say why.

26: Do you think violent films can be blamed for violence in society at large?

27: Do you think *Basic Instinct* can be blamed for violence in society at large?

28: Is there anything else you would like to say about *Basic Instinct*?

29: Do you think there should be changes to censorship and age restrictions on films in Britain? (please tick or ring answers)
    films in cinemas:
     a. More censorship of sex/violence/swearing/other (please specify)
     b. Less censorship of sex/violence/swearing/other (please specify)
     c. No change in censorship
     d. Tighter age restrictions
     e. Looser age restrictions
     f. No change in age restrictions
    films on video:
     a. More censorship of sex/violence/swearing/other (please specify)
     b. Less censorship of sex/violence/swearing/other (please specify)
     c. No change in censorship
     d. Tighter age restrictions
     e. Looser age restrictions
     f. No change in age restrictions
    films on television:

a. More censorship of sex/violence/swearing/other (please specify)
b. Less censorship of sex/violence/swearing/other (please specify)
c. No change in censorship
d. Later showings of 'adult' films
e. Earlier showings of 'adult' films
f. No change in programming times

Part Three

This section covers details about you. Of course, I would be grateful if you could answer all the questions, but I understand if you would prefer not to answer some.

30: Name:
31: Address:
32: Are you:
    a. Female
    b. Male
33: Age:
34: Would you describe yourself as:
    a. Afro-Caribbean
    b. Asian
    c. White European
    d. other (please specify)
35: Would you describe yourself as religious? (If yes, please give details)
36: Would you describe yourself as:
    a. heterosexual
    b. lesbian
    c. gay (male)
    d. bisexual
    e. other (please specify)
37: Are you:
    a. in full-time employment
    b. in part-time employment
    c. in full-time or part-time education
    d. unemployed
    e. retired
    f. other (please specify)
38. If you are in full- or part-time employment, please give details.
39: If you are in full- or part-time education, please give details.
40: Would you be prepared to be quoted in my research findings?
    a   Yes, by name
    b. Yes, anonymously
    c. No

41: Would you be prepared to be quoted if this research is published as a
    book?
    a. Yes, by name
    b. Yes, anonymously
    c. No

Unless you have agreed to the contrary, I shall treat this questionnaire in the
strictest confidence.

Thank you very much for your time.

Appendix 3

Basic Instinct research sample details

Empire:	62 letters followed by 40 completed questionnaires
The Guardian:	12 letters followed by 7 questionnaires
Everywoman:	5 letters followed by 3 questionnaires
Gay Times:	4 letters followed by 4 questionnaires
Pink Paper:	3 letters followed by 3 questionnaires
source unclear:	3 letters followed by 3 questionnaires

Age on return of questionnaire

age 14–17:	4
age 18–24:	26
age 25–35:	19
age 36–45:	6
age 46–55:	3
age 56+:	1 (aged 57)
no age given:	1
total:	60

Occupations

(As described in part three of questionnaire.) (E: *Empire*; Ev: *Everywoman*; G: *The Guardian*; GT: *Gay Times*; P: *Pink Paper*):

25 college and university students	(18 E; 2 GT; 1 G; 2 Ev; 1 P; 1 unknown)
6 unemployed	(4 E; 1 Ev; 1 G)
3 school pupils	(3 E)
3 teachers or in teacher training	(2 G; 1 E)
2 lecturers	(1 E; 1 unknown)
2 housewife and/or mother	(2 E)
2 part-time secretary/admin. assistant	(1E; 1 G)

1 medical-legal consultant   (G)
1 public sector policy manager   (G)
1 fine arts consultant   (P)
1 director of US gay and lesbian centre   (GT)
1 rape counsellor   (unknown)
1 life model   (G)
1 estimator   (GT)
1 library worker   (E)
1 lab assistant   (E)
1 civil servant   (E)
1 publisher's PA   (E)
1 computer operator   (E)
1 university media technician   (E)
1 bank clerk   (E)
1 hairdresser   (E)
1 groom   (E)
1 "retired early' (aged 39)   (E)

Appendix 4

Basic Instinct audience research respondents

All members of the questionnaire sample described themselves as white, with the exception of *57, who described himself as 'black Indian'

*1: anon. female, no details given, *Guardian* sample, letter only.

*2: Susan, female, age 33, lecturer, bisexual, unknown sample .

*3: Barbara, female, age 48, rape counsellor, lesbian, unknown sample.

*4: anon. female, age 20, student, heterosexual, *Guardian* sample.

*5: Jim, male, age 47, director of gay and lesbian centre, gay, *Gay Times* sample.

*6: Wim, male, age 33, student, 'biologically male, gender mixed, sexuality gay or lesbian', *Gay Times* sample.

*7: James, male, age 19, student, gay, *Gay Times* sample.

*8: anon. male, age 26, estimator, gay, *Gay Times* sample.

*9: Helen, female, age 26, student, lesbian, *Pink Paper* sample.

*10: Steve, male, no age given, arts consultant, gay, *Pink Paper* sample.

*11: Michael, male, age 23, administration assistant, gay, *Pink Paper* sample.

*12: John, male, age 57, medical-legal consultant, heterosexual, *Guardian* sample.

*13: anon. female, age 44, life model, heterosexual, *Guardian* sample.

*14: Megan, female, age 25, school teacher, heterosexual, *Guardian* sample.

*15: anon. female, age 31, public sector policy manager, heterosexual, *Guardian* sample.

*16: Joanna, female, age 24, unemployed, heterosexual, *Guardian* sample.

*17: Jacqueline, female, age 26, film studies teacher, heterosexual, *Guardian* sample.

*18: anon. female, age 32, student/civil servant, 'celibate' heterosexual, unknown sample.

*19: anon. female, age 22, student, bisexual, *Everywoman* sample.

*20: anon. female, age 22, unemployed, bisexual, *Everywoman* sample.

*21: Arwen, female, age 22, student, bisexual, *Everywoman* sample.

*22:   anon. female, age 21, student, heterosexual, *Empire* sample.
*23:   Bronwen, female, age 22, student, heterosexual, *Empire* sample.
*24:   Nicholas, male, age 20, student, heterosexual, *Empire* sample.
*25:   Deborah, female, age 19, trainee teacher, heterosexual, *Empire* sample.
*26:   Peter, male, age 36, unemployed, heterosexual, *Empire* sample.
*27:   Karen, female, age 29, film student, heterosexual, *Empire* sample.
*28:   James, male, age 18, year off before university, heterosexual, *Empire* sample.
*29:   anon. female, age 19, student, heterosexual, *Empire* sample.
*30:   David, male, age 25, student, heterosexual, *Empire* sample.
*31:   James, male, age 39, 'retired early in life', heterosexual, *Empire* sample.
*32:   Philip, male, age 21, unemployed, heterosexual, *Empire* sample.
*33:   Nina, female, age 22, part-time A-level student, heterosexual, *Empire* sample.
*34:   Teresa, female, age 23, librarian, heterosexual, *Empire* sample.
*35:   Louise, female, age 26, groom/riding instructor, heterosexual, *Empire* sample.
*36:   anon. male, age 33, unemployed, heterosexual, *Empire* sample.
*37:   anon. female, age 25, housewife and mother, heterosexual, *Empire* sample.
*38:   Robert, male, age 21, student, heterosexual, *Empire* sample.
*39:   Rachel, female, age 19, English student, heterosexual, *Empire* sample.
*40:   Rebecca, female, age 19, student, heterosexual, *Empire* sample.
*41:   anon. female, age 17, school pupil, heterosexual, *Empire* sample.
*42:   anon. female, age 14, school pupil, heterosexual, *Empire* sample.
*43:   Duncan, male, age 22, student, heterosexual, *Empire* sample.
*44:   Lydia, female, age 26, media technician, heterosexual, *Empire* sample.
*45:   Nicky, female, age 30, bank clerk, heterosexual, *Empire* sample.
*46:   Paul, school pupil 'doing A levels', no age or sexuality given, *Empire* sample.
*47:   Donna, female, age 20, student, heterosexual, *Empire* sample.
*48:   Kathryn, female, age 26, computer operator 'and part-time photographer and poet', heterosexual, *Empire* sample.
*49:   Robbie, male, age 29, personal assistant in publishing, heterosexual, *Empire* sample.
*50:   Ian, male, age 21, student, heterosexual, *Empire* sample.
*51:   Stephen, male, age 51, unemployed, heterosexual, *Empire* sample.
*52:   anon. male, age 43, civil servant, heterosexual, *Empire* sample.
*53:   anon. female, age 34, lecturer, heterosexual, *Empire* sample.
*54:   anon. male, age 21, student, heterosexual, *Empire* sample.
*55:   anon. female, age 34, housewife, heterosexual, *Empire* sample.

*56: anon. male, age 18, lab assistant, heterosexual, *Empire* sample.

*57: David, age 17, student, heterosexual, *Empire* sample.

*58: Geraldine, female, age 46, part-time secretary, 'mother, etc', heterosexual, *Empire* sample.

*59: anon. female, age 31, hairdresser, heterosexual 'but have had lesbian partner', *Empire* sample.

*60: Anthony, male, age 21, student, heterosexual, *Empire* sample.

*61: David, male, age 23, student, heterosexual, *Empire* sample.

*63: Ann, female, age 57, no other details given, *Guardian* sample, letter only.

*64: Rosa, female, age 31, student, lesbian, *Empire* sample.

*65: Charlotte, female, no details given, *Empire* sample.

*66: Angie, female, student, no other details given, *Empire* sample.

*67: anon. female, student, no other details given, *Guardian* sample.

*68: anon. female, student, no other details given, *Everywoman* sample, letter only.

*69: anon. female, student, no other details given, *Everywoman* sample, letter only.

*70: Alexander, male, age 19, film studies student, no sexuality stated, *Empire* sample.

*71: Shane, male, age 15, no other details given, *Empire* sample, letter only.

*72: Basil, male, no details given, *Empire* sample, letter only.

*73: Tony, male, no details given, *Empire* sample, letter only.

*74: Jason, male, no details given, *Empire* sample, letter only.

*75: Mick, male, no details given, *Empire* sample, letter only.

*76: Sean, male, student, no other details given, *Empire* sample, letter only.

*77: Nick, no other details given, *Empire* sample, letter only.

*78: anon. male, no details given, *Empire* sample, letter only.

*79: anon. male, no details given, *Empire* sample, letter only.

*80: anon. female, no details given, *Guardian* sample, letter only.

*81: Angela, female, no details given, *Guardian* sample, letter only.

*82: anon. male, age 20, student, no other details given, *Empire* sample, letter only.

*83: anon. female, no details given, *Empire* sample, letter only.

*84: anon. female, film student, no other details given, *Empire* sample, letter only.

*85: anon. male, no details given, *Empire* sample, letter only.

*86: anon. male, no details given, *Empire* sample, letter only.

*87: anon. male, no details given, *Empire* sample, letter only.

*88: anon. male, no details given, *Empire* sample, letter only.

*89: anon. male, no details given, *Empire* sample, letter only.

Appendix 5

Questionnaire used for *Bram Stoker's Dracula* case study

Questionnaire

Thank you for taking a questionnaire. I am researching cinema audiences at the University of Sussex. I would be very grateful if you could fill in this questionnaire and return it to me using the envelope provided.

Please note that the questionnaire is in three sections. Part One covers basic details about you, including your interests and film preferences. Part Two is left blank for you to write about your own reactions to a film I'm particularly interested in – *Bram Stoker's Dracula*.

You may have seen the film recently on ITV. If you have not seen it at all, or not for some time, please do still fill in the questionnaire, as I'm interested in what you remember about the film, and/or why you didn't see it.

Part Three contains some specific questions about why you watched *Bram Stoker's Dracula* (or why you didn't) and your responses to it.

The questions are a mixture of multiple choice and open-ended questions where you can write what you think. If you think not enough space has been provided for your response, please feel free to use an additional page.

Your reply will remain confidential unless you agree otherwise in Part One.

Thanks again for your help, I look forward to hearing from you.

Thomas Austin

Part One

This section covers details about you. Of course, I would be grateful if you could answer all the questions, but I understand if you would prefer not to answer some. Unless you agree to the contrary below, I shall treat this questionnaire in the strictest confidence.

1: Name:
2: Address:
3: Are you:
   a. Female
   b. Male
4: Age:
5: Would you describe yourself as:
   a. Afro-Caribbean
   b. Asian
   c. White European
   d. other (please give details)
6: Are you:
   a. in full-time employment
   b. in part-time employment
   c. in full- or part-time education
   d. unemployed
   e. retired
   f. other (please give details)
7: If you are in full- or part-time employment, please give details.
8: At what age did you leave full-time education?
9: If you are in full- or part-time education, please give details.
10: On average, how many films would you say you watch a month:
   a. at the cinema
   b. on video
   c. on television
11: What sorts of films do you enjoy most? Please give examples.
12: What sorts of films do you dislike most? Please give examples.
13: Please list the last three films you saw at the cinema, or on video.
14: Do you read reviews and articles on films? Is so, please give details.
15: Do you watch tv programmes about the cinema? If so, please give details.
16: Which of these factors influence you in deciding whether or not to see a film? (Please tick.)

	Very important:	Quite important:	Not important:
a. What friends/ relatives say			
b. Reading reviews or articles			
c. Seeing reviews or features on tv			
d. Seeing adverts in newspapers			
e. Seeing adverts on television			
f. Seeing previews/trailers at the cinema			

   g. Seeing posters
   h. Whatever is on the night I go out
   i. Knowing the director
   j. Knowing the stars/actors
   k. Other (please give details
17: Please list your hobbies and leisure activities in order of preference.
    Where would you include watching films on your list?
18: What television programmes do you enjoy watching?
19: What magazines or newspapers do you read? How often do you read
    them?
20: Which radio station(s) do you listen to?
21: Do you ever read books for pleasure? (Not for school or work..)
    If so, please list the last two books you read.
22: Would you be prepared to be quoted in my research findings?
   a. Yes, by name
   b. Yes, anonymously
   c. No

Part Two
PLEASE COMPLETE THIS SECTION BEFORE READING PART
THREE.

Please use this page to write about (i) why you watched *Bram Stoker's Dracula*.

(* If you haven't seen the film, please state why not, and then go on to question 35.)

If you have seen the film, please also write about your reactions to it at (ii).

If you saw the film more than once, did your opinion of it change over time?

Feel free to use an additional page if required.
   (i)
   (ii)

Part Three
This section asks some more questions about your response to *Bram Stoker's Dracula*. Don't worry if you repeat some of your response to Part Two.

23: How many times have you seen *Bram Stoker's Dracula*?
   a. at the cinema
   b. on video
   c. on television
24: Where and when did you see it for the first time?
25: Who did you see the film with the first time you saw it? (Please tick an
    answer.)

    a. No one else
    b. Mother/father
    c. Sister/brother
    d. Husband/wife
    e. Boyfriend/girlfriend
    f. Children
    g. Friends (same sex) (please say how many)
    h. Friends (opposite sex) (please say how many)
    i. Other (please give details)

26: Who chose to see the film? (Please tick an answer.)
    a. Me
    b. Mother/father
    c. Sister/brother
    d. Husband/wife
    e. Boyfriend/girlfriend
    f. Children
    g. Friends
    h. Other (please give details)

27: Did you talk about the film with anyone else before or after seeing it? If so, please say who, and what you talked about.

28: Please say what you knew about *Bram Stoker's Dracula* before you saw it.

29: Where did you get this information about the film from?

30: How would you describe the film?

31: Did it fulfil your expectations? Please give details.

32: What did you think of the film? (Please tick a response for each category on the list.)

	Very:	A bit:	Not at all:
How enjoyable/entertaining?			
How frightening/horrific?			
How romantic?			
How sexy?			
How funny?			
How exciting?			
How stylish?			
How believable/realistic?			
How seriously did you take it?			

33: Did *Bram Stoker's Dracula* remind you of any other films? Please give details.

34: What elements of the film did you particularly like or dislike? Please give details
    (i) liked:
    (ii) disliked:

35: Who do you think *Bram Stoker's Dracula* appeals to most?

36: Do you own any *Bram Stoker's Dracula* merchandise? Please give details.

37: Have you read the novel, *Dracula*? If so, when? Was it before or after seeing the film? How did the film compare with the book?

38:   Is there anything else you would like to say about the film?

Thank you very much for your time.

Bram Stoker's Dracula research sample details

Age on return of questionnaire

age 16–17:   2
age 18–24:   16
age 25–35:   8
age 36–45:   3
age over 45:   1 (48)
total: 30

Occupations

9 students
2 school students
2 local government workers
1 publisher
1 tax consultant
1 doctor
1 biomedical scientist
1 social worker
1 insurance worker
1 medical librarian
1 charity worker
1 media worker
1 graphic designer
1 taxi driver
1 hairdresser
1 worker in family business
1 au pair
1 unemployed/voluntary worker
2 no details given

Film preferences

Each respondent's code number is given in brackets. The symbol @ denotes that the respondent did not see *Bram Stoker's Dracula*.

'What sort of films do you enjoy most?':

Female respondents:
'v. wide variety': 1M+F (*26)
'action, thriller, romance, musicals: all sort really, as long as they are well directed/acted': 1F (*17)
'Disney, true stories, murder, action. Most films': 1F (*27)
'action, horror, thrillers/fantasy, cartoons, science fiction, epics': 1F (*11)
'horror sometimes, comedy, science fiction, Channel 4 films': 1F (*9)
'cult, comedies, fantasy/science fiction, dramas, action, Disney films':1F (*25)
'science fiction, crime/action, comedies': 1F (*7)
'*Silence of the Lambs, Interview with the Vampire, Die Hard*': 1F (*4)
'clever films: *Seven, Silence of the Lambs, The Shining, Natural Born Killers, Menace to Society*': 1F (*15)
'Tarantino films, psychological thrillers': 1F (*31)
'thrillers, comedy': 1F (*40) @
'sci-fi, Disney, dramas, particularly women-centred': 1F (*8)
'*The Crow, Star Trek, Independence Day*': 1F (*38) @
'science fiction, British films, true life stories': 1F (*10)
'classics, British films, humorous films, 'cute' films': 1F (*18)
'historical/"classics", modern films with social/political content': 1F (*21)
'*The Big Blue, Betty Blue, Cinema Paradiso*': 1F (*28)
'Art films, also 50s camp films': 1F (*29)
'romance, thriller, comedy': 1F (*23)
'comedy, romantic drama': 1F (*13)
'light entertainment, foreign films, period drama': 1F (*30)
'period drama, *Emma, Sense and Sensibility*' 1F (*31)
'*Sex, Lies and Videotape*': 1F (*32) @
'*Pride and Prejudice, Independence Day*': 1F (*33) @
'nice gentle stories, films with happy endings, preferably romantic': 1F (*35) @
'feel-good: *Breakfast Club*, Steve Martin': 1F (*37) @
'comedy': 1F (*41) @

Male respondents:
'horror, science fiction, and fantasy': 1M (*2) (*Samhain* sample)
'horror and science fiction': 1M (*3)
'horror and thrillers': 1M (*16)
'science fiction, action, fantasy': 1M (*22)

'science fiction, period dramas, action': 1M (*34)
'science fiction': 1M (*39) @
'action, intrigue': 1M (*5)
'adventure, comedy, science fiction, romance': 1M (*20)
'intelligent, cool films: *Star Trek*, gangster, *Pulp Fiction*': 1M (*24)
'films with a strong storyline which do not insult the intelligence of the audience': 1M (*12)
'clever, bright, intriguing, entertaining, *Shallow Grave*, *Usual Suspects*': 1M (*14)
'director's cut of *Blade Runner*': 1M (*19)
'costume drama, real lives, comedy, miscellaneous contemporary, British': 1M (*36) @

'What sort of films do you dislike most?':

none listed, 'no real dislikes', etc: 1F, 1M, 1M+F (*27, 2, 26)
'horror': 2F (*38, 41) @ @
'horror, gory things, psychological': 1F (*37) @
'violent films, horror': 1F (*30)
'westerns, horror': 1F (*13)
'horror, sci-fi, anything with Schwarzenegger in it!': 1F (*18)
'Anything with Arnie [Schwarzenegger] or Stallone in' 1F (*28)
'violent, "cops and robbers", anything with Schwarzenegger or Stallone in': 1F (*33) @
'action, James Bond, anything with Stallone': 1F (*8)
'cowboy movies and kung fu testosterone motivated movies for highly sexed 13 year olds (boys usually)': 1F (*17)
'Anything with Emma Thompson! Tarantino movies, black gangland hip hop movies, anything glorifying violence, especially violence to women/children': 1F (*10)
'mindless (misogynistic) violence, e.g. *Seven*': 1F (*32) @
'violent, sex–rape type films': 1F (*35) @
'violent and sexually explicit': 1F (*31)
'horror, war, costume/period dramas': 1F (*40) @
'sci-fi, *Star Trek*': 1F (*31)
'war/political, *Schindler's List*': 1F (*11)
'romantic comedies': 1F (*7)
'X-films and romantic films': 1F (*4)
'westerns, children's animal films': 1F (*25)
'Hollywood inspirational films': 1F (*29)
'"Family" comedy, *Father of the Bride*': 1F (*23)
'stupid American comedies, *The Nutty Professor*': 1F (*9)
'comedy': 1F (*15)
'romantic, period': 1M (*22)

'crap thrillers when you know what will happen': 1M (*24)

'Nineties "thrillers", [comedies like]*Airplane* and its kind': 1M (*3)

'cheap American comedy, anything with Van Damme [or] Emma Thompson': 1M (*12)

'Stereotyped, bland, unimaginative. Any Stallone film': 1M (*14)

'epic and martial art': 1M (*16)

'most British films after 1970, most comedies': 1M (*34)

'comedy where it gets annoying, movies without plots where they just spend loads of money instead, anything with Goldie Hawn in!': 1M (*20)

'*Four Weddings and a Funeral*': 1M (*5)

'*Bram Stoker's Dracula*': 1M (*19)

'action movies, horror/fantasy (except good sci-fi, *Star Wars* etc)': 1M (*36) @

'horror, some romance': 1M (*39)

Appendix 7

Bram Stoker's Dracula audience research respondents

The vast majority of the questionnaire sample was white. The only exceptions were one self-described Eur-asian and one self-described Asian.

Respondents who saw the film:
  *1   anon. male, no other details given (*Samhain* sample)
  *2: anon. male, self-employed, age 34 (*Samhain* sample)
  *3: anon. male, media worker, age 26
  *4: Alex, female, insurance worker, age 24
  *5: anon. male student, age 19
  *6: anon. female, student, age 20
  *7: anon. female, school student, age 16
  *8: anon. female, unemployed/voluntary worker, age 24
  *9: anon. female, student, age 21
 *10: anon. female, biomedical scientist, age 33
 *11: Evonne, female, student, age 21
 *12: anon. male, no job details given, age 32
 *13: anon. female, publisher, age 39
 *14: anon. male, student, age 20
 *15: Jessica, female, French au pair, age 20
 *16: anon. male, school student, age 16
 *17: anon. female, charity worker, age 22
 *18: anon. female, medical librarian, age 29
 *19: anon. male, student, age 23
 *20: anon. male, student, age 20
 *21: anon. female, tax consultant, age 35
 *22: anon. male, graphic designer, age 23
 *23: anon. female, worker in family business, age 34
 *24: John, male, taxi driver, age 25
 *25: Tessa, female, student, age 20
 *26: anon. couple (male and female), in local government, 'mid-thirties'
 *27: anon. female, hairdresser, age 20
 *28: anon. female, social worker, age 26

*29: Allison, female, student, age 20
*30: anon. female, doctor, age 29
*31: anon. female, no job details, age 48

Respondents who did not see the film:
*32: Julie, female, social worker, age 31
*33: anon. male, retired, age 45
*34: anon. male, no job details given, age 34
*35: Carmel, female, teacher, age 31
*36: anon. male, local government officer, age 26
*37: Emma, female, town planner, age 27
*38: anon. female, receptionist, age 23
*39: Michael, male, shoe repairer, age 18
*40: anon. female, occupational therapist, age 37
*41: anon. female, childminder/part-time student, age 16

Appendix 8

Questionnaire used for *Natural Born Killers* case study: first batch

Cinema questionnaire

Thank you for taking a questionnaire. I am researching cinema audiences at the University of East Anglia, Norwich. I would be very grateful if you could fill in this questionnaire and return it to me using the envelope provided.

Please note that the questionnaire is in three parts. Part One asks questions about your general cinemagoing habits. Part Two asks questions about a film I'm particularly interested in. Part Three covers some basic details about you. The questions are a mixture of multiple choice and open-ended questions where you can write what you think. If you think not enough space has been provided for your response, please feel free to use an additional page.

Your reply will remain confidential, unless you agree otherwise in Part Three.

Thanks again for your help, I look forward to hearing from you.

Thomas Austin

EAS (PG)

University of East Anglia

Norwich NR4 7TJ

Part One
Questions about your general cinemagoing habits.

  1: What film have you just seen?
  2: Who did you go to see the film with?
    (Please tick an answer. Please tick who you normally go with twice.)
    a. No one else
    b. Mother

    c. Father
    d. Sister
    e. Brother
    f. Husband/wife
    g. Boyfriend/girlfriend
    h. Children (please say their sex and age)
    i. Friends (same sex) (please say how many)
    j. Friends (opposite sex) (please say how many)
    k. Other (please give details)

3: Who chose the film on this occasion?
   (Please tick an answer. Please tick who normally chooses twice.)
    a. Me
    b. Mother
    c. Father
    d. Sister
    e. Brother
    f. Husband/wife
    g. Boyfriend/girlfriend
    h. Children
    i. Friends (same sex)
    j. Friends (opposite sex)
    k. Other (please give details)

4: When did you last go to the cinema before today?
   (Please tick an answer.)
    a. Within the last week
    b. Within the last month
    c. Within the last three months
    d. Within the last year
    e. other (please give details)

5: Why did you go to the cinema today? Please give details

6: Do you always go to the_____? If not, please state the other cinema(s) you normally go to.

7: In your own words, please say what you enjoy about going to the cinema.

8: On average, how many films would you say you watch a month:
    a. at the cinema
    b. on video
    c. on television

9: What sorts of films do you enjoy most? Please give examples.

10: What sorts of films do you dislike most? Please give examples.

11: Please list the last three films you saw at the cinema, not counting today.

12: Which of these factors influence you in deciding whether or not to see a film?

(Please tick.)

	Very important:	Quite important:	Not important:
a. Presence of film stars			
b. Type of film/genre			
c. Plot/storyline			
d. Director			
e. Acting			
f. Photography			
g. Special effects			
h. Music			
i. Scenery/setting			
j. Other (please give details)			

13: Do you read reviews of films? If so, please give details.

14: Do you watch tv programmes about the cinema? If so, please give details.

15: Do you like to talk about a coming film before you see it? If so, who with?

16: Do you like to talk about a film after you have seen it? If so, who with?

17: Which of these factors influence you in deciding whether or not to see a film?

(Please tick.)

	Very important:	Quite important:	Not important:
a. What friends/relatives say			
b. Reading reviews or articles			
c. Seeing reviews or features on tv			
d. Seeing adverts in newspapers			
e. Seeing adverts on television			
f. Seeing previews/trailers at the cinema			
g. Seeing posters			
h. Whatever is on the night I go out			
i. Other (please give details)			

18: When you go to the cinema, which of the following factors are important to you?

(Please tick.)

	Very important:	Quite important:	Not important:
a. Cinema decor and comfort			
b. Availability of refreshments			
c. The quality of the film			

d. Presence of partner/friends/relatives
e. Price of tickets
f. Spending time out of the house
g. Other (please give details)

Part Two

This section asks questions about a film I'm particularly interested in, *Natural Born Killers*. I would like to find out if you have seen it, and if not, whether you are planning to see it or not.

19: Have you seen *Natural Born Killers*?
a. Yes
b. No
(If you answered no, please go on to question 22.)

20: If you have seen *Natural Born Killers*, please say (i) why you went to see it, and (ii) what you thought of it.
(i)
(ii)

21: Would you recommend *Natural Born Killers* to a friend?
Please give reasons for your answer. Please now go on to question 26.

22: Have you heard of *Natural Born Killers*?
a. Yes
b. No
If you answered yes, please say what you know about it.

23: Where did you get this information from?

24: Do you intend to see *Natural Born Killers*?(Please tick an answer.)
a. No
b. Yes
c. Perhaps/don't know
Please give reasons for your answer.

25: If you intend to see the film, will you go to see it with anybody else, or on your own? (If with somebody else, please give details.)

26: Have you spoken to anybody who has seen *Natural Born Killers*?
a. Yes
b. No
If you answered yes, please say who you talked to, and what they said about the film.

27: Have you seen or read any of the following? (If so, please tick.)
a. The poster for *Natural Born Killers*
b. Newspaper or magazine review(s) of the film
c. Newspaper or magazine article(s) about the film
d. Television coverage about the film
e. Cinema preview/trailer for the film
f. Advert for the film in newspapers/magazines

g. Advert for the film on television

28: Do you think *Natural Born Killers* will be a commercial success?
(Please tick an answer.)
a. No
b. Yes
c. Perhaps/don't know
Please give reasons for your answer.

29: Who do you think *Natural Born Killers* will appeal to? (Please tick an answer.)
a. Young women
b. Women of all ages
c. Young men
d. Men of all ages
e. Young men and women
f. Men and women of all ages
g. other (please give details)

30: Are films getting more violent?
a. Yes
b. No

31: If so, does this matter?
a. Yes
b. No
Please say why.

32: Do you think violent films can be blamed for violence in society at large?

33: Do you think there should be changes to censorship and/or age restrictions for (a) cinema films (b) rented and bought videos in Britain? If so, please give details.

Part Three

This section covers details about you. Of course, I would be grateful if you could answer all the questions, but I understand if you would prefer not to answer some.

Unless you agree to the contrary below, I shall treat this questionnaire in the strictest confidence.

35: Name:
(Give just a first name or made-up name if you wish)

36: Address:
(Leave this blank if you wish)

37: Are you:
a. Female
b. Male

38: Age:
39: Would you describe yourself as:
    a. Afro-Caribbean
    b. Asian
    c. White European
    d. other (please give details)
40: Would you describe yourself as religious? (If yes, please give details.)
41: Are you:
    a. in full-time employment
    b. in part-time employment
    c. in full- or part-time education
    d. unemployed
    e. retired
    f. other (please give details)
42: If you are in full or part-time employment, please give details.
43: At what age did you leave full-time education?
44: If you are in full- or part-time education, please give details.
45: Who do you live with?
    (Please tick one or more answers.)
    a. On my own
    b. Wife/husband
    c. Girlfriend/boyfriend
    d. Children (* Please state their ages)
    e. Friends (same sex)
    f. Friends (opposite sex)
    g. Parent(s)
    h. Brother/sister
    i. other (please give details)
46: Is your home rented or owned?
    a. Rented
    b. Owned
47: Please list your hobbies and leisure activities in order of preference. Would you include going to the cinema in your list?
48: What television programmes do you enjoy watching? How often do you watch these programmes?
49: Do you read any magazines or newspapers? Please give details. How often do you read them?
50: Which radio station(s) do you listen to?
51: Do you ever read books for pleasure? (Not for school or work..) If so, please list the last two books you read.
52: Would you be prepared to be quoted in my research findings?
    a. Yes, by name

b. Yes, anonymously
c. No

Unless you have agreed to the contrary, I shall treat this questionnaire in the strictest confidence. Thank you very much for your time.

Questionnaire used for *Natural Born Killers* case study: second batch

Natural Born Killers Questionnaire

Thank you for taking a questionnaire. I am researching cinema audiences at the University of East Anglia, Norwich. I would be very grateful if you could fill in this questionnaire and return it to me using the envelope provided.

Please note that the questionnaire is in three sections. Part One is left blank for you to write about your own reaction to *Natural Born Killers*. Please answer this section first. Part Two contains some specific questions about why you watched the film and your response to it. Part Three covers basic details about you.

The questions are a mixture of multiple choice and open-ended questions where you can write what you think. If you think not enough space has been provided for your response, please feel free to use an additional page. (If you have already completed the general questionnaire on going to the cinema which was handed out earlier this month, please complete Parts One and Two here, then at Part Three fill in your name and ignore the other questions in that section.) Your reply will remain confidential, unless you agree otherwise in Part Three.

Thanks again for your help, I look forward to hearing from you.
Thomas Austin
EAS (PG)
University of East Anglia
Norwich NR4 7TJ

Part One
PLEASE COMPLETE THIS SECTION BEFORE READING PART TWO.
Please use this page to write about (i) why you went to see *Natural Born Killers*, and (ii) your reactions to it.
(i):
(ii):

Part Two

This section asks some more questions about your response to the film, and about the publicity and promotion around it. Don't worry if you repeat some of your response to Part One.

1: Who did you go to see *Natural Born Killers* with?
   (Please tick an answer. Please also tick who you normally go to the cinema with <u>twice</u>.)
   a. No one else
   b. Mother
   c. Father
   d. Sister
   e. Brother
   f. Husband/wife
   g. Boyfriend/girlfriend
   h. Children
   i. Friends (same sex) (please say how many)
   j. Friends (opposite sex) (please say how many)
   k. Other (please give details)

2: Who chose the film on this occasion?
   (Please tick an answer. Please also tick who normally chooses which film to see *twice*.)
   a. Me
   b. Mother
   c. Father
   d. Sister
   e. Brother
   f. Husband/wife
   g. Boyfriend/girlfriend
   h. Children
   i. Friends (same sex)
   j. Friends (opposite sex)
   k. Other (please give details)

3: Did you talk about the film with anyone else before or after seeing it? If so, please say who, and what you talked about.

4: If you watched it alone, was this because someone refused to see it with you? If so, please give details.

5: Please say what you knew about *Natural Born Killers* before you saw it.

6: Where did you get this information about the film from?

7: Was the film what you expected or not? Please say how.

8: What did you think of the film? (Please tick a response for each category on the list.)

Very :   A bit: Not at all:

How enjoyable/entertaining?
How funny?
How exciting?
How believable/realistic?
How offensive?
How violent?
How seriously did you take it?

9: Did *Natural Born Killers* remind you of any other films? If so, please give details.

10: Would you say *Natural Born Killers* has a message? If so, what is it?

11: Are there any elements of the film that you particularly liked or disliked? Please give details.

12: Have you seen or read any of the following? (If so, please tick.)
   a. The poster for *Natural Born Killers*
   b. Newspaper or magazine review(s) of the film
   c. Newspaper or magazine article(s) about the film
   d. Television coverage about the film
   e. Cinema preview/trailer for the film
   f. Advert for the film in a newspaper or magazine
   g. Advert for the film on television

13: Do you think *Natural Born Killers* will be a commercial success? (Please tick an answer.)
   a. No
   b. Yes
   c. Perhaps/don't know
   Please give reasons for your answer.

14: Who do you think *Natural Born Killers* will appeal to? (Please tick an answer.)
   a. Young women
   b. Women of all ages
   c. Young men
   d. Men of all ages
   e. Young men and women
   f. Men and women of all ages
   g. other (please give details)

15: Are films getting more violent?
   a. Yes
   b. No

16: If so, does this matter?
   a. Yes
   b. No
   Please say why

17: Do you think violent films can be blamed for violence in society?

18: Do you think *Natural Born Killers* can be blamed for violence in society?

19: Were you aware of protests against the film by censorship and anti-violence campaigners? If so, how?

20: What was your reaction to the protests? Did it change after watching the film?
Please give details.

21: Should *Natural Born Killers* have been banned in this country, as some newspapers have suggested?

22: Do you think there should be any changes to censorship and/or age restrictions for (a) cinema films (b) rented and bought videos in Britain? If so, please give details.

Part Three

This section covers details about you. Of course, I would be grateful if you could answer all the questions, but I understand if you would prefer not to answer some.

Unless you agree to the contrary below, I shall treat this questionnaire in the strictest confidence.

25: Name:
(Give just a first name or made up name if you wish)

26: Address: (Leave this blank if you wish)

27: Are you:
a. Female
b. Male

28: Age:

29: Would you describe yourself as:
a. Afro-Caribbean
b. Asian
c. White European
d. other (please give details)

30: Would you describe yourself as religious? (If yes, please give details.)

31: Are you:
a. in full-time employment
b. in part-time employment
c. in full- or part-time education
d. unemployed
e. retired
f. other (please give details)

32: If you are in full- or part-time employment, please give details.

33: At what age did you leave full-time education?

34: If you are in full- or part-time education, please give details

35: Who do you live with? (Please tick one or more answers.)
   a. On my own
   b. Wife/husband
   c. Girlfriend/boyfriend
   d. Children (* Please state their sex and ages)
   e. Friends (same sex)
   f. Friends (opposite sex)
   g. Parent(s)
   h. Brother/sister
   i. other (please give details)

36: Is your home rented or owned?
   a. Rented
   b. Owned

37: When did you last go to the cinema before today? (Please tick an answer.)
   a. Within the last week
   b. Within the last month
   c. Within the last three months
   d. Within the last year
   e. other (please give details)

38: Why did you go to the cinema today, as opposed to any other day?

39: On average, how many films would you say you watch a month:
   a. a. at the cinema
   b. on video
   c. on television

40: What sorts of films do you enjoy most? Please give examples.

41: What sorts of films do you dislike most? Please give examples.

42: Please list the last three films you saw at the cinema, not counting today.

43: Do you read reviews of films? If so, please give details.

44: Do you watch tv programmes about the cinema? If so, please give details.

45: Which of these factors influence you in deciding whether or not to see a film?
   (Please tick.)

	Very important:	Quite important:	Not important:
a. What friends/relatives say			
b. Reading reviews or articles			
c. Seeing reviews or features on tv			
d. Seeing adverts in newspapers			

    e. Seeing adverts on television
    f. Seeing previews/ trailers at the cinema
    g. Seeing posters
    h. Whatever is on the night I go out
    i. Other (please give details)

46: When you go to the cinema, which of the following factors are important to you?
(Please tick.)

	Very important:	Quite important:	Not important:
a. Cinema decor and comfort			
b. Availability of refreshments			
c. The quality of the film			
d. Presence of partner/friends relatives			
e. Price of tickets			
f. Spending time out of the house			
g. Other (please give details)			

47: Please list your hobbies and leisure activities in order of preference. Would you include going to the cinema on your list?

48: What television programmes do you enjoy watching?

49: Do you read any magazines or newspapers? If so, please give details. How often do you read them?

50: Which radio station(s) do you listen to?

51: Do you ever read books for pleasure? (Not for school or work..) If so, please list the last two books you read.

52: Would you be prepared to be quoted in my research findings?
    a. Yes, by name
    b. Yes, anonymously
    c. No

Unless you have agreed to the contrary, I shall treat this questionnaire in the strictest confidence. Thank you very much for your time.

Appendix 10

Research sample details

Age on return of questionnaire

age 14–17:   6
age 18–24:   55
age 25–35:   29
age 36–45:   13
age 46–55:   1
total   104

Occupations

25 students
15 sixth-form-college and school students
 1 housewife and student
 2 housewives
 3 teachers
 1 college lecturer
 1 cleric
 1 financial software consultant
 1 business manager
 1 information manager
 1 shipbroker
 1 marketing manager
 1 marketing employee
 1 bookseller
 1 reporter
 1 social worker
 1 nurse
 1 quantity surveyor
 1 graphic designer
 1 British Telecom internet worker
 1 new media

1 shop manager
1 pub manager
1 paramedic
1 civil servant
1 insurance worker
1 advice centre worker
1 post office worker
1 secretary/computer operator
1 typist/salesperson
1 army officer
3 soldiers
1 firefighter
1 security officer
1 beauty therapist
1 motor mechanic
1 butcher
2 builders
1 decorator
1 chef
1 gardener
1 kitchen porter
1 lifeguard
2 factory workers
4 employed, no details given
6 unemployed
5 no details given

Appendix 11

Natural Born Killers audience research respondents

The overwhelming majority of respondents described themselves as 'white European'. Three respondents called themselves 'white British', and one 'African/European'.

First batch

*1:1: David, male, age 23, unemployed
*1:2: Samantha, female, age 14, school pupil
*1:3: Robert, male, age 30, bookseller
*1:4: Juliette, female, age 26, journalist
*1:5: Shoshana, female, age 22, pub manager
*1:6: Javiera, female, age 38, student
*1:7: Beverley, female, age 22, student
*1:8: anon. female, age 30, no job details given
*1:9: anon. male, age 25, factory worker
*1:10: Ruth, female, age 22, student
*1:11: Peter, male, age 44, paramedic
*1:12: Malcolm, male, age 34, builder
*1:13: anon. female, age 43, teaching assistant
*1:14: anon. female, age 42, lecturer
*1:15: anon. male, age 26, quantity surveyor
*1:16: Chris, male, age 18, sixth-form student
*1:17: Cecilia, female, age 18, sixth-form student
*1:18: anon. male, age 39, soldier
*1:19: anon. female, age 17, sixth-form student
*1:20: anon. male, age 45, builder
*1:21: anon. female, age 29, housewife
*1:22: anon. female, age 41, typist/salesperson
*1:23: Tina, female, age 18, student
*1:24: anon. female, age 20, student
*1:25: anon. female, age 23, advice centre worker

*1:26: anon. male, age 32, gardener
*1:27: Anna, female, age 15, school pupil
*1:28: anon. female, age 16, school pupil
*1:29: James, male, age 26, marketing manager
*1:30: anon. female, age 37, student
*1:31: Charlotte, female, age 18, marketing employee
*1:32: Stephen, male, age 25, student
*1:33: anon. female, age 23, student
*1:34: anon. male, age 21, student
*1:35: anon. male, age 27, financial software consultant
*1:36: David, male, age 19, student
*1:37: Steve, male, age 28, student
*1:38: Jennifer, female, age 49, teacher
*1:39: David, male, age 43, no job details given
*1:40: anon. male, age 39, shipbroker
*1:41: anon. male, age 40, unemployed
*1:42: anon. male, age 23, student
*1:43: Alison, female, age 17, sixth-form student
*1:44: anon. female, age 32, information manager
*1:45: Catherine, female, age 14, school pupil

Second batch

*2:1: Dave, male, age 20, kitchen porter
*2:2: anon. female, age 18, sixth-form student
*2:3: Ben, male, age 17, sixth-form student
*2:4: anon. male, age 20, student
*2:5: Anthony, male, age 19, lifeguard
*2:6: Jonathan, male, age 28, business manager
*2:7: anon. male, age 24, firefighter
*2:8: David, male, age 19, student
*2:9: Richard, male, age 28, factory worker
*2:10: anon. male, age 22, student
*2:11: Duncan, male, age 23, student
*2:12: James, male, age 27, army officer
*2:13: anon. male, age 24, no job details given
*2:14: David, male, age 19, student
*2:15: anon. female, age 18, student
*2:16: anon. female, age 20, student
*2:17: anon. female, age 38, illustrator
*2:18: Martin, male, age 23, student
*2:19: Ed, male, age 28, British Telecom employee
*2:20: anon. male, age 32, local authority employee

*2:21: David, male, age 35, security officer
*2:22: anon. female, age 30, civil servant
*2:23: anon. female, age 21, beauty therapist
*2:24: Duanne, male, age 25, shop manager
*2:25: anon. female, age 30, civil servant
*2:26: anon. male, age 27, soldier
*2:27: Catherine, female, age 23, post office worker
*2:28: Cecilia, female, age 18, sixth-form student
*2:29: anon. female, age 27, homeless worker
*2:30: Heidi, female, age 18, sixth-form student
*2:31: anon. female, age 18, unemployed
*2:32: Edward, male, age 29, student
*2:33: anon. male, age 18, unemployed
*2:34: anon. female, age 23, housewife
*2:35: Sid, male, age 24, motor mechanic
*2:36: anon. male, age 39, no job details given
*2:37: anon. male, age 22, student
*2:38: Jude, male, age 30, decorator
*2:39: anon. male, age 20, student
*2:40: anon. male, age 19, student
*2:41: Chris, male, age 22, insurance worker
*2:42: anon. male, age 25, graphic designer
*2:43: Georgia, female, age 20, student
*2:44: Mark, male, age 28, butcher
*2:45: anon. female, age 24, teacher
*2:46: Christine, female, age 25, secretary/computer operator
*2:47: anon. female, age 24, unemployed
*2:48: Jacqueline, female, age 25, housewife and student
*2:49: Simon, male, age 15, school pupil
*2:50: anon. female, age 24, cleric
*2:51: Scott, male, age 18, sixth-form student
*2:52: Jolene, female, age 19, student
*2:53: LP, female, age 18, care worker
*2:54: Steven, male, age 22, unemployed
*2:55: Karen, female, age 20, student
*2:56: anon. female, age 24, chef
*2:57: anon. female, age 37, nurse
*2:58: anon. male, age 25, student
*2:59: Melanie, female, age 21, social worker

Select bibliography

Allen, Robert C., 'From exhibition to reception: reflections on the audience in film history', *Screen*, 31:4 (1990), 347–56.

Allen, Robert C., 'Home alone together: Hollywood and the "family film"', in Melvyn Stokes and Richard Maltby (eds), *Identifying Hollywood's Audiences: Cultural Identity and the Movies* (London, British Film Institute, 1999).

Allen, Robert C. and Douglas Gomery, *Film History: Theory and Practice* (New York, McGraw-Hill, 1985).

Allor, Martin, 'Review' (on Ien Ang, *Desperately Seeking the Audience*, and James Lull, *Inside Family Viewing*), *Screen*, 34:1 (1993),99–102.

Altman, Rick, *The American Film Musical* (Bloomington, Indiana University Press, 1987).

Altman, Rick, *Film/Genre* (London, British Film Institute, 1999).

Ang, Ien, *Desperately Seeking the Audience* (New York and London, Routledge, 1991).

Ang, Ien, 'Wanted. Audiences. On the politics of empirical audience studies', in Ellen Seiter, Hans Borchers, Gabriele Kreutzner and Eva-Maria Warth (eds), *Remote Control: Television, Audiences and Cultural Power* (London, Routledge, 1989).

Ang, Ien, *Watching 'Dallas': Soap Opera and the Melodramatic Imagination* (New York, Methuen, 1985).

Ang, Ien and Joke Hermes, 'Gender and/in media consumption', in James Curran and Michael Gurevitch (eds), *Mass Media and Society* (London, Edward Arnold, 1991).

Austin, Bruce A., *Immediate Seating: A Look at Movie Audiences* (Belmont, Wadsworth, 1989).

Bacon-Smith, Camille, with Tyrone Yarbrough, 'Batman: the ethnography', in Roberta E. Pearson and William Uricchio (eds), *The Many Lives of the Batman: Critical Approaches to a Superhero and His Media* (New York, Routledge, 1991).

Balio, Tino, 'Adjusting to the new global economy: Hollywood in the 1990s', in Albert Moran (ed.), *Film Policy: International, National and Regional Perspectives* (New York, Routledge, 1996).

Balio, Tino, '"A major presence in all of the world's important markets": the globalization of Hollywood in the 1990s', in Steve Neale and Murray Smith (eds), *Contemporary Hollywood Cinema* (London, Routledge, 1998).

Balio, Tino, (ed.), *Hollywood in the Age of Television* (London, Unwin, 1990).

Barker, Martin, 'Seeing how far you can see: on being a "fan" of *2000AD*', in David Buckingham (ed.), *Reading Audiences: Young People and the Media* (Manchester, Manchester University Press, 1993).

Barker, Martin, 'Violence', *Sight and Sound*, 5:6 (NS) (1995), 10–13.

Barker, Martin, with Thomas Austin, *From Antz to Titanic: Reinventing Film Analysis* (London, Pluto Press, 2000).

Barker, Martin and Kate Brooks, *Knowing Audiences: Judge Dredd, its Friends, Fans and Foes* (Luton, University of Luton Press, 1998).

Barker, Martin and Julian Petley (eds), *Ill Effects: The Media/Violence Debate* (London, Routledge, 1997).

Bausinger, Hermann, 'Media, technology and daily life', *Media, Culture, Society*, 6:4 (October 1984), 343–51.

Bennett, Tony, 'Texts in history: the determinations of readings and their texts', in Derek Attridge, Geoff Bennington and Robert Young (eds), *Post-structuralism and the Question of History* (Cambridge, Cambridge University Press, 1987).

Bennett, Tony and Janet Woollacott, *Bond and Beyond: The Political Career of a Popular Hero* (London, Macmillan, 1987).

BFI Film and Television Handbook 1993 (London, British Film Institute, 1992).

BFI Film and Television Handbook 1994 (London, British Film Institute, 1993).

BFI Film and Television Handbook 1997 (London, British Film Institute, 1996).

BFI Film and Television Handbook 2000 (London, British Film Institute, 1999).

Bordwell, David, *Making Meaning: Inference and Rhetoric in the Interpretation of Cinema* (Cambridge, Mass. and London, Harvard University Press, 1989).

Bordwell, David, Janet Staiger and Kristin Thompson, *The Classical Hollywood Cinema: Film Style and Mode of Production to 1960* (New York, Routledge, 1985).

Bourdieu, Pierre, 'The aristocracy of culture', in Richard Collins, James Curran, Nicholas Garnham, Paddy Scannell, Philip Schlesinger and Colin Sparks (eds), *Media, Culture and Society: A Critical Reader* (London, Sage, 1986).

Bourdieu, Pierre, *Distinction: A Social Critique of the Judgement of Taste* (trans. Richard Nice) (London, Routledge & Kegan Paul, 1984).

Brod, Harry, 'Pornography and the alienation of male sexuality', in Jeff Hearn and David Morgan (eds), *Men, Masculinities and Social Theory* (London, Unwin Hyman, 1990).

Brunsdon, Charlotte, '"Crossroads": notes on soap opera', *Screen*, 22:4 (1981), 32–7.

Brunsdon, Charlotte, 'Post-feminism and shopping films', in Brunsdon, *Screen Tastes: Soap Opera to Satellite Dishes* (London, Routledge, 1997).

Brunsdon, Charlotte, 'Text and audience', in Ellen Seiter, Hans Borchers, Gabriele Kreutzner and Eva-Maria Warth (eds), *Remote Control: Television, Audiences and Cultural Power* (London, Routledge, 1989).

Brunsdon, Charlotte and David Morley, *Everyday Television: 'Nationwide'* (London, British Film Institute, 1978).

Brunt, Rosalind, 'Engaging with the popular: audiences for mass culture and what to say about them', in Lawrence Grossberg *et al.* (eds), *Cultural Studies* (London, Routledge, 1992).

Buckingham, David, 'Boys' talk: television and the policing of masculinity', 'Conclusion: re-reading audiences', 'Introduction: young people and the media', in Buckingham (ed), *Reading Audiences: Young People and the Media* (Manchester, Manchester University Press, 1993).

Buckingham, David, 'What are words worth? Interpreting children's talk about television', *Cultural Studies*, 5:2 (May 1991), 228–45.

de Certeau, Michel, *The Practice of Everyday Life* (Berkeley, University of California Press, 1984).

Cherry, Brigid, 'Refusing to refuse to look: female viewers of the horror film', in Melvyn Stokes and Richard Maltby (eds), *Identifying Hollywood's Audiences: Cultural Identity and the Movies* (London, British Film Institute, 1999).

Clover, Carol, 'Introduction', in Pamela Church Gibson and Roma Gibson (eds), *Dirty Looks: Women, Pornography, Power* (London, British Film Institute, 1993).

Clover, Carol, *Men, Women and Chainsaws: Gender in the Modern Horror Film* (London, British Film Institute, 1992).

Clover, Carol, 'White noise', *Sight and Sound*, 3:5 (1993), 6–9.

Collins, Jim, 'Batman: the movie, narrative: the hyperconscious', in Roberta E. Pearson and William Uricchio (eds), *The Many Lives of the Batman: Critical Approaches to a Superhero and His Media* (New York, Routledge, 1991).

Collins, Jim, 'Genericity in the nineties: eclectic irony and the new sincerity', in Jim Collins, Hilary Radner and Ava Preacher Collins (eds), *Film Theory Goes to the Movies* (New York, Routledge, 1993).

Corner, John, 'Meaning, genre and context: the problematics of "public knowledge" in the new audience studies', in James Curran and Michael Gurevitch (eds), *Mass Media and Society* (London, Edward Arnold, 1991).

Corner, John, 'Media studies and the "knowledge problem"', *Screen*, 36:2 (1995), 147–55.

Corrigan, Timothy, 'Auteurs and the new Hollywood' in Jon Lewis (ed.), *The New American Cinema* (Durham, Duke University Press, 1998).

Cruz, Jon and Justin Lewis (eds), *Viewing, Reading, Listening: Audiences and Cultural Reception* (Boulder, Westview Press, 1994).

Curran, James, 'Rethinking mass communications', in James Curran, David Morley and Valerie Walkerdine (eds), *Cultural Studies and Communications* (London, Arnold, 1996).

Dale, Martin, *The Movie Game: The Film Business in Britain, Europe and America* (London, Cassell, 1997).

Denisoff, Serge R. and George Plasketes, 'Synergy in 1980s film and music: formula for success of industry mythology?' *Film History*, 4 (1990), 257–76.

van Dijk, Teun A., *News as Discourse* (Hillsdale, New Jersey, Erlbaum, 1988).

van Dijk, Teun A., *Racism and the Press* (London, Routledge, 1991).

Docherty, David, David Morrison and Michael Tracey, *The Last Picture Show? Britain's Changing Film Audiences* (London, British Film Institute, 1987).

Doty, Alexander, 'Music sells movies: (Re)new(ed) conservatism in film marketing', *Wide Angle*, 10:2 (1988), 70–9.

Dunant, Sarah (ed.), *War of the Words: The Political Correctness Debate* (London, Virago, 1994).

Dyer, Richard, *Heavenly Bodies: Film Stars and Society* (Basingstoke, Macmillan, 1986).

Dyer, Richard, *The Matter of Images: Essays on Representations* (London, Routledge, 1993).

Dyer, Richard, *Stars* (London, British Film Institute, 1979).

Earnest, Olen J., '*Star Wars*: a case study of motion picture marketing', *Current Research in Film: Audiences, Economics, and Law*, 1 (1985), 1–18.

Ellis, John, *Visible Fictions: Cinema: Television: Video* (London, Routledge and Kegan Paul, 1982).

Ellsworth, Elizabeth, 'Illicit pleasures: feminist spectators and *Personal Best*', *Wide Angle*, 8:2 (1986), 45–56.

Faludi, Susan, *Backlash: The Undeclared War Against Women* (New York, Chatto and Windus, 1991, and London, 1992).

Fiske, John, 'British cultural studies and television', in Robert C. Allen (ed.), *Channels of Discourse: Television and Contemporary Criticism* (London, Methuen, 1987).

Fiske, John, 'The cultural economy of fandom' in Lisa Lewis (ed.), *The Adoring Audience* (London, Routledge, 1992).

Fiske, John, 'Moments of television: neither the text nor the audience', in

Ellen Seiter, Hans Borchers, Gabriele Kreutzner and Eva-Maria Warth (eds), *Remote Control: Television, Audiences and Cultural Power* (London, Routledge, 1989).

Fiske, John, *Television Culture* (London, New York, Methuen, 1987).

Fiske, John, *Understanding Popular Culture* (Boston, Unwin Hyman, 1989).

Foucault, Michel, *The History of Sexuality, Volume 1: An Introduction*, trans. Robert Hurley (London, Allen Lane, 1979).

Foucault, Michel, *Power/Knowledge: Selected Interviews and Other Writings, 1972–77*, ed. Colin Gordon (Brighton, Harvester Press, 1980).

Fowler, Roger, *Language in the News: Discourse and Ideology in the Press* (London, Routledge, 1991).

French, Karl (ed.), *Screen Violence* (London, Bloomsbury, 1996).

Gabriel, John, 'What do you do when minority means you? *Falling Down* and the construction of "whiteness"', *Screen*, 37:2 (1996), 129–51.

Galvin, Angela, '*Basic Instinct*: damning dykes', in Diane Hamer and Belinda Budge (eds), *The Good the Bad and the Gorgeous: Popular Culture's Romance with Lesbianism* (London, Pandora, 1994).

Garnham, Nicholas, *Capitalism and Communication: Global Culture and the Economics of Information* (London, Sage, 1990).

Geraghty, Christine, 'Re-examining stardom: questions of texts, bodies and performance', in Christine Gledhill and Linda Williams (eds), *Reinventing Film Studies* (London, Arnold, 2000).

Gibson, Pamela Church and Roma Gibson (eds), *Dirty Looks: Women, Pornography, Power* (London, British Film Institute, 1993).

Gillespie, Marie, '*The Mahabharata*: from Sanskrit to sacred soap. A case study of two contemporary televisual versions', in David Buckingham (ed.), *Reading Audiences: Young People and the Media* (Manchester, Manchester University Press, 1993).

Gillespie, Marie, *Television, Ethnicity and Cultural Change* (London, Routledge, 1995).

Gledhill, Christine, 'Pleasurable negotiations', in E. Deidre Pribram (ed.), *Female Spectators: Looking at Film and Television* (London, Verso, 1988).

Gledhill, Christine, (ed.), *Stardom: Industry of Desire* (London, Routledge, 1992).

Gomery, Douglas, *Shared Pleasures: A History of Movie Presentation in the United States* (London, British Film Institute, 1992).

Graham, Paula, 'Girl's camp? The politics of parody', in Tamsin Wilton (ed.), *Immortal Invisible: Lesbians and the Moving Image* (London, Routledge, 1995).

Gray, Ann, 'Behind closed doors: video recorders in the home', in Helen Baehr and Gillian Dyer (eds), *Boxed In: Women and Television* (London, Pandora, 1987).

Gray, Ann, 'Reading the audience', *Screen*, 28:3 (1987), 24–35.

Gray, Ann, *Video Playtime: The Gendering of a Leisure Technology* (London, Routledge, 1992).

Gripsrud, Jostein, 'Film Audiences', in John Hill and Pamela Church Gibson (eds), *The Oxford Guide to Film Studies* (Oxford, Oxford University Press 1998).

Gripsrud, Jostein, *The Dynasty Years: Hollywood Television and Critical Media Studies* (London, Routledge 1995).

Gripsrud, Jostein, '"High culture" revisited', *Cultural Studies*, 3:2 (1989), 194–207.

Gross, Larry, 'Out of the mainstream: sexual minorities and the mass media', in Ellen Seiter, Hans Borchers, Gabriele Kreutzner and Eva-Maria Warth (eds), *Remote Control: Television, Audiences and Cultural Power* (London, Routledge, 1989).

Grossberg, Lawrence, Cary Nelson, Paula A. Treichler (eds), *Cultural Studies* (London, Routledge, 1992).

Hacker, Jonathan and David Price, 'A British film culture? A British film industry?', in Hacker and Price, *Take Ten: Contemporary British Film Director* (Oxford, Clarendon Press, 1991).

Hall, Stuart, 'Cultural studies and its theoretical legacies', in Lawrence Grossberg, Cary Nelson, Paula A. Treichler (eds), *Cultural Studies* (London, Routledge, 1992).

Hall, Stuart, 'Encoding/decoding', in Stuart Hall, Dorothy Hobson, Andrew Lowe and Paul Willis (eds), *Culture, Media Language: Working Papers in Cultural Studies, 1972–79* (London, Hutchinson, 1980).

Hall, Stuart, 'Introduction', in David Morley, *Family Television: Cultural Power and Domestic Leisure* (London, Comedia, 1986).

Hall, Stuart, 'Reflections upon the encoding/decoding model: an interview with Stuart Hall', in Jon Cruz and Justin Lewis (eds), *Viewing, Reading, Listening: Audiences and Cultural Reception* (Boulder, Westview Press, 1994).

Hansen, Miriam, *Babel and Babylon: Spectatorship in American Silent Film* (Cambridge, Mass., Harvard University Press, 1991).

Hansen, Miriam, 'Early cinema, late cinema: transformations of the public sphere', *Screen*, 34:3 (1993), 197–210.

Harding, Sandra, 'Is there a feminist method?' in Harding (ed.), *Feminism and Methodology* (Milton Keynes, Open University Press, 1987).

Harper, Sue, 'Review', *Screen*, 35:2 (1994), 199–203 (on Douglas Gomery, *Shared Pleasures: A History of Movie Presentation in the United States*).

Harper, Sue and Vincent Porter, 'Moved to tears: weeping in the cinema in postwar Britain', *Screen*, 37:2 (1996), 152–73.

Hermes, Joke, 'Media, meaning and everyday life', *Cultural Studies*, 7 (1993), 493–506.

Hermes, Joke, *Reading Women's Magazines* (Cambridge, Polity Press,

1995).

Hill, Annette, *Shocking Entertainment: Viewer Response to Violent Movies* (Luton, University of Luton Press, 1997).

Hillier, Jim, *The New Hollywood* (London, Studio Vista, 1993).

Hills, Matthew, 'The media cult: what, when and why?' unpublished paper (University of Sussex, 1996).

Holmlund, Chris, 'Reading character with a vengeance: the *Fatal Attraction* phenomenon', *The Velvet Light Trap*, 27 (1991), 25–36.

Hutchings, Peter, 'Genre theory and criticism', in Joanne Hollows and Mark Jancovich (eds), *Approaches to Popular Film* (Manchester, Manchester University Press, 1995).

Jancovich, Mark, 'Genre and the audience: genre classifications and cultural distinctions in the mediation of *The Silence of the Lambs*', in Melvyn Stokes and Richard Maltby (eds), *Hollywood Spectatorship: Changing Perceptions of Cinema Audiences* (London, British Film Institute, forthcoming, 2001).

Jenkins, Henry, 'Historical poetics', in Joanne Hollows and Mark Jancovich (eds), *Approaches to Popular Film* (Manchester, Manchester University Press, 1995).

Jenkins, Henry, *Textual Poachers: Television Fans and Participatory Culture* (New York, Routledge, 1992).

Jenkins, Steve, 'A critical impasse', in Martyn Auty and Nick Roddick (eds), *British Cinema Now* (London, British Film Institute, 1985).

Jensen, Klaus Bruhn, 'Introduction: the qualitative turn', in Klaus Bruhn Jensen and Nicholas W. Jankowsi (eds), *A Handbook of Qualitative Methods for Mass Communications Research* (London, Routledge, 1991).

Kapsis, Robert E., *Hitchcock: The Making of a Reputation* (Chicago, University of Chicago Press, 1992).

King, Barry, 'Articulating stardom', *Screen*, 26:5 (1985), 27–50.

Karpf, Ann, 'The unbearable rightness of being PC', *The Guardian*, 24 September 1992, 34.

Kitzinger, Jenny, 'A sociology of media power: key issues in audience reception research', in Greg Philo (ed), *Message Received: Glasgow Media Group Research 1993–1998* (Harlow, Longman).

Klinger, Barbara, 'Cinema/ideology/criticism revisited: the progressive text', *Screen* 25:1 (1984), 30–44.

Klinger, Barbara, 'Digressions at the cinema: reception and mass culture', *Cinema Journal*, 28:4 (1989), 3–19.

Klinger, Barbara, 'Film history terminable and interminable: recovering the past in reception studies', *Screen*, 38:2 (1997), 107–28.

Klinger, Barbara, 'In retrospect: film studies today', *Yale Journal of Criticism*, 2:1 (1988), 129–51.

Klinger, Barbara, *Melodrama and Meaning: History, Culture and the Films of Douglas Sirk* (Bloomington, Indiana University Press, 1994).

Kramer, Peter, 'The lure of the big picture: film, television and Hollywood', in John Hill and Martin McLoone (eds), *Big Picture, Small Screen: The Relations Between Film and Television* (Luton, University of Luton Press, 1997).

Kramer, Peter, 'Women first: *Titanic* (1997), action-adventure films and Hollywood's female audience', *Historical Journal of Film, Radio and Television* 18:4 (1998), 599–618.

Kramer, Peter, 'Would you take your child to see this film? The cultural and social work of the family-adventure movie', in Steve Neale and Murray Smith (eds), *Contemporary Hollywood Cinema* (London, Routledge, 1998).

Kuhn, Annette, *Family Secrets: Acts of Memory and Imagination* (London, Verso, 1995).

Lacey, Joanne, 'Seeing through happiness: Hollywood musicals and the construction of the American dream in Liverpool', *Journal of Popular British Cinema*, 2 (1999), 54–65.

Lewis, Justin, *The Ideological Octopus: An exploration of television and its audience* (New York and London, Routledge, 1991).

Lewis, Justin, 'What counts in cultural studies', *Media, Culture and Society*, 19:1 (1997), 83–97.

Lull, James, *Inside Family Viewing: Ethnographic Research on Television's Audiences* (London, Routledge, 1990).

Maltby, Richard, '"A brief romantic interlude": Dick and Jane go to $3^{1}/_{2}$ seconds of the classical Hollywood cinema', in David Bordwell and Noel Carroll (eds), *Post-Theory: Reconstructing Film Studies* (Madison, University of Wisconsin Press, 1996).

Maltby, Richard, '"Sticks, hicks and flaps": Classical Hollywood's generic conception of its audiences', in Melvyn Stokes and Richard Maltby (eds), *Identifying Hollywood's Audiences: Cultural Identity and the Movies* (London, British Film Institute).

Maltby, Richard and Ian Craven, *Hollywood Cinema: An Introduction* (Oxford, Blackwell, 1995).

Marchetti, Gina, 'Subcultural studies and the film audience: rethinking the film viewing context', *Current Research in Film: Audiences, Economics, and Law*, 2 (1986), 62–79.

Mayne, Judith. *Cinema and Spectatorship* (London, Routledge, 1993).

McDonald, Paul, 'Star Studies', in Joanne Hollows and Mark Jancovich (eds), *Approaches to Popular Film* (Manchester, Manchester University Press, 1995).

McLeod, Jack M., Gerald M. Kosicki and Zhongdang Pan, 'On understanding and misunderstanding media effects', in James Curran and

Michael Gurevitch (eds), *Mass Media and Society* (London, Edward Arnold, 1991).

McRobbie, Angela, 'The moral panic in the age of the postmodern mass media', in McRobbie, *Postmodernism and Popular Culture* (London and New York, Routledge, 1994).

McRobbie, Angela, 'The politics of feminist research: between talk, text and action', *Feminist Review*, 12 (October 1982), reprinted in Angela McRobbie, *Feminism and Youth Culture: From Jackie to Just Seventeen* (Basingstoke, Macmillan, 1991).

Medved, Michael, *Hollywood vs. America* (London, Harper Collins, 1992).

Meehan, Eileen R., '"Holy commodity fetish, Batman!": the political economy of a commercial intertext', in Roberta E. Pearson and William Uricchio (eds), *The Many Lives of the Batman: Critical Approaches to a Superhero and His Media* (New York, Routledge, 1991.

Melucci, Alberto, *Nomads of the Present: Social Movements and Individual Needs in Contemporary Society*, eds J. Keane, P. Mier (London, Hutchinson Radius, 1989).

Miller, David, and Greg Philo, 'Against orthodoxy: the media do influence us', *Sight and Sound*, 6:12 (NS) (1996), 18–20.

Modleski, Tania, *Feminism Without Women: Culture and Criticism in a 'Postfeminist' Age* (New York, Routledge, 1991).

Modleski, Tania, 'Introduction' in Modleski (ed.), *Studies in Entertainment: Critical Approaches to Mass Culture* (Bloomington, Indiana University Press, 1986).

Monk, Claire, 'Heritage films and the British cinema audience in the 1990s' *Journal of Popular British Cinema*, 2 (1999), 22–38.

Moores, Shaun, *Interpreting Audiences: The Ethnography of Mass Consumption* (London, Sage, 1993).

Morley, David, 'Between the public and the private: the domestic uses of information and communications technologies', in Jon Cruz and Justin Lewis (eds), *Viewing, Reading, Listening: Audiences and Cultural Reception* (Boulder, Westview Press, 1994).

Morley, David, 'Changing paradigms in audience studies', in Ellen Seiter, Hans Borchers, Gabriele Kreutzner and Eva-Maria Warth (eds), *Remote Control: Television, Audiences and Cultural Power* (London, Routledge, 1989).

Morley, David, *Family Television: Cultural Power and Domestic Leisure* (London, Comedia, 1986).

Morley, David, *The 'Nationwide' Audience: Structure and Decoding* (London, British Film Institute, 1980).

Morley, David, 'The "Nationwide" audience: a critical postscript', *Screen Education*, 39 (1981), 3–14.

Morley, David, 'Where the global meets the local: notes from the sitting room', *Screen*, 32:1 (1991), 1–15.

Morley, David, *Television, Audiences and Cultural Studies* (London, Routledge, 1992).

Morris, Meaghan, 'Banality in Cultural Studies', *Discourse*, 10:2 (1988), 3–29.

Morris, Meaghan, 'Indigestion: a rhetoric of reviewing', *Filmnews*, 12:6 (1982), reprinted in Meaghan Morris, *The Pirate's Fiancee: Feminism, Reading, Postmodernism* (London, Verso, 1988).

Moss, Gemma, 'Girls tell the teen romance: four reading histories', in David Buckingham (ed.), *Reading Audiences: Young People and the Media* (Manchester, Manchester University Press, 1993).

Mulvey, Laura, 'Afterthoughts on "Visual pleasure and narrative cinema" inspired by *Duel in the Sun*', *Framework*, 6:15/16/17(1981), 12–15.

Mulvey, Laura, 'Visual pleasure and narrative cinema', *Screen*, 16:3 (Autumn 1975), 6–18.

Murdock, Graham, 'Critical inquiry and audience activity', in Brenda Dervin, Lawrence Grossberg, Barbara J.O'Keefe and Ellen Wartella (eds), *Rethinking Communication: Volume 2: Paradigm Exemplars* (Newbury Park, London, New Delhi, Sage, 1989).

Myers, Kathy, 'Television previewers: no critical comment', in Len Masterman (ed.), *Television Mythologies* (London, Comedia, 1984).

National Viewer's and Listeners' Association, *Newsbrief*, 64–93 (January 1995–June 1997).

Neale, Steve, 'Art cinema as institution', *Screen*, 22:1 (1981), 11–39.

Neale, Steve, *Genre* (London, British Film Institute, 1980).

Neale, Steve, *Genre and Hollywood* (London, Routledge, 2000)

Neale, Steve, 'Masculinity as spectacle', *Screen*, 24:6 (1983), 2–17.

Neale, Steve, 'Questions of genre', *Screen*, 31:1 (1990), 45–66.

Norris, Pippa, 'Introduction: Women, Media, and Politics', in Norris (ed.), *Women, Media, and Politics* (New York and Oxford, Oxford University Press, 1997).

Oakley, Ann, 'Interviewing women: a contradiction in terms', in Helen Roberts (ed.), *Doing Feminist Research* (London, Routledge and Kegan Paul, 1981).

Ohmer, Susan, 'Measuring desire: George Gallup and audience research in Hollywood', *Journal of Film and Video*, 43:1–2 (Spring–Summer 1991), 3–28.

Ohmer, Susan, 'The science of pleasure: George Gallup and audience research in Hollywood', in Melvyn Stokes and Richard Maltby (eds), *Identifying Hollywood's Audiences: Cultural Identity and the Movies* (London, British Film Institute, 1999).

Paul, William, 'The K-mart audience at the mall movies', *Film History*, 6 (1994), 487–501.

Philo, Greg, 'Children and film/video/TV violence', in Greg Philo (ed.),

Message Received: Glasgow Media Group Research 1993–1998 (Harlow, Longman).

Pidduck, Julianne, 'The 1990s Hollywood fatal femme: (dis)figuring feminism, family, irony, violence', *CineAction*, 38 (1995), 63–72.

Radway, Janice, *Reading the Romance: Women, Patriarchy, and Popular Literature* (Chapel Hill, University of North Carolina Press, 1984).

Radway, Janice, 'Reception study: ethnography and the problems of dispersed audiences and nomadic subjects', *Cultural Studies*, 2:3 (1988), 359–67.

Radway, Janice, 'Romance and the work of fantasy: struggles over feminine sexuality and subjectivity at century's end', in Jon Cruz and Justin Lewis (eds), *Viewing, Reading, Listening: Audiences and Cultural Reception* (Boulder, Westview Press, 1994).

Rutherford, Jonathan, 'Who's that man?' in Rowena Chapman and Jonathan Rutherford (eds), *Male Order: Unwrapping Masculinity* (London, Lawrence and Wishart, 1988).

Rutherford, Jonathan and Rowena Chapman, 'The forward march of men halted' in Rowena Chapman and Jonathan Rutherford (eds), *Male Order: Unwrapping Masculinity* (London, Lawrence and Wishart, 1988).

Schatz, Thomas, 'The New Hollywood', in Jim Collins, Hilary Radner and Ava Preacher Collins (eds), *Film Theory Goes to the Movies* (New York, Routledge, 1993).

Schlesinger, Philip, R. Emerson Dobash, Russell P. Dobash and C. Kay Weaver, *Women Viewing Violence* (London, British Film Institute, 1992).

Schroder, Kim Christian, 'Audience semiotics, interpretive communities and the "ethnographic turn" in media research', *Media Culture and Society*, 16:2 (1994), 337–47.

Sconce, Jeffrey, 'Trashing the academy: taste, excess, and an emerging politics of cinematic style', *Screen*, 36:4 (Winter 1995), 371–93.

Seaman, William R., 'Active audience theory: pointless populism', *Media, Culture and Society*, 14 (1992), 301–11.

Sedgwick, Eve Kosofsky, *Epistemology of the Closet* (New York, Harvester Wheatsheaf, 1990).

Segal, Lynne, *Slow Motion: Changing Masculinities, Changing Men* (London, Virago, 1990).

Seiter, Ellen, 'Making distinctions in TV audience research: case study of a troubling interview', *Cultural Studies*, 4:1 (1990), 61–84.

Seiter, Ellen, Hans Borchers, Gabriele Kreutzner and Eva-Maria Warth, 'Introduction', and '"Don't Treat Us Like We're So Stupid and Naive"': towards an ethnography of soap opera viewers', in Seiter *et al.* (eds), *Remote Control: Television, Audiences and Cultural Power* (London, Routledge, 1989).

Silverstone, Roger, *Television and Everyday Life* (London, Routledge, 1994).

Skeggs, Beverley, *Formations of Class and Gender* (London, Sage, 1997).

Smith, Jeff, *The Sounds of Commerce: Marketing Popular Film Music* (New York, Columbia University Press, 1998).

Smith, Murray, *Engaging Characters: Fiction, Emotion, and the Cinema* (Oxford, Clarendon Press, 1995).

Stacey, Jackie, 'Hollywood Memories', *Screen*, 35:4 (1994), 317–35.

Stacey, Jackie, *Star Gazing: Hollywood Cinema and Female Spectatorship* (London, Routledge, 1994).

Stacey, Jackie, 'Textual obsessions: methodology, history and researching female spectatorship', *Screen*, 34:3 (1993), 260–74.

Staiger, Janet, 'The handmaiden of villainy: methods and problems in studying the historical reception of film', *Wide Angle*, 8:1 (1986), 19–27.

Staiger, Janet, *Interpreting Films: Studies in the Historical Reception of American Cinema* (Princeton, Princeton University Press, 1992).

Staiger, Janet, 'Taboos and totems: cultural meanings of *The Silence of the Lambs*', in Jim Collins, Hilary Radner and Ava Preacher Collins (eds), *Film Theory Goes to the Movies* (New York, Routledge, 1993).

Stokes, Melvyn and Richard Maltby (eds), *Identifying Hollywood's Audiences: Cultural Identity and the Movies* (London, British Film Institute, 1999).

Street, Sarah, *British National Cinema* (London and New York, Routledge, 1997).

Strinati, Dominic. 'The taste of America: Americanization and popular culture in Britain', in Strinati and Stephen Wagg (eds), *Come on Down? Popular Media Culture in Post-War Britain* (London, Routledge, 1992).

Studlar, Gaylyn, 'The perils of pleasure? Fan magazine discourse as women's commodified culture in the 1920s', *Wide Angle*, 13:1 (1991), 6–33.

Studlar, Gaylyn, 'Valentino, "Optic intoxication", and dance madness', in Steven Cohan and Ina Rae Hark (eds), *Screening the Male: Exploring Masculinities in Hollywood Cinema* (London, Routledge, 1993).

Tasker, Yvonne, 'Pussy Galore: lesbian images and lesbian desire in the popular cinema', in Diane Hamer and Belinda Budge (eds), *The Good the Bad and the Gorgeous: Popular Culture's Romance with Lesbianism* (London, Pandora, 1994).

Tasker, Yvonne, *Spectacular Bodies: Gender, Genre and the Action Cinema* (London, Routledge, 1993).

Taylor, Helen, *Scarlett's Women: Gone With The Wind and its Female Fans* (London, Virago, 1989).

Taylor, Lisa, 'From psychoanalytic feminism to popular feminism', in Joanne Hollows and Mark Jancovich (eds), *Approaches to Popular Film* (Manchester, Manchester University Press, 1995).

Telotte, J.P. (ed.), *The Cult Film Experience: Beyond All Reason* (Austin, University of Texas Press, 1991).

Thornton, Sarah, *Club Cultures: Music, Media and Subcultural Capital* (Cambridge, Polity Press, 1995).

Uricchio, William and Roberta E. Pearson, 'I'm not fooled by that cheap disguise', in Roberta E. Pearson and William Uricchio (eds), *The Many Lives of the Batman: Critical Approaches to a Superhero and His Media* (New York, Routledge, 1991).

Uricchio, William and Roberta E. Pearson, *Reframing Culture: The Case of the Vitagraph Quality Films* (Princeton, Princeton University Press, 1993).

Vasey, Ruth, *The World According to Hollywood, 1918–1939* (Exeter, University of Exeter Press, 1997).

Volosinov, V.N., *Marxism and the Philosophy of Language*, 1929, trans. Ladislav Matejka and I.R. Titunik (New York, Seminar Press, 1973).

Walkerdine, Valerie, *Daddy's Girl: Young Girls and Popular Culture* (Basingstoke, Macmillan, 1997).

Walkerdine, Valerie, 'Video replay: families, films and fantasy', in Victor Burgin, James Donald and Cora Kaplan (eds), *Formations of Fantasy* (London, Methuen, 1986).

Waller, Gregory A., *The Living and the Undead: From Stoker's Dracula to Romero's Dawn of the Dead* (Urbana, University of Illinois Press, 1986).

Wasko, Janet, *Hollywood in the Information Age: Beyond the Silver Screen* (Cambridge, Polity Press, 1994).

Weeks, Jeffrey, *Coming Out: Homosexual Politics in Britain from the Nineteenth Century to the Present*, revised edition (London, Quartet, 1990).

Weiss, Andrea, '"A queer feeling when I look at you", Hollywood stars and lesbian spectatorship in the 1930s', in Christine Gledhill (ed.), *Stardom: Industry of Desire* (London, Routledge, 1992).

Whatling, Clare, 'Fostering the illusion', in Diane Hamer and Belinda Budge (eds), *The Good, the Bad and the Gorgeous: Popular Culture's Romance with Lesbianism* (London, Pandora, 1994).

Willemen, Paul, 'Letter to John', *Screen* 21:2 (1980), 53–66.

Williams, Alan, 'Is a radical genre criticism possible?' *Quarterly Review of Film Studies*, 9:2 (1984), 121–5.

Williams, Linda, 'Discipline and fun: *Psycho* and postmodern cinema', in Christine Geraghty and Linda Williams (eds), *Reinventing Film Studies* (London, Arnold, 2000).

Williams, Linda, *Hard Core: Power, Pleasure, and the 'Frenzy of the Visible'* (Berkeley, University of California Press, 1989).

Williams, Linda, 'Learning to scream', *Sight and Sound*, 4:12 (NS) (1994), 14–17.

Williams, Linda, 'Pornographies on/scene or Diff'rent strokes for diff'rent folks', in Lynne Segal and Mary McIntosh (eds), *Sex Exposed* (London, Virago, 1992).

Williams, Linda (ed.), *Viewing Positions: Ways of Seeing Film* (New Brunswick, Rutgers University Press, 1995).

Williams, Linda Ruth, 'Erotic thrillers and rude women', *Sight and Sound*, 3:7 (NS) (1993), 12–14.

Wolfe, Charles, 'The return of Jimmy Stewart: the publicity photograph as text', in Christine Gledhill (ed.), *Stardom: Industry of Desire* (London, Routledge, 1991).

Wood, Julian, 'Repeatable pleasures: notes on young people's use of video', in David Buckingham (ed.), *Reading Audiences: Young People and the Media* (Manchester, Manchester University Press, 1993).

Wyatt, Justin, *High Concept: Movies and Marketing in Hollywood* (Austin, University of Texas Press, 1994).

van Zoonen, Liesbet, *Feminist Media Studies* (London, Sage, 1994).

Index